With the Master In The Fiery Furnace

A Ladies' Bible Study of 1 Peter

By
Susan J. Heck

*Holy Bible
You version*

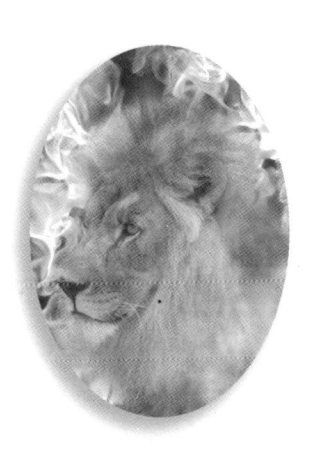

With the Master in the Fiery Furnace
A Ladies' Bible Study of 1 Peter
By Susan J. Heck

©2022 Focus Publishing, Bemidji, Minnesota
All rights reserved

No part of this book may be reproduced by any means without written consent of the publisher except for brief quotes used in reviews written specifically for use in a magazine or newspaper.

Scripture taken from
The New King James Version® of the Bible
Copyright©1982, by Thomas Nelson, Inc
Used by permission
All rights reserved

Cover design by Kymm Tingum

ISBN 978-1-936141-66-1

Printed in the United States of America

Dedication

This book is dedicated to a dear woman whose now in glory, Elisabeth Elliott. She went through many fiery trials in her pilgrimage on earth, and yet came forth as gold. Her legacy lives on. To God be the glory!

Endorsements

In Susan's newest study, she brings her rich knowledge and experience to Peter's first epistle. Here is a work saturated not only with the Scriptures, but also with the spiritual wisdom from Susan's deep study of the Word, and her years of walking with the Savior as a pastor's wife and certified Biblical Counselor. Each chapter is a beneficial study of the text of First Peter. All the chapters end with a summary, but all chapters end with a series of excellent and in depth study questions. You hold in your hands an ideal resource for individual study, Ladies Bible Study, and a most helpful counseling and discipleship resource. As a pastor, I not only will recommend this study to the ladies of our church, I also gladly recommend this book to you!

Dr. Glenn Dunn
Pastor, Cornerstone Bible Fellowship
Executive Director of the Biblical Counseling Institute

Uncertainty is all around us but, this study in I Peter shows us biblically that our times are not uncertain to the Savior. Susan systematically shows us from this epistle how we can be biblically equipped for the living of these days. Probing, personal questions supported by solid theology and doctrine make this in-depth study an essential tool for women wanting to grow in their walk with the Lord. As a pastor's wife I have been part of many bible studies. This study in I Peter is by far the most personally probing and biblically convicting study I have read. Susan carefully exposits God's Word to equip, edify and encourage the reader. I can't wait for the ladies in our church to begin this study.

Beth Dunn
ACBC Certified Biblical Counselor

As a Christian, there are times when you come across bible study tools that are significantly helpful. This is one of those resources. Susan's love and devotion for the word of God is clearly evident through her careful handling of His word. As she walks through the profound wisdom of God in 1st Peter, the meaning and implications of each portion are handled with exegetical precision in order to help the reader put into practice what they have learned. We could not more highly recommend this for your own library.

> **Terry and Rebecca Wragg** (Terry is the Pastor of Fellowship Bible Church, Chester, NH. Rebecca is Susan's personal friend and disciple & Terry's faithful wife of 35 years.)

Table of Contents

1. Grace in the Midst of the Fiery Furnace
   1 Peter 1:1-2 1

2. Four Blessings of Our Redemption
   1 Peter 1:3-7 15

3. The Importance of the Prophets
   1 Peter 1:8-12 31

4. A Call to Holy Living
   1 Peter 1:13-16 45

5. The Cost of Eternal Life
   1 Peter 1:17-21 61

6. Genuine Believers Possess Genuine Love for Others
   1 Peter 1:22-25 77

7. Get Rid of Sin and Grow!
   1 Peter 2:1-3 91

8. Is Jesus Precious or Offensive to You?
   1 Peter 2:4-8 107

9. Priests, Pilgrims and Peculiar People Giving Praises to God!
   1 Peter 2:9-12 125

10. The Christian's Response to Government
    1 Peter 2:13-17 141

11. Our Supreme Example in Suffering, Christ our Lord!
    1 Peter 2:18-25 157

Jan 9

12. ...at Does a Beautiful Woman Look Like? *Dec 12*
    1 Peter 3:1-6 175

13. The Rest of the Story! *Jan 16*
    1 Peter 3:7-9 191

14. Five Keys to Loving Life *Jan 23*
    1 Peter 3:10-12 207

15. Six Keys to Being an Effective Witness *Jan 30*
    1 Peter 3:13-17 221

16. The Suffering and Longsuffering of Christ and God *Feb 6*
    1 Peter 3:18-22 237

17. The Past, the Present, and the Future Life of a Believer *Feb 13*
    1 Peter 4:1-6 253

18. How to Occupy Until He Comes *Feb 20*
    1 Peter 4:7-8 269

19. Knowing and Using Your Spiritual Gifts for the Glory of God *Feb 27*
    1 Peter 4:9-11 283

20. What to Do in the Furnace: Part 1 *March 5*
    1 Peter 4:12-14 301

21. What to Do in the Furnace: Part 2 *Mar 13*
    1 Peter 4:15-19 315

22. What Does a Good Pastor Look Like? *Mar 20*
    1 Peter 5:1-4 331

23. Four Reasons to Avoid Pride *27*
    1 Peter 5:5-9 349

24. A Hopeful End *April 3*
    1 Peter 5:10-14 367

April 10

Chapter 1

Grace in the Midst of the Fiery Furnace
1 Peter 1:1-2

The date was April 20, 1999. The place was Columbine High School, in Littleton, Colorado. Most of us remember what happened. Two high school students, Eric Harris and Dylan Klebold, murdered 12 students and 1 teacher, injured 24 others, and then committed suicide. This particular school shooting seems to have set off a disturbing trend that continues to this day. Mass shootings have become commonplace in our society. There were more mass shootings in 2019 than there were days in the year—the total for that year was 417.

But there is one detail that sets the shooting at Columbine High School apart from the school shootings which have taken place since. As explosions and gunfire thundered through the halls of Columbine High, Cassie Bernall closed her eyes and clasped her hands in prayer. And, as she bowed her head in prayer, Eric Harris pointed a shotgun at her and asked whether she believed in God. "Yes," she said. And then he killed her. In the days and weeks following Cassie's death, it became widely known that this 17-year-old had been a young woman of incredible faith. Many even called her a martyr. In a statement made at her funeral, Cassie's parents said of her, "Her life was rightly centered around our Lord Jesus. It was for her strong faith in God and His promise of eternal life that she made her stand."

Perhaps some of you, like me, have asked yourself, "Would I have said 'yes' if that gun was pointed at my face?" "Just how strong is my faith in Christ?" "Would I deny Christ if such an opportunity presented itself?" As we get closer to the end of the age, and as persecution against Christians begins to grow in America, we would all do well to ponder these types of questions. There may come a time, if our Lord tarries, that we be required to suffer for the name of Christ. Are we ready? I am not a prophetess, by any means, nor am I the daughter of a prophet, but if we are reading the times and seasons correctly, the end seems to be at hand. As we face the uncertainties of life, and as situations happen like this one in Colorado, will you and I be ready to suffer for The Name? Are you teaching your children to stand fast in their faith as Cassie Bernall did?

As we begin our study in 1 Peter, it is my desire that we approach it with an attitude of sobermindedness. The men and women to whom this letter was originally written were enduring incredible suffering, the kind of suffering that is far different from what most of us have gone through. Peter wrote to these persecuted Christians in order to give them hope and help in the midst of their suffering. In fact, Peter was known as the apostle of hope. His is a letter of great encouragement for men and women of all ages and for all times.

Before we begin examining the first few verses of Peter's letter, I want to share with you some background material that you will find far from boring and perhaps even a bit sobering. It is imperative before we begin studying this book, as well as any book of God's Word, that we answer some basic questions that will aid us in understanding the book.

The first question we ought to ask is: Who wrote 1 Peter? The answer to this question is pretty simple: Peter wrote it. It was the first of two letters Peter wrote, 2 Peter being the other one, which was written toward the end of his life. But even though Peter actually authored the words of this epistle, it is probable that Silvanus or Silas actually penned the words as Peter dictated them. Consider 1 Peter 5:12: "By Silvanus, our faithful brother as I consider him, I have written to you briefly, exhorting and testifying that this is the true grace of God in which you stand." It was not uncommon among New Testament writers to utilize an amanuensis, a person who writes down the words another person speaks. This is probably the situation in Peter's case, because Acts 4:13 states that Peter and John were perceived to be unlearned and ignorant men. Many scholars believe that Peter could not have known classical Greek well enough to write the letter of 1 Peter, so he would have needed an amanuensis.

A second question we should pose is: When was 1 Peter written? Though there are varying ideas concerning when 1 Peter was penned, the most probable date seems to be sometime around AD 65. We do know that within about two years of writing this epistle Peter followed James and Paul in martyrdom, dying for his faith.

Another question to ask, which is actually answered in the epistle itself, is: Where was Peter when he wrote 1 Peter? It appears that Peter was in Babylon, as he states in 1 Peter 5:13, "She who is in Babylon, elect together with you, greets you; and so does Mark, my son." Unlike the apostle Paul, it seems that Peter was not in prison, at least not yet.

A question I often find helpful to ask and answer when interpreting a book of the Bible is: To whom was this particular book written? For the answer to this question, we have only to search as far as the very first verse: "Peter, an apostle of Jesus Christ, To the pilgrims of the Dispersion in Pontus, Galatia, Cappadocia, Asia, and Bithynia." This epistle was written to the pilgrims, or sojourners as your translation might say, who were in the cities of Pontus, Galatia, Cappadocia, Asia and Bithynia. We will discuss this more when we unpack verse 1, but suffice to say here that some scholars think these believers were Jews and Gentiles, yet others think Peter's readers were only Gentiles. We know for sure, though, that it was written to Christians because of Peter's use of the term "elect," found in 1:2 as well as 5:13.

A question that is a personal favorite of mine is the "why" question: Why did Peter write this epistle? Peter's purpose statement is found in 1 Peter 5:10-12. There, he says, "But may the God of all grace, who called us to His eternal glory by Christ Jesus, after you have suffered a while, perfect, establish, strengthen, and settle you. To Him be the glory and the dominion forever and ever. Amen. By

Silvanus, our faithful brother as I consider him, I have written to you briefly, exhorting and testifying that this is the true grace of God in which you stand." Peter desired that his readers remain steadfast amidst their intense suffering and persecution, and he knew this would only be possible by the grace of God. Peter wrote to exhort them and to encourage them as they faced the suffering that was taking place among the Christians.

My friend, the persecution these believers were enduring wasn't like the persecution you and I face in America. Their persecution came under the wicked rule of the emperor Nero. As most rulers do, Nero had a serious problem with pride. He was obsessed with building. But in order to be able to continue his obsession with building, he had to destroy what was already there. So, in AD 64, he set the city of Rome on fire. This man was so determined to burn the city completely to ashes that it has been said that those who tried to extinguish the fire were deliberately stopped, and then he would have men rekindle the fire when it would start to subside. The fire lasted for three days and three nights, and everything was destroyed—homes, idols, temples, everything. So many people became homeless due to the destruction that they began to become resentful toward Nero. But Nero could not have his pride deflated, so he devised an evil plan to use the Christians as a scapegoat; he actually accused them of starting the fire.

Why would Nero blame Christians for this monstrosity? Well, simply put, the Christians were already hated, so it seemed to him like the logical thing to do. But why were Christians hated? There were many reasons, and most of them were the result of slander and rumors circulating at the time. One false report claimed that when Christians partook of the Lord's Supper, they were actually practicing cannibalism, that they were literally eating someone's body and drinking the blood. Another false report claimed that Christians were practicing sexual orgies, which was surmised from the fact that Christians greeted one another with a "holy kiss." Christians were also accused of separating families, which was to some extent true, due to the division that arose within families when some family members chose to follow Christ. Of course, this was something that Christ said would happen, when He said in Matthew 10:34-36, "Do not think that I came to bring peace on earth. I did not come to bring peace but a sword. For I have come to 'set a man against his father, a daughter against her mother, and a daughter-in-law against her mother-in-law'; and 'a man's enemies will be those of his own household.'"

With these rumors already prevalent, and Christians already hated, Nero thought it would be a good idea to just go ahead and blame believers for the destruction of Rome. This false accusation against Christians began a terrible outbreak of persecution against them. It was the most horrible persecution the church had yet faced. It was sadistic. Many Christians were rolled in pitch and set on fire to be used as living torches to light Nero's gardens. He even had some Christians sewed up in the skins of wild animals and would let his dogs tear them from limb to limb while they were still living. One historian writes of this: "Mockery of every sort was added to their deaths. Covered with the skins of beasts, they were torn by dogs and perished, or were nailed to crosses, or were doomed to the flames and burned, to serve as a nightly illumination, when daylight had expired. Nero offered his gardens for the spectacle and was exhibiting a show in the circus, while he mingled with the people in the dress of a charioteer or stood aloft on a car. There arose not a feeling of compassion. It was for one man's cruelty that they were being destroyed."[1]

The persecution became so severe that it was said to be considered illegal to even be a Christian. Christians were considered social misfits. Christian wives were often persecuted by their unsaved heathen husbands, and unsaved masters were cruel to their Christian slaves. Many were executed for the sole reason that they claimed to be Christians. It was under Nero's rule both Peter and Paul lost their lives.

---

[1] William Barclay, *The Letters of James and Peter* (Louisville: John Knox Press, 1976), 160.

The suffering these believers endured was quite different from the suffering most of us endure today. They were persecuted for their faith; they were hated because of their attachment to Christ. Most of our suffering comes in the form of illness, the loss of a loved one, the loss of finances or friendships, and trials like that. And while those experiences are indeed forms of suffering, few of us in this country have experienced the kind of persecution-type-suffering that they endured. We might be called to suffer for the name of Christ! Christ promised we would, and Paul says in 2 Timothy 3:12 that "all who desire to live godly in Christ Jesus will suffer persecution."

As we study this epistle together, maybe the Lord will grant us the privilege of suffering for His name. Paul says in Philippians 1:29 that suffering for Christ is a gift; some of us may soon be given that "gift." It is under these conditions of suffering that Peter writes this letter to encourage believers during their time of distress. Peter's message of hope and courage in the midst of suffering is as applicable to his original readers as it is to us today.

This leads us to the final question: What is the theme of 1 Peter? The theme is steadfastness in time of suffering—thus the name of this study: With the Master in the Fiery Furnace!

I would like to share some brief quotes about 1 Peter and then we will cover the first two verses. One man has said of 1 Peter that, "It is written out of the love of a pastor's heart to help people who were experiencing troubled times and for whom worse things still lay ahead."[2] Another has said, "1 Peter is one of the most moving pieces of persecution literature."[3] Still another, that 1 Peter is "one of the easiest letters in the New Testament to read, for it has never lost its winsome appeal to the human heart."[4] With all these things in mind, let's begin our study of the letter's first two verses.

---

[2] Ibid, 160.
[3] Ibid, 206.
[4] D. Edmond Hiebert, First Peter: *An Expositional Commentary* (Chicago: Moody Press, 1984), 1.

1 Peter 1:1-2

> Peter, an apostle of Jesus Christ, To the pilgrims of the Dispersion in Pontus, Galatia, Cappadocia, Asia, and Bithynia, ²elect according to the foreknowledge of God the Father, in sanctification of the Spirit, for obedience and sprinkling of the blood of Jesus Christ: Grace to you and peace be multiplied.

We have already answered some very important questions about 1 Peter as we considered some of the background material, and as we move into these first two verses we will continue to ask and answer some more questions. I have outlined these verses in this way:

> *Who Wrote 1 Peter?* (v 1a)
> *To Whom was 1 Peter Written?* (vv 1b-2a)
> *What is the Greeting of 1 Peter?* (v 2b)

Let's begin by considering who wrote this epistle, in verse 1.

Who Wrote 1 Peter?

1 Peter 1:1a

> Peter, an apostle of Jesus Christ, (1 Peter 1:1a)

Peter begins this epistle with his name, which is how most of the New Testament books are written. I've often thought that these New Testament writers had a better way of beginning their letters than we do today, because we have to wait till the end of a letter before we know who it's from! In fact, I've noticed the first thing my husband does when he gets a card or letter is look at the end of it to see who it's from. In biblical times, the very beginning of a letter would contain the name of the person sending the letter, then the name or names of the letter's recipients, and then a greeting of some sort. This is exactly the pattern we find here at the beginning of 1 Peter.

So, we know that Peter wrote this letter, but who is Peter exactly? According to John 1:40-42, he was the son of Jonah and the brother of Andrew: "One of the two who heard John speak, and followed Him, was Andrew, Simon Peter's brother. He first found his own brother Simon, and said to him, 'We have found the Messiah' (which is translated, the Christ). And he brought him to Jesus. Now when Jesus looked at him, He said, 'You are Simon the son of Jonah. You shall be called Cephas' (which is translated, A Stone)."

It was Andrew who brought Simon Peter, the fisherman, to the Lord. Peter was married and his wife, evidently, went along with him on his ministry journeys (see Mark 1:29-31 and 1 Corinthians 9:5). Peter's name in the Greek is Petros, which means the rock; this is the name given to him by Jesus in John 1:42 at the beginning of their discipling time together. Prior to that, he was known as Simon. In fact, in Matthew 16:18 Christ tells Simon that he is Peter and upon that rock He will build His church. The Lord called Simon Peter to follow Him and later appointed him to be an apostle. He was certainly one of the leaders among the 12 disciples and seemed to be one of the three closest friends of the Lord, James and John being the other two. Peter was the disciple who seemed to ask all the questions; he was present on the Mount of Transfiguration; he walked on water to meet his Lord, until he became frightened and started to sink and cried out for the Lord to save him; he was present at the Last Supper with the other disciples; he fell asleep during His Lord's final hours of suffering; and he was the one who vowed he would never deny his Lord, and yet he did.

But after Christ's death, resurrection, and ascension, Peter is a changed man, as we read in the book of Acts. By the power of the Holy Spirit, Peter changed from being impulsive and unsteady, to being courageous, a bold preacher of the faith, one who was ready to go to prison for the cause of Christ. The end of his life was marked by suffering, and under Nero's rule Peter was crucified upside down because he felt unworthy to be crucified in the same manner as his Lord. Before Peter's own crucifixion, he watched as his wife was crucified, and as he did, he comforted her with these words: "Remember the Lord! Remember the Lord!"

Another interesting fact about Peter is that he is the only person called by that name in the entire New Testament. There is quite a bit more we can learn about Peter from the Scriptures, but according to our text here, Peter is an apostle of Jesus Christ. The word apostle in the Greek is apostolos, which means to send, and is used to describe one sent from someone else, with appropriate credentials, on a specific mission. Apostles were given special authority from God to do mighty works, and often those mighty works involved doing miraculous things. Peter, of course, was sent from Jesus Christ with the mission of proclaiming the gospel. But notice that Peter does not call attention to himself here in his letter, but to the One who sent him, His Lord and Savior Jesus Christ.

To Whom is 1 Peter Written?

1 Peter 1:1b-2a

> To the pilgrims of the Dispersion in Pontus, Galatia, Cappadocia, Asia, and Bithynia, (1 Peter 1:1b)

We mentioned already that Peter has written this letter *to the pilgrims of the Dispersion in Pontus, Galatia, Cappadocia, Asia, and Bithynia*. To call his readers *pilgrims* is to say that they are strangers who are scattered throughout these areas, those who are dwelling in a strange land and whose thoughts are turned toward home. This Greek word was used to describe Christians who had settled down alongside the unsaved. As God's children, we often feel like strangers in this world, but it really can be even more vivid in our minds if we ever travel internationally. I have been to many countries now, and I've sensed in my travels that I am in heathen nations which are very unfriendly and spiritually dark. It is an odd feeling of being alone and, strangely, it makes the United States look good! And yet, think what heaven will be like compared to the United States? This term, pilgrims, comes up again later in this letter, in 2:11, and the writer to the Hebrews also uses this term in Hebrews 11:13 when he refers to men and woman of great faith as strangers and pilgrims.

Peter says that his readers are pilgrims *of the Dispersion*, which comes from the Greek word diaspora, which means to be scattered. This was the Jews' way of referring to Jews who were living among Gentiles outside of their homeland. It was also used to describe Christians who are not only scattered but also away from their true home, heaven. James uses this term in his greeting in James 1:1 when he writes, "to the twelve tribes which are scattered abroad." Often in scripture the term scattering is used to describe a result of God's judgment. For example, in Ezekiel 20:23, when God is describing the judgment He is going to pour out because of Israel's disobedience, He says He will scatter and disperse them throughout the countries.

Pontus, Galatia, Cappadocia, Asia, and Bithynia were all Roman providences in Asia Minor, what is now present-day Turkey. They're listed in this particular order probably because this would have been the route that was taken as the letter was delivered to its recipients. This area, for some reason, was more prone to attacks on Christians than other areas. We know from verse 2 that these are believers Peter is writing to because he mentions that they are elect.

> elect according to the foreknowledge of God the Father, in sanctification of the Spirit, for obedience and sprinkling of the blood of Jesus Christ: Grace to you and peace be multiplied. (1 Peter 2a)

The term elect *means "to pick out or to select out of a number." And Peter* says that this selecting is *according to the foreknowledge of God the Father*. In the Old Testament, the term elect is used, in Deuteronomy 7:6-8, to describe God selecting Israel from among all the other nations to be His chosen, beloved ones: "For you are a holy people to the LORD your God; the LORD your God has chosen you to be a people for Himself, a special treasure above all the peoples on the face of the earth. The LORD did not set His love on you nor choose you because you were more in number than any other people, for you were the least of all peoples; but because the LORD loves you, and because He would keep the oath which He swore to your fathers, the LORD has brought you out with a mighty hand, and redeemed you from the house of bondage, from the hand of Pharaoh king of Egypt."

Like Israel, we who are followers of the Lord Jesus Christ have been elected before the foundation of the world. John MacArthur puts it this way: "Before the foundation of the world, God placed His love on you, then brought you into His kingdom by granting you saving grace. That's the doctrine of election."[5] The doctrine of election is a wonderful doctrine that should bring humility to all of us. God demonstrated His love to a portion of mankind whom He chose, a people who do not deserve anything but hell.

Peter says that God elected us according to the *foreknowledge* of God. Some people will say that this means God looked ahead in time and saw that we would choose Him and so He based his choosing of us on the knowledge that we would choose Him. Of course, God knew that we would be saved, but that is not the meaning of the text here. For God to choose us based on His foreknowledge does not mean that God chose simply because He knew that some would respond to His call. It means that He took the initiative to choose before and apart from anyone doing anything to deserve it or to influence His decision. None of us would choose God if left to ourselves, but He chooses some for His glory and because of His mercy. We were dead in our trespasses and sins and none of us were seeking after God. In fact, Jesus is very clear in John 6:44, when He says, "No one can come to Me unless the Father who sent Me draws him; and I will raise him up at the last day." Also, the word foreordained, which occurs in verse 20, speaks of a predetermined relationship in the knowledge of God. We get our English word prognosis from this word. God brought you and I salvation by decreeing it ahead of time. He knew before the world was created whom He had elected for salvation, just as it was foreordained for Jesus Christ to come and die for our sins (Acts 2:23).

---

[5]http://www.gty.org/resources/print/daily-devotion/DN562

Peter goes on to say that this electing is *in sanctification of the Spirit, for obedience and sprinkling of the blood of Jesus Christ*. It is a precious thing that all three of the Godhead are involved in our salvation. God the Father chooses us; The Holy Spirit sets us apart from a life of unbelief to a life of faith in the Lord Jesus; and Jesus Christ cleanses us and consecrates us through His blood.

That act of faith is referred to here as *obedience*. This obedience is not the obedience that is required of us after salvation, though. Rather, this obedience is the work of the Holy Spirit in bringing the sinner to the act of faith. It involves both listening to and submitting to what has been heard. Acts 6:7 helps us with this, when it says that "a great many of the priests were obedient to the faith."

What does Peter mean by the *sprinkling of the blood*? In the Old Testament, Moses sprinkled the altar and the people of Israel with the blood of a sacrifice, which was to symbolize the sealing of the covenant between them and God. This practice was a sign of being set apart for service to God. However, Hebrews 9 speaks of a new and better covenant which is not made of the blood of goats and bulls, but of the blood of Christ, which was shed on the cross once and for all to provide eternal redemption for us. This is the wonderful sprinkling of the blood that Peter is referring to, the precious blood of Jesus which washes away our sins!

As we close, let's answer the question, "What is the greeting of Peter's letter?"

What is the Greeting of 1 Peter?

1 Peter 1:2b

Grace to you, and peace be multiplied. (1 Peter 1:2b)

Grace is God's unmerited favor toward us. It is the divine enabling that He grants to those who have yielded to His Lordship. Peter is going to mention grace 10 times in this epistle alone. Peace is one of the blessings of salvation, one of the results of receiving God's grace, and is produced by the Holy Spirit. It is interesting that Peter sends greetings for both grace and peace and adds that they be *multiplied*. Why? Because these readers would need an abundance of both grace and peace as they go through intense suffering and persecution. What a great beginning to a great letter of hope and encouragement.

As we close this lesson, I want to give you a brief preview of what we will be studying together in the coming lessons, the Lord willing. Some of the *doctrinal* questions we will be answering include: What is election? (Hopefully, we answered that some in this lesson!) What is the believer's hope? What does it mean that we are living stones and a spiritual priesthood? Did God really create some of mankind solely for the purpose of destruction? What in the world does 1 Peter 3:18-22 mean? What does it mean that judgment must begin at the house of God?

We will also answer some *practical* questions: How should believers face suffering? Why do we suffer? How does one live holy, as He is holy? How does a Christian submit to a wicked government? How does a Christian wife win her lost husband to Christ? Should women wear jewelry? How is it possible to rejoice during persecution? How do I live in a God-honoring way under persecution and opposition? Does God really use suffering for our good? Why should I cover another person's sin? How do I discovering my spiritual gifts and use them? Do I really need to be hospitable without complaining? Why it is better to suffer for Christ, than to suffer for being a busybody? What does a good pastor look like? How do I fight the devil?

If you are a child of the Lord, then it's likely that sometime during our study you will be called on to suffer for His sake. Are you ready? Are you willing? Regardless of what you think may happen this year or in the near future, we all must agree that the world is becoming morally corrupt at a rapid pace. When will God's patience with us turn into God's wrath upon us? And what will you do if that day comes that you might have to die for your faith? Let's commit ourselves to be with the Master in the Fiery Furnace!

Questions to Consider
Grace in the Midst of the Fiery Furnace
1 Peter 1:1-2

1. Read all of 1 Peter and write down the verses that are difficult for you to understand. (Hold on to this list; it will be important come the end of our study!)

2. What facts do you already know about the apostle Peter?

3. Memorize 1 Peter 1:2.

4. (a) Look up *at least* 10 of the following references, and list some of the facts you discover about Peter. (b) What do you glean about his character from these verses?
Matthew 4:18-22; 10:2; 14:22-33; 17:1-13, 24-27; 18:21; 19:27-30; 26:30-75; Mark 5:35-43; 8:27-33; 16:6-7; Luke 5:1-11; 12:35-41; 22:7-13; 24:1-12; John 1:40-42; 6:66-71; 13:1-38; 18:10-11; 20:1-10; 21:1-25; Galatians 1:18; 2:1-14.

5. *Skim* the first 12 chapters of Acts to gain more knowledge of the apostle Peter and write down what you learn about him.

6. Locate the places mentioned in 1 Peter 1:1 on a biblical map.

7. How would you explain the doctrine of election?

8. (a) What do you hope to glean from this study in 1 Peter? (b) Why not pause now and ask God to help you to grow in the areas that He so desires. Write a request to be shared with your group.

9. Spend some time this week thanking God that He elected you to salvation. Be prepared to share how this election (so great salvation) has blessed and changed your life.

Chapter 2

Four Blessings of Our Redemption
1 Peter 1:3-7

The gospel of Jesus Christ is amazing! To think that Christ died for our sins and that He was buried and raised again according to the Scriptures is marvelous indeed! To think that if we repent of our sins and turn our lives over to His Lordship, we will have eternal life in heaven with Him is amazing!

It is likely that each of us has heard of this amazing gospel at some point in our lives. Perhaps for you, the gospel was shared like this: "God has a wonderful plan for your life!" or "Come to Jesus and your life will be full of peace and joy, and you will receive the added bonus of eternal life!" or "Repent and embrace the Lordship of Christ and be saved from eternal damnation!" How many of you heard something like this: "Turn to Christ and get ready for persecution!" or "Embracing Christ as Lord means taking up your cross, and even the possibility of separation from family and close friends!"? Which of these presentations is true?

Really, they're both true! When you think about the life of a Christian, there are indeed many wonderful and rich blessings, and yet there are many trials, troubles, and persecutions! In this second lesson in our study of 1 Peter, Peter will remind his readers of four blessings that come as a result of their redemption. Peter is not unbalanced in what the Christian faith is all about. Christianity involves blessings beyond measure, but it also involves difficulties at times, as these readers well knew. Let's read verses 3-7 to see what Peter says.

1 Peter 1:3-7

> Blessed be the God and Father of our Lord Jesus Christ, who according to His abundant mercy has begotten us again to a living hope through the resurrection of Jesus Christ from the dead, ⁴to an inheritance incorruptible and undefiled and that does not fade away, reserved in heaven for you, ⁵who are kept by the power of God through faith for salvation ready to be revealed in the last time. ⁶In this you greatly rejoice, though now for a little while, if need be, you have been grieved by various trials, ⁷that the genuineness of your faith, being much more precious than gold that perishes, though it is tested by fire, may be found to praise, honor, and glory at the revelation of Jesus Christ.

In this lesson, we'll learn of four blessings of our redemption:

> *Promised Hope* (v 3)
> *Perpetual Inheritance* (v 4)
> *Powerful Protection* (v 5)
> *Precious Trials* (vv 6-7)

Promised Hope

1 Peter 1:3

> Blessed be the God and Father of our Lord Jesus Christ, who according to His abundant mercy has begotten us again to a living hope through the resurrection of Jesus Christ from the dead. (1 Peter 1:3)

Peter begins verse 3 by saying *blessed be the God and Father of our Lord Jesus Christ*. What does it mean to be *blessed*? The Greek word is eulogetos, from which we get our English word eulogize or eulogy. It refers to a person or thing being well spoken of, and it would involve praise or celebration with praises. We all have probably been to funerals where a eulogy is given. This event is a time to speak well (hopefully) of the deceased, to tell of the good things that person did or said in his or her lifetime. The Jews of Peter's day began most of their prayers with the introductory thought: "Blessed art Thou, O God." But Peter modifies that blessing a bit; he says blessed be the *God and Father of our Lord Jesus Christ*. This particular phrase was used to describe God, and it was distinctly used by the Christian. *God* is our Father, and He is the *Father of the Lord Jesus Christ*.

Peter goes on to give the reason behind the blessing that we give to God: our living hope because of His resurrection. Peter puts it this way: *who according to His abundant mercy has begotten us again to a living hope through the resurrection of Jesus Christ from the dead*. Ladies, this is the first blessing of our redemption: our promised hope. Peter states that it is by *His abundant mercy*, or compassion, that we have been given this promised hope. It was God's kindness that brought salvation to you and me. God saw our miserable condition and felt compassion and pity toward us. As Titus 3:5 says, "not by works of righteousness which we have done, but according to His mercy He saved us, through the washing of regeneration and renewing of the Holy Spirit." Peter could have simply used the word *mercy*, but instead he uses the words *abundant* mercy, which means that God's mercy is large and plenteous. As the songwriter says, "There's a wideness in God's mercy, like the wideness in the sea." [6] If we know Christ as our Savior, then we know that His mercy is abundant, especially as we grow in understanding the depth of our sin.

Peter helps us see that this mercy is active. He says that in God's abundant mercy He has *begotten us again to a living hope*. The word *begotten* means to be born again. This is a term Peter uses again in verse 23, where he says, "having been born again, not of corruptible seed but incorruptible, through the word of God which lives and abides forever." If you are a Christian, then you have not only experienced being born in the physical realm, but you have also been born again in the spiritual realm by God the Father unto a *living hope. Hope* is a word that means confident expectancy. This hope is active because it is alive! It is also a living hope because it is forever, it is eternal, and it will never die.

---

[6] Words by Frederick W. Faber.

This reality of the believer possessing living hope is in stark contrast to the unbeliever who has no hope, whose life is meaningless, cold and dead. Paul describes the state of the unbeliever in Ephesians 2:12 as "having no hope, and without God in the world." In contrast, in 1 Thessalonians 4:13, Paul writes regarding those who have died in Christ, and he tells the church to not sorrow as those who have no hope. People of the world have no hope, but those who are in Christ are born again, and because of that, they have a living hope, and for them the best is yet to come! One man has said, "A child of God has no right to look on the dark side of things, and to look for the worst to happen to him. As the object of God's care and love, he has the right to look for the best to come to him and to look on the bright side of things."[7] The hope of eternal life in a true Christian is a hope that keeps him alive spiritually, quickens him, supports him, and encourages him on his journey toward heaven.

How was this living hope provided? This living hope is made possible because of *the resurrection of Jesus Christ*, as Peter says. Peter knew about this personally because he was one of the disciples who had witnessed the resurrection of Jesus Christ. Up until the time of Christ's death, the disciples had great hope that Jesus was the Messiah that would redeem Israel, but when Christ died on the cross and was buried, the disciples appeared to have lost all hope. The hope they'd had died with their Master, but after His resurrection, all their hope was restored! Ladies, our living hope is possible because of the resurrection of Jesus Christ. Christianity is the only "religion" who has a risen Savior. Jesus said in John 14:19, "Because I live, you will live also." Paul explains in 1 Corinthians 15:14, "if Christ is not risen, then our preaching is empty and your faith is also empty." And in verse 19, he says, "If in this life only we have hope in Christ, we are of all men the most pitiable" (1 Corinthians 15:19). It is interesting that Peter was known as the apostle of hope. Paul was known as the apostle of faith; John, as the apostle of love; and Peter, as the apostle of hope. In verse four, Peter elaborates on what this living hope entails. He also gives his readers the second blessing of their redemption.

---

[7] Kenneth S. Wuest, *Wuest's Word Studies from the Greek New Testament* (Grand Rapids: Wm.B. Eerdmans Publishing Company, 1980), 21.

Perpetual Inheritance

1 Peter 1:4

> to an inheritance incorruptible and undefiled and that does not fade away, reserved in heaven for you, (1 Peter 1:4)

The second blessing of our redemption is that we have a perpetual inheritance. When Peter says we have *an inheritance*, it means both we have a title to our inheritance and that we have the full possession of the inheritance. We have that inheritance now—it's ours—and will realize the full possession of it when we get to heaven. Paul says in Romans 8:17 that if we are children of God, then we are joint heirs of God and Christ.

Peter goes on to list four characteristics of this inheritance. First, he says this inheritance is *incorruptible*, a word which means undecaying or unravaged by any invading army. This means that absolutely nothing can get to our inheritance! Jesus put it well in Matthew 6:19-20 when he said, "Do not lay up for yourselves treasures on earth, where moth and rust destroy and where thieves break in and steal; but lay up for yourselves treasures in heaven, where neither moth nor rust destroys and where thieves do not break in and steal." And Paul explains in 1 Corinthians 9:25 that our crown in heaven is incorruptible.

The second characteristic of our inheritance is that it is *undefiled*. The word defiled means to color something by painting or staining it. So, to say that something is undefiled is to say that it is free from any stain. It is not polluted, not soiled, not stained with evil; it is pure. Revelation 21:27 says that in heaven, "there shall by no means enter it anything that defiles."

Thirdly, our inheritance does *not fade away*. This means that it cannot be extinguished, like a fire that will not go out. Our inheritance will not pass away or wither and die like the grass and flowers do (see verses 23-25!). Our inheritance cannot wither; it is always in bloom, and it never loses its beauty.

The fourth characteristic of our blessed inheritance is that it is *reserved in heaven for you*. This literally reads, "which has been reserved," indicating that our inheritance has been reserved by God for His own from the beginning of time down to the present. It has the idea of being laid up and kept, being guarded in safe deposit. It is under constant surveillance. Jesus told his disciples when they were going through a troubling time that He was going to heaven to prepare a place just for them (John 14:1-3), and, ladies, He has done the same for us! Do you know that you have a place in heaven reserved just for you, that is incorruptible, undefiled, and will never fade away?

It's likely that Peter's readers would have understood these terms because of their own understanding of the Promised Land, which was their inheritance passed down from their forefathers. Unlike that land, which was corruptible and ravaged many times by invading armies, their eternal inheritance was one of lasting peace and joy. Unlike the Promised Land, which would be often defiled by the impure worship of idols, their inheritance had a purity which sin cannot touch. The Promised Land had beautiful flowers, but even the most beautiful flowers would fade and die, but the inheritance in glory will never fade and never change. Their inheritance in the Promised Land was only a temporary reservation, limited to this earthly life, but the eternal Promise Land in Glory is a permanent reservation with no end. And Peter says at the end of this verse that all of this is *for you*. All of this is for you and for me! Incredible! Sounds wonderful, doesn't it? Can't wait to get there? It sounds too good to be true, doesn't it? And it is without the power of God, as Peter writes in verse 5. Here, he gives us the third blessing of our redemption.

Powerful Protection

1 Peter 1:5

> who are kept by the power of God through faith for salvation ready to be revealed in the last time. (1 Peter 1:5)

The third blessing of our redemption is that it is powerfully protected. Peter tells us in this verse that our salvation is *kept,* or preserved, by God's power. The word kept is a military term which means to guard or protect. The present participle indicates something that is continually protected. The guard never goes off duty or changes his position with another guard. Rather, He is on duty 24 hours a day, year in and year out, until we arrive to our reserved place. These words would be so encouraging to the suffering Christians Peter was writing to; they could take courage in the fact that no matter what happened to them physically, it did not matter because their souls and their salvation were preserved until glory. No harm can come to a believer that God does not allow; no harm can come to a believer that is not under His watchful eye and for His glory. This keeping is by a powerful God. In fact, the word *power* is dunamis, from which we get our English word dynamite. It is a miraculous power that keeps us, the same power that resurrected God's Son. And this same power will protect His people until they come to a full possession of their inheritance.

Now, Peter says that even though we are kept by God's power, we have a responsibility, and that responsibility is faith. He puts it this way: *through faith for salvation.* How are we kept or guarded? By *faith.* Our faith lays hold of this power. Our faith is the means by which God's dynamite power is activated, and this faith is exercised until we get to heaven. We have a human responsibility to act on our faith as God gives out His protective power. Hebrews 11:6 says, "But without faith it is impossible to please Him, for he who comes to God must believe that He is, and that He is a rewarder of those who diligently seek Him."

Peter goes on to say that the outcome of our faith, which releases God's power, is *salvation* which *is ready to be revealed in the last time.* What does it mean that this salvation is ready to be revealed in the last time? To be *revealed* means to take off the cover; to disclose; to unveil. Who or what is it that is ready to be revealed? This is a reference to our salvation, which is a term that is synonymous with inheritance. Our inheritance is ready to be unveiled when He will draw back the veil that hides our human eyes from salvation. As 1 John 3:2 states: "Beloved, now we are God; and it has not yet been revealed what we shall be, but we know that when He is revealed, we shall be like Him, for we shall see Him as He is." And 1 Corinthians 2:9 says, "But as it is written: 'Eye has not seen, nor ear heard, nor have entered into the heart of man the things which God has prepared for those who love Him.'" The inheritance is prepared for us, but its glories will not be revealed until the last time.

Peter now ends this section with a fourth blessing of our eternal redemption—one we may not realize is a blessing but, in fact, it is.

Precious Trials

1 Peter 1:6-7

> In this you greatly rejoice, though now for a little while, if need be, you have been grieved by various trials, (1 Peter 1:6)

When we read this verse, the question naturally comes to mind, "In what are we to rejoice?" Some think the rejoicing mentioned here is referring to the last time when we shall have our glorified bodies; others think it is referring to our salvation. Both are true. Either way, we are to *greatly rejoice*, which means to be exceedingly glad, to jump for joy, to be exuberantly jubilant. And Peter calls his readers to rejoice even though they were going through various trials! He puts it this way, "though now for a little while, if need be, you have been grieved by various trials."

Like some of us, it's possible that some in Peter's audience were beginning to wonder if trials were simply a constant part of everyday life. Peter assures them that these trials are just for *a little while*, just for a season. I often tell people that I long for some normalcy in life, and then I am reminded that trials are the normalcy of this life. But our life here is just a season compared to eternity in Heaven. Second Corinthians 4:17 tells us that "our light affliction, which is but for a moment, is working for us a far more exceeding and eternal weight of glory." Our trials are brief, especially when we consider that the Bible says our life is but a vapor that appears for a little while and then vanishes away.

Peter adds to this statement a strange little phrase, *if need be*, which means if it is needed. This is not a hypothetical statement Peter is making; it is an affirmative statement. In other words, it is a reality that we need trials. In fact, some of us need more trials than others. Let's take, for example, the case of one who slips away from their devotion to God; it may be that God deems it necessary to chasten that person by some form of suffering to bring them back into right relationship to Him. Psalm 119:67 and 71 say, "Before I was afflicted I went astray, but now I keep Your word," and "It is good for me that I have been afflicted, that I may learn Your statutes." The writer to the Hebrews tells us that those whom the Lord loves He chastens (Hebrews 12:6). Now, of course, not all trials are a result of sin, not all trials are for our chastening; many are for the testing of our faith, which we will see in a moment.

Peter describes these trials not as a picnic but as *grievous* or heavy, which means to be sad. Hebrews 12:11 says that no chastening is joyful but is grievous. Paul says in 2 Corinthians 1:8 that he was undergoing so much hardship and under such pressure, even beyond his ability to endure, that he despaired even of life. Even our Lord, during the greatest trial of His life, facing the cross, experienced this; it states in Matthew 26:37 that He was sorrowful and deeply distressed. Trials can produce a real heaviness in our spirit. They can produce genuine mental distress. But a true Christian can also take delight in that heaviness of trials knowing that those trials can be used by God for His glory.

Peter goes on to say that these trials are *various*, or manifold, which means many-colored or variegated. The word is used to describe the skin of a leopard, which has different-colored veining, like marble, or an embroidered robe, like Joseph's coat of many colors. It is not necessarily referring to the number of trials, but to the different kinds of trials. Trials are diverse. James 1:2 says, "My brethren, count it all joy when you fall into various trials." We differ in the type of trials we go through. If we took a poll of a hundred believers as to the sufferings and trials they were going through, we would probably get many different answers. Some may be going through dark gray or black trials, like the loss of a loved one, a divorce, or the loss of a job. Some are going through what we might call pale yellow trials, like a broken-down car, an argument with a spouse, or a sick child. Our trials are indeed varied.

Since we're talking about trials, it would be good for us to define just what they are. A trial means a putting to proof and to examine. A trial is a test to see if something or someone can stand up to strain or pressure. These may come directly from God or may be allowed under His permissive will to come to us from Satan, or they may come to us as the natural result of our own sinful choices. All are intended to prove our faith, to see if it is genuine. If trials prompt you to doubt God or to waver in your faith, that is a real danger. Trials are sent to push us closer to Him, not to doubt Him or to drive us further away from Him. Many of us respond to our trials with fear, and yet we should welcome them as opportunities to prove that our faith is real. Paul tells us in Philippians 1:29 that trials are gifts: "For to you it has been granted on behalf of Christ, not only to believe in Him, but also to suffer for His sake." Remember Abraham and his son Isaac? It says in Genesis 22:1 that God tested Abraham. God was testing Abraham to see if he really believed God, and the test God gave Abraham was to offer his son Isaac as a sacrifice on the altar. Abraham obeyed; he took Isaac to the top of the mountain and prepared the fire and the wood, and then took his son and laid him on the altar. Abraham was about to kill Isaac with the knife when God stopped him and told him not to do it, because by his willingness to obey God, even to the point of killing his own son, God knew—and Abraham knew—that Abraham feared God.

Job is another good example. God allowed Satan to come and wreak havoc in Job's life—as a test. Satan was allowed by God to take Job's children, his wealth, and his health. Even his dear wife told him to curse God and die. And yet, the Scriptures tell us that in all this Job did not sin with his mouth (Job 2:10). This was a test for Job, specifically instituted by God. Now, I am not saying that God is going to ask you to endure such severe testing, but He may; the question you and I should ponder is, "Will we pass the test?"

At this point, you may be wondering why we even have to have trials. Why can't life just be a big bowl of cherries? How come trials have to be a part of this redemption package? There is a purpose for our sufferings and Peter gives two reasons for it, in verse 7.

> that the genuineness of your faith, being much more precious than gold that perishes, though it is tested by fire, may be found to praise, honor, and glory at the revelation of Jesus Christ. (1 Peter 1:7)

Here, Peter gives the first purpose of our trials, and that is to test the reality of our faith. A genuine Christian will go through a trial and in the end, however rocky the journey may be to get there, he or she will still be holding on to their faith in God. In fact, James in his epistle talks about a man who goes through a trial wavering in his faith, and James says that man won't receive anything from the Lord. And in the larger context, James is talking about that man's salvation. That man isn't even redeemed. I have seen some "Christians" go through trials and it is heartbreaking to watch them stumble and fall, often getting mad at God or even abandoning faith in God altogether. My friend, we need to keep in mind that these Christians were undergoing tremendous suffering for the name of Christ. Their trials were not sick kids, broken washing machines or air conditioners or cars, or an argument with their mate. Their trials included slander, being robbed of their homes, losing their employment, being tortured and even, for some, facing certain death.

Peter says this suffering you are going through is *much more precious than gold that perishes*, which means that trials are extremely valuable to our faith. Gold can be destroyed, but our faith cannot. The picture Peter puts before us is of a goldsmith who would liquify gold in intense heat. The impurities would then rise to the top and be skimmed off. And when the goldsmith had so refined the gold that he would be able to see his own reflection in the liquid, then he would remove the gold from the fire, for then it would be truly pure gold. So it is with trials. God puts us through sufferings, through intense heat, so to speak, with the intent that as the ugly sin rises to the top it is removed from our lives. Then our faith is purified, and then we mirror the reflection of Jesus Christ. In fact, later on in 1 Peter 4:12, Peter refers to trials as being fiery. The Psalmist describes it like this, in Psalm 66:10-12: "For You, O God, have tested us; you have refined us as silver is refined. You brought us into the net; you laid affliction on our backs. You have caused men to ride over our heads; we went through fire and through water; but You brought us out to rich fulfillment." A favorite verse of mine that I like to use to encourage others during their trials is Job 23:10 where Job states, "But He knows the way that I take; when He has tested me, I shall come forth as gold." Now, here is a guy who has lost all his children, his health, and his wealth, even his friends were nothing but a bunch of miserable comforters, and his dear wife told him to curse God and die. And yet, Job says, "God knows what He is doing, and when He is finished I will come forth as gold." Can you say that about what you are going through? Do you believe it? Can you look at past sufferings in your life and say, "Yes, I came forth as gold through that!"? Granted, sometimes we can look back and see the purpose of our trials and other times we don't see the purpose, but we can be confident that heaven will reveal to us what God's divine purpose was.

Not only are trials sent to test us, but trials are also too sent for the glory of God. Peter puts it this way: *that we may be found to praise, honor, and glory at the revelation of Jesus Christ.* Genuine faith will produce *praise, honor, and glory* to the Lord even as we are going through trials. I have seen Christians go through tremendous suffering and bring such glory to God that it encourages me deeply and I stand amazed. I also have seen Christians going through trials complaining all the way and bringing such dishonor to the Lord.

We can also endure any trial knowing that we will someday receive praise, honor, and glory from our Lord. Peter perhaps is recalling here what the Lord said in Matthew 5:11-12, "Blessed are you when they revile and persecute you, and say all kinds of evil against you falsely for My sake. Rejoice and be exceedingly glad, for great is your reward in heaven, for so they persecuted the prophets who were before you." What does Romans 8:18 say? "For I consider that the sufferings of this present time are not worthy to be compared with the glory which shall be revealed in us."

Peter encourages the believers he is writing to that the trials they're enduring have been sent to test the reality of their faith and to bring glory to God, and that in the passing of these tests, the reality of their commitment to follow Christ will be proven, and one day they will receive their great reward in heaven, their eternal inheritance.

Summary

In Peter's opening words, we find four blessings of our inheritance:

1. *Promised Hope* (v 3): When you consider your salvation do you focus on the fact that you have a promised living hope? Our living hope isn't an "I hope so," but an "I know so!"

2. *Perpetual Inheritance* (v 4): Are you laying up treasure for that eternal inheritance? Are you known as a woman who is investing her life in the eternal or the temporal? Or is your focus on some earthy inheritance that you hope to get someday?

3. *Powerful Protection* (v 5): Do you believe that God has the power to keep you until that day? Have you thanked him for the fact He is keeping you until that day?

4. *Precious Trials* (vv 6-7): Do you look at your trials as precious gifts from God or as dirty rotten deals? How do you respond to your trials? Do you grit your teeth and bear it? Or do you look at trials as opportunities to reflect Christ, as opportunities to be joyful in the Lord, as opportunities to praise him, and as opportunities to prove your faith is the real thing? For most of us, our trials really do not

compare to the ones these readers were going through, and yet the challenge was the same for them. Every Christian reading this letter in Peter's day was in continual danger of losing his life. For the word was then, "Renounce Jesus and live; cleave to him and die!" Have you thanked God for the tests he has brought you through and those He will bring you through?

What wonderful blessings we can thank God for—promised hope, perpetual inheritance, powerful protection, and precious trials! No wonder Peter began with "Blessed be the God and Father of our Lord Jesus Christ!" It is that same God and Father who is also our Master and He is with us every step of the way as we walk with the Master through the fiery furnace!

Questions to Consider

Four Blessings of our Redemption
1 Peter 1:3-7

1. (a) Read 1 Peter 1:3-7. What do you learn about God the Father from this passage? (b) What do you learn about God the Son?

2. Peter says in 1 Peter 1:3 that we have been begotten or born again. Read John 3:1-21 and answer the following questions. (a) Who did not understand this concept? (b) How did Jesus answer his troubling questions? (c) What example from nature did Jesus use to help Nicodemus understand? (d) According to John 3:15-16, how is one born again? (e) Have you been born again?

3. Memorize 1 Peter 1:6.

4. (a) What does Peter say in 1 Peter 1:4 about our inheritance? (b) Read Revelation 21 and 22 and make note of the characteristics of our inheritance.

5. (a) Why should we rejoice in our trials, according to 2 Corinthians 12:9-10; Galatians 5:22; Philippians 3:3; Philippians 4:4; James 1:2-3; and 1 Peter 4:12-14? (b) Does the word rejoice describe you when going through trials?

6. What do you think it means to be kept by the power of God? (1 Peter 1:5)

7. (a) If you were under terrible persecution, as the early Christians were, how do you think you would receive 1 Peter 1:6-7? (b) How would it be an encouragement? (c) How is it an encouragement now in your trials?

8. (a) Recall a time in your life when you went through a trial. (b) How was it used to glorify God and strengthen your faith?

9. Using 1 Peter 1:6-7, write a prayer asking God to help you in your current trial. For example: "Dear Lord, help me to greatly rejoice as I am undergoing persecution for sharing my faith with my family member," or, "Help me, Lord, to see this trial as part of your refining process in my life."

Chapter 3

The Importance of the Prophets
1 Peter 1:8-12

One of the things I remember from my childhood growing up in a Baptist minister's home was the New Year's Eve services. They were always an enjoyable time for me, and a great way to bring in the New Year! I recall that my father would ask how many of us had ever read through the entire Bible. The show of hands was usually pathetic. He would then go on to challenge his flock to read through the Bible in the coming year. Since then, I've been places where the same question has been asked that my dad asked on New Year's Eve, and, unfortunately, the response is usually that only a few individuals claim they have read the 66 letters that God wrote to them. These books are what we call the Holy Bible. In fact, the first time I meet with a woman for the purpose of discipleship, one of the first things I generally ask is whether she's ever read through the Scriptures. I have been sorely disappointed over the years to find that it is rare for me to meet a woman who has ever read those 66 letters God wrote her, prior to me challenging her to do so. Some say they've read the New Testament or portions of it, but when I bring up the Old Testament, they look bewildered at the thought! The Old Testament?! You must be kidding, right?!

Perhaps you also have never read through the Bible. Perhaps you're even wondering why you should read the Old Testament. Why is it so important? Don't we live under the New Covenant? Yes. Yes, we do. But God's revelation of Himself to you and me is progressive. In other words, He starts revealing Himself in the pages of Genesis, not Matthew, and He ends His revelation of Himself in the book of Revelation. If you only read the New Testament, then did you know that you are missing out on more than half of God's revelation of Himself? The Old Testament is rich with examples of God's character; the doctrine of salvation; numerous examples for us to follow, as well as many to avoid; the history and genealogy of Israel; various prophecies, some which have already been fulfilled and some which are still to be fulfilled in the future. There are more than 1200 prophecies in the Old Testament alone, and 26% of our Bible is prophetic. The prophets were a major part of the Old Testament. Some of the most exciting things that those prophets predicted were the sufferings and the glory of our Lord Jesus Christ, as well as the grace that would come to us through Him. Consider how Peter puts it in verses 8-12.

1 Peter 1:8-12

> whom having not seen you love. Though now you do not see Him, yet believing, you rejoice with joy inexpressible and full of glory, ^{9}receiving the end of your faith—the salvation of your souls. ^{10}Of this salvation the prophets have inquired and searched carefully, who prophesied of the grace that would come to you, ^{11}searching what, or what manner of time, the Spirit of Christ who was in them was indicating when He testified beforehand the sufferings of Christ and the glories that would follow. ^{12}To them it was revealed that, not to themselves, but to us they were ministering the things which now have been reported to you through those who have preached the gospel to you by the Holy Spirit sent from heaven—things which angels desire to look into.

In these verses, we'll learn what should be

> *Our Attitudes toward the Risen Christ* (vv 8-9) *and Our Attitude toward the Righteous Prophets* (vv 10-12).

Peter ended verse 7 by talking about the appearing of Jesus Christ, and he continues in verse 8 by telling us what our attitudes should be toward this risen Christ.

Our Attitudes toward the Risen Christ

1 Peter 1:8-9

> whom having not seen you love. Though now you do not see Him, yet believing, you rejoice with joy inexpressible and full of glory, (1 Peter 1:8)

Peter begins verse 8 with the word *whom*, which is a reference back to Jesus Christ, who is mentioned in verse 7. Peter says you *have not seen Him*, which means you have never even had a glimpse of Him. Most, if not all, of Peter's readers would never have seen the Lord Jesus Christ. But as Peter penned these words, he may have been thinking back to some words Jesus spoke after His resurrection. John 20 tells us that Jesus appeared to the disciples after His resurrection. Thomas wasn't present the first time Jesus appeared, but he was when Jesus came back eight days later. When Jesus appeared to Thomas, he didn't believe that it was really Jesus, so Jesus encouraged him to not only look upon His wounds but to put his hand on them. When Thomas did as Jesus asked, Thomas responded with, "My Lord and my God!" (John 20:28), and Jesus responded, "Thomas, because you have seen Me, you have believed. Blessed are those who have not seen and yet have believed" (John 20:29). Peter and Thomas had seen Jesus, but most of those to whom Peter was writing had never seen Jesus in the flesh. And yet, we do not have to see Him to love Him. Paul says in 2 Corinthians 5:7, "For we walk by faith, not by sight." And John tells us in 1 John 4:19-20, "We love Him because He first loved us. If someone says, 'I love God,' and hates his brother, he is a liar; for he who does not love his brother whom he has seen, how can he love God whom he has not seen?"

So, Peter says, even though you haven't seen Him, you *love* Him. This word for love is agape, and it refers to a love that outwardly demonstrates the preciousness of the person being loved. My friend, just like Peter's first readers, you and I have not seen Jesus either, but if we know Him, then we too love Him. Do you love Him? Oh, I pray that your love for the Lord is genuine and that it will grow more and more with each passing day! *This should be our first attitude toward the risen Christ—we should love Him.* Every once in a while, you'll have someone tell you about a family member or a friend of theirs that you've never met, and yet even before you meet them you feel like you know them and already love them. Most of the time it is difficult to love someone whom you've never met, but to love the Lord who loved us first and gave His life for us that we might live forever—how can we not love someone like that?

Perhaps you're reading this, and you know that you don't really love the Lord. If that is the case, then it is likely that you do not know Him because loving the Lord is one of the signs of a true believer. The apostle John states in 1 John 5:1, "Whoever believes that Jesus is the Christ is born of God, and everyone who loves Him who begot also loves him who is begotten of Him." Jesus said in John 8:42, "If God were your Father, you would love Me, for I proceeded forth and came from God; nor have I come of Myself, but He sent Me." And Paul tells us in 1 Corinthians 16:22, "If anyone does not love the Lord Jesus Christ, let him be accursed. O Lord, come!"

There is a second attitude Peter tells us that we must have toward the risen Christ. Not only do we love Him, but Peter says even though we cannot see Him, we believe. *Belief is the second attitude we are to have toward the risen Christ. To believe* in Christ means to entrust one's spiritual well-being to Christ. Believing here is in the present tense, which describes a habitual activity. It is not simply a mental assent to the works of Christ; it is belief that changes the nature of who you are from the inside out. It is a belief that submits to His Lordship! It is a faith that trusts Him in the midst of suffering and difficulties, in the good times and in the bad.

Because of one's love for Christ, because of one's belief in Him, Peter says something wonderful is produced in us. He says *you rejoice with joy inexpressible and full of glory!* To *rejoice* is to jump for joy, and *joy inexpressible* is a cheerfulness or calm delight that is incapable of being put into words. Our affection for Christ, Whom we have not seen but we love and believe in, should cause us to have such joy that we cannot even describe it. The song on our lips should be, "Oh, for a thousand tongues to sing my great

Redeemer's praise!" which was inspired by Charles Wesley when another Christian brother expressed his spiritual joy in this manner: "Oh, Brother Wesley, the Lord has done so much for my life. Had I a thousand tongues, I would praise Christ Jesus with every one of them!"[8] *My dear sister, this is the third attitude we should have towards the risen Christ—we should rejoice in Him!*

Peter says this joy is also *full of glory.* You might wonder what that means. It is a term which means glorified joy. The word is used in Exodus 34:29 to describe the glory of Moses's countenance after he received the 10 commandments, which was so bright that the people could not look upon his face. Just as Moses' encounter with God on the mount left him full of glory, so also should our walk with God fill us with glory. People should look at us and see a difference in not only our attitude, which is joyful, but also our countenance. I have been around people that radiate with the glory of God—and, my friend, that joy is possible in the midst of trials and suffering. When we were going through the Coronavirus Pandemic, it was amazing to see so many believers not living in fear but in joy. Remember, these believers Peter was writing to were undergoing severe persecution and yet he tells them to walk in joy.

What is this source of this joy? Is it a hot fudge sundae or a day at the beach? No, it is something that is not a temporal pleasure but an eternal pleasure. Peter says in verse 9 it is the salvation of our souls. He writes,

> receiving the end of your faith—the salvation of your souls. (1 Peter 1:9)

The idea behind the term *receiving* is that we receive what has been promised to us. It has the idea of taking care of or providing for someone, bringing them home with a view to take care of them. This salvation is something that is promised to us because of our faith in Christ. We Christians right now possess our salvation, but the full possession of it will be in the future (v 5)—as Peter puts it,

---

[8] Kenneth W. Osbeck, *Amazing Grace: 365 Inspiring Hymn Stories for Daily Devotions* (Grand Rapids: Kregel Publications, 1990). Pg 274.

the end of your faith, the salvation of your souls. So, *the salvation of your souls* refers to the prize or the reward that these believers would someday receive. This is also the reward for which you and I are waiting for. *The end of your faith* is that which will culminate in glory with the salvation of our souls from eternal damnation. It's what the writer to the Hebrews is referring to in Hebrews 12:2, when he says, "Looking unto Jesus, the author and finisher of our faith." What an encouragement this would be to these believers as they were undergoing such suffering—to know that the end result would be eternal glory!

What are the attitudes that we should have toward the Risen Christ? Peter says we should love Him, believe in Him, and rejoice in Him. And all of this is not just for right now, but it is for all eternity; the end result will be the salvation of our souls for all eternity! Peter now elaborates on this salvation, in verse 10, and shifts from focusing upon the risen Christ to the righteous prophets, in verses 10-12.

Our Attitude toward the Righteous Prophets

1 Peter 1:10-12

> Of this salvation the prophets have inquired and searched carefully, who prophesied of the grace that would come to you, (1 Peter 1:10)

As Peter is continuing to write about salvation, he mentions the *prophets* inquired and searched carefully about this salvation. Since Peter is talking about prophets, let's define who they were. A prophet was one who spoke forth openly and proclaimed a divine message, and often in the Old Testament they would foretell future events. There were three functions of the prophets:
1. Divine revelation, in which they would warn of judgment to come and plead for repentance;
2. Revelation of God's will for their day; and
3. Prediction of future events. (By the way, this third area was a very small part of what they did.)

These prophets, Peter says, *inquired and searched carefully*, which means they searched out, investigated, and explored. These words were often used to describe the tenacity of miners who would dig and dig to break not only through the earth but also through rock to get to the ore they were seeking. In this same manner, these holy prophets had an earnest desire to know, and were equally as diligent in their inquiry and search to understand this mysterious grace of God, the salvation of our souls. John Wesley says, "Like miners searching after precious ore, they searched after the meaning of the prophecies which they delivered."[9] These were not easy tasks these prophets had. They were not lazy guys. Even their own revelation required study, meditation, and prayer because many of their prophecies had double meaning. Their prophecies were often aimed at some person or event near at hand, but in many instances their ultimate design was to describe the person, sufferings, or kingdom of Christ. The prophets searched and inquired as the Spirit of God revealed to them certain things that were to come. Many times prophets had no idea the significance of the things they spoke, but nonetheless they persisted.

These prophets, Peter says, prophesied *of the grace that would come to us*. This *grace* would not only include our salvation, but would also include the end, or the time in which Christ returns for His own and when we will be physically present with Him forever. Peter says this was part of God's divine plan, and it was destined to come unto you. Some in those days did not receive that grace, unfortunately, just as some in our day will not. They do not see the Messiah revealed in the Old Testament. Jesus said it well in John 5:46-47: "if you believed Moses, you would believe Me; for he wrote about Me. But if you do not believe his writings, how will you believe My words?" (For further reading, see Acts 3:18-26 and Luke 24:19-31.)

Peter goes on in verse 11 to mention several things for which these prophets diligently searched.

---

[9] Quote from Charles Wesley; taken from http://bible.chrisitansunite.com/wes.cgi?b-1Pe&c=1

> searching what, or what manner of time, the Spirit of Christ who was in them was indicating when He testified beforehand the sufferings of Christ and the glories that would follow. (1 Peter 1:11)

The prophets searched or investigated *what manner of time*, or when, Messiah would come. The Greek word here indicates the character or condition of the age in which Messiah would come. The prophets were searching diligently to find out who Messiah would be, *what* would happen to Him, and when all of this would occur. Jesus indicated these things when He was speaking to His disciples in Matthew 13:17. He said, "For assuredly, I say to you that many prophets and righteous men desired to see what you see, and did not see it, and to hear what you hear, and did not hear it." The prophets wanted to understand the time and the circumstances in which their prophecies would be fulfilled. The prophets knew to some extent what they prophesied, but not at what time the messianic prophecies would be fulfilled. What they saw dimly, you and I see clearly.

Have you ever wondered how they received this revelation? Did they have weird dreams? No! They received it by divine revelation; Peter says it was *the Spirit of Christ who was in them*. Peter makes this clear in 2 Peter 1:20-21: "Knowing this first, that no prophecy of Scripture is of any private interpretation, for prophecy never came by the will of man, but holy men of God spoke as they were moved by the Holy Spirit."

There are two specific things Peter points out that the prophets predicted about the Lord, that is, His sufferings and His glory. The *sufferings of Christ* would include His hardships and His pain, which were horrendous, as we know from the Scriptures. The Jews wanted a king, but not one that would suffer. Rather, they wanted a king that would set up his rule and reign here on earth. They did not want a crucified Christ; they wanted deliverance from their present situation. Sadly, this is similar to what we often see in Christendom today—men and women don't want to take up their cross and follow a crucified Lord; they want health, wealth and prosperity, and to be delivered from all their trials!

In addition to prophesying about Christ's suffering, the prophets also predicted the glories that would follow that suffering. This would include His resurrection, His ascension, and His coming kingdom (see Isaiah 11; Daniel 7:13-14; and Zechariah 14:9 for some examples). Jesus Himself said to the two on the road to Emmaus, in Luke 24:25-26, "O foolish ones, and slow of heart to believe in all that the prophets have spoken! Ought not the Christ to have suffered these things and to enter into His glory?" Peter's readers—including you and me—should find encouragement in remembering that after Christ suffered there was glory to follow. He'll even remind us of this again in 1 Peter 4:13 and 5:1 and 5:10. We can take great encouragement in these verses because they remind us that we also may suffer in this life, but oh, my friend, the glory that is to come will be inexpressible! Peter goes on in verse 12 to make an interesting statement about these prophets of old. He says:

> To them it was revealed that, not to themselves, but to us they were ministering the things which now have been reported to you through those who have preached the gospel to you by the Holy Spirit sent from heaven—things which angels desire to look into. (1 Peter 1:12)

Peter says that it was *revealed* to the prophets that these prophecies were not for *themselves*. The prophets understood that they were not writing for themselves, but for those who in the future would hear the gospel. The word *ministering* means to be an attendant, to wait upon, as a Christian deacon. The prophets' ministry would mostly benefit the age to come, the age of grace. There is a principle here I want to draw out, and that is this: some of you may think that the work you are doing now for the Lord is of no value (raising kids, doing dishes, teaching a Sunday School class, discipling young women, or various other things that God has called you to). But have you stopped to consider that what you are doing now may have impact and profit in years to come? Raising children to love God and instilling a desire in them to serve Him is a wonderful contribution to the Kingdom. Mentoring young women who will pass on what they've learned to other women is also an investment in the Kingdom to come. These prophets did not minister for themselves, but for those in the future.

Peter goes on to say the things the prophets ministered *now have been reported* to them *through those who have preached the gospel to you.* By using the word now, Peter is indicating that the gospel was being preached in his day. The things the prophets predicted in the Old Testament were being preached to the people of Peter's day in the gospel of the New Testament! Peter is linking the message of the Old Testament with that of the New Testament. He's looking at the Old Testament prophecies in light of their New Testament fulfillment. In this, we see that the Old Testament is vitally important. As one man says, "The whole New Testament gospel rests on the Spirit's Old Testament testimony that was made through the Old Testament prophets. Cancel that testimony, and you remove the basis of the gospel of Christ."[10] Ladies, it behooves us to read and study the whole council of God!

These prophecies took place through the Holy Spirit who was *sent from heaven.* In the Old Testament period, the Holy Spirit did not permanently and perpetually indwell the prophets. According to Acts 2, the Spirit's continual indwelling of believers did not take place until the Day of Pentecost. However, in the Old Testament, the Holy Spirit did descend upon men for various purposes and for various periods of time. The Holy Spirit was sent from heaven to guide and direct the prophets, and it was He who revealed these truths to their hearts. It is the Holy Spirit that inspired the prophets, and it is the same Holy Spirit that led the apostles to evangelize, and it is the same Holy Spirit which would take the truth of the gospel and bring its truth to the hearts of Peter's readers.

Peter ends verse 12 with a curious statement: *things which angels desire to look into. Angels*, evidently, have longing, or an intense *desire*, to understand the mysteries of the gospels and the things the prophets predicted concerning Christ and His sufferings and glory. In fact, the word *look* means to bend down and lean over so as to peer in to look at something. It means to look at with one's body stooped over, gazing with an outstretched neck in order to gaze upon some

---

[10]R.C. H. Lenski. Commentary on the New Testament—1-2 Peter, 1-3 John, Jude (Peabody: Hendrickson Publishers, Inc. Edition, 1998), 49.

wonderful sight. This word is used in James 1:25 when James is describing an individual who looks intently into the Word of God as he does in a mirror, so much so, that James says this person is not a forgetful hearer, but a doer of the work. It is also used in Luke 24:12 and John 20:5 and 11, of Peter, John, and Mary, who stooped down and looked into the empty tomb. This wasn't just a casual glance; it was a long, lingering look. Peter is saying that the mysteries of the gospel and the methods of man's salvation are so glorious that the angels earnestly desire to look into them. He's saying that the angels consider the whole plan of man's redemption with deep attention and admiration; they're curious about it. They're intently watching the plan of salvation unfold, yet they themselves do not participate in it in the sense that Christ did not die for them, but for the ungodly.

So, what should be our attitude toward the righteous prophets? Peter doesn't tell us specifically, but when we consider how we have benefited from the prophets' ministry, I think it's safe to say that we should be thankful for them. Have you stopped to consider what the prophets suffered on your behalf? What they went through for the generations to come was not an easy task. They endured persecution for their stand and for their uncompromising prophecies, especially of impending judgment. Isaiah went naked and barefoot for 3 years. Ezekiel laid on his left side for 390 days and on his right side for 40 more. Jeremiah was thrown into a pit. And these are just a few examples. My friend, we should be grateful to the Lord for sending these prophets as ministers of His grace.

Summary

There are two lessons I'd like for you to consider as you meditate on this text.

1. *Thank God for His gift of the Old Testament.* The Old Testament Scriptures so beautifully tell of the coming of Christ, His sufferings, and His glory. So often, we're quick to thank God for His Word, but when is the last time you thanked Him specifically for the Old Testament and for the prophets?

2. *Embrace the doctrine of suffering.* How do you do that?! And what does this lesson have to do with suffering? How should this lesson give me hope in the midst of my trials? Well, here are four principles from this lesson that you can live by in the midst of your trials:

   a. *Love Christ* (v 8). In the midst of trials, love the Lord, as Peter says in verse 8. When you are in the midst of difficulty, turn your heart to Christ in true love and worship! This will ease the pain and difficulty of your hardship and replace it with healing.

   b. *Trust Christ* (v 8). My dear sister, walk by faith and not by sight. How can we grow in faith in the midst of trials? By feeding on God's Word and communicating with Him.

   c. *Rejoice in Christ* (v 8). You may not be able to rejoice in the hardships, but you can rejoice in the Lord and set your mind on Him and the glory to come. With every trial, we should come away with some new knowledge and understanding of our Lord, and that should bring us great joy.

   d. *Receive from Christ* (v 9). In the midst of our trials, we can receive from the Lord all that we need for victory over the temptations that come with our situation. Turn your trials into dwelling on the fact that one day you will receive future glory. Charles Spurgeon said, "Little faith will take your soul to heaven, but great faith will bring heaven to your soul."[11]

I don't know what suffering you are experiencing this day, but I encourage you to love Him, trust Him, rejoice in Him, and receive from Him all that He has to offer. By doing so, you can experience a taste of glory here and now. No matter what you face now, you can have joy unspeakable and be full of glory as you go with the Master through the Fiery Furnace!

---

[11] Warren Weirsbe, Be Hopeful (Colorado Springs: David C. Cook, 2009, pg. 37.)

Questions to Consider
The Importance of the Prophets
1 Peter 1:8-12

1. (a) Read 1 Peter 1:8-12 and write down at least five things you do not understand. (b) Now, take some time and do some searching to find out the answers to those five things you do not understand.

2. Memorize 1 Peter 1:8.

3. First Peter 1:10 mentions the prophets of old who prophesied of the grace that should come. (a) According to Acts 28:23-24, what were the responses that the people had concerning these prophecies? (b) Why did some not believe the words of the prophets? See verses 25-29. (c) What did Jesus say in John 5:46-47 to those who would not believe the prophets?

4. (a) How were the prophecies revealed to the Old Testament prophets, according to 2 Peter 1:19-21? (b) What is the "more sure word of prophecy" (KJV) that Peter mentions in verse 19? (c) What should be our response to this word of prophecy?

5. (a) After His resurrection, to whom did Jesus expound the prophets? See Luke 24:13-32, 44-45. (b) What was their response? See verse 32.

6. The following passages are some prophecies from the Old Testament concerning the sufferings of Christ: Psalm 22; Psalm 69; Psalm 88; Isaiah 52:13-14; Isaiah 53; Zechariah 13:7. (a) Skim these passages and list the sufferings you find predicted about our Lord. (b) Who is the prophet that is prophesying in each passage? (c) What is the "glory that should follow," according to Isaiah 11?

7. (a) Would you be able to explain from the New Testament how some Old Testament prophecies have been fulfilled? (b) Do you spend as much time in the Old Testament as you do in the New Testament? Why or why not? (c) After studying this lesson, do you see any importance in familiarizing yourself with the whole counsel of God?

8. (a) If you were an Old Testament Prophet, how do you think you would react to a prophecy revealed to you? (b) What was Daniel's reaction? See Daniel 2:19-23 and Daniel 10.

9. After carefully considering this week's lesson, write down a prayer request to share with others.

What happened
The Holiness

Chapter 4

A Call to Holy Living

1 Peter 1:13-16

We have come to a subject in our study of 1 Peter that should be of great importance to all of us—one that ought to weigh heavy upon our hearts. However, in the decades I've been a believer, I've noticed that it is a subject not often spoken of, one that makes people very uncomfortable. The subject is holiness. When was the last time you really thought about holiness—holiness in your personal life, holiness in the life of your family, holiness in your church, holiness in our country? Are we a holy people? Are you a holy person? Are your children holy?

As I grow older in the Lord and older in age, I am more and more grieved as I watch good Christian friends fall prey to compromises of all kinds. (It actually seems like this is happening more rapidly these days.) To them the Bible is not really a book to live by. It is a comfort in their affliction, it has some good stories to read, and it's even a good book for ladies to study together! But live by the book? For some, this notion of living by the Bible's teachings isn't in vogue unless it happens to be convenient at the moment.

I have witnessed countless such compromises over the years, and each has troubled my heart. One woman told me, "I have lived in this marriage for x amount of years, and it hasn't worked out. I am not happy, so I think divorce is better." "But you don't have grounds for divorce," I warned her, "I would be cautious about committing willful sin, as it will not go well with you!" Unfortunately, my words didn't seem to reach her hardened heart; it didn't seem to matter to her that God is more interested in her holiness than in her happiness.

Unforgiveness and bitterness is another very common issue with many believers. "Me ask forgiveness?! No way! If you knew what so-and-so did to me, well then you would understand why I'm bitter and won't forgive them!" One person told me, "I am done with her!" as she talked with me of her personal struggle with bitterness. Another told me that she only wanted to be around people who would talk about the Lord, excusing her own unforgiving attitude toward another individual.

One woman we were trying to help was working 70 hours a week with school-aged children in the home; her marriage was falling apart, her children were rebellious, and eventually they all stopped going to church. We urged her to cut back on her hours and to be present at home. Her response was that she had done the "Titus 2 thing"! Done the Titus 2 thing?! What does that even mean?

I could literally take this entire lesson and give you example after example of unholy living I have witnessed among professing believers, but that would not bring much profit to any of us. What will profit us is to look into the Scriptures and see what the Holy Spirit says through the apostle Peter regarding this most important subject of holiness. What is holiness anyway? Is holiness really attainable in this life? Let's read how Peter answers these questions.

1 Peter 1:13-16

> [13]Therefore gird up the loins of your mind, be sober, and rest your hope fully upon the grace that is to be brought to you at the revelation of Jesus Christ; [14]as obedient children, not conforming yourselves to the former lusts, as in your ignorance; [15]but as He who called you is holy, you also be holy in all your conduct, [16]because it is written, "Be holy, for I am holy."

Our outline for this lesson will include:

> *The Means to Holiness* (vv 13-14)
> *The Mandate for Holiness* (v 15)
> *The Motivation for Holiness* (v 16)

Peter now moves from the message of the gospel to the means by which we live out the gospel, in verse 13.

The Means to Holiness

1 Peter 1:13-14

> Therefore gird up the loins of your mind, be sober, and rest your hope fully upon the grace that is to be brought to you at the revelation of Jesus Christ (1 Peter 1:13)

When the word *therefore* is mentioned in the Word of God, it is there for a reason. The word therefore is mentioned in this verse because of what has been written in verses 3-12. Because of the grace that has been offered to you; because you have an inheritance that is incorruptible, undefiled, unfading, and reserved in heaven for you; because you have been elected before the foundation of the world; because the prophets ministered unto you and not unto themselves; and, finally, because even angels desire to look into these things, then how earnest and watchful you ought to be! Because of all this, we have a responsibility, and that responsibility, Peter says, is to *gird up the loins of your mind*. We are to put out of the way, once for all, anything that would obstruct the action of our mind. The term therefore also marks the turning point in the tone of 1 Peter, as it is the transition from the doctrinal portion of the letter to the practical portion of the letter. From now on, the bulk of the letter will focus on our duty as believers and how we are to live.

The call to gird up the loins of our minds is in the aorist tense in the Greek language, so that it conveys the idea of having already girded up the loins of our mind. This would indicate that this action was a once for all act that happened in the past. If we don't gird up the loins of our minds and get ourselves ready for mental battle, we will fail. We might put it this way "Roll up your shirtsleeves and get to work!" or "Pull your thoughts together!" This is an obligation for us as believers and not something that is an option.

Peter is using a physical metaphor to describe a mental act. His readers would understand the wordage here. The image they would likely have in their minds would be found in Exodus 12:11, where the Israelites were told to eat the Passover with their loins girded, with their shoes on their feet, and with their staff in their hands. The reason for doing all this was so that they would be ready to move at a moment's notice for their journey. They would gather up their long flowing garments and tuck them under their belt in preparation for vigorous activity. This would keep them from falling and getting tripped up; it would also lend support to their loins. Now, what would have happened if they had not gathered their garments but tried to run with them loose? They would have tripped and fallen because their clothes would have gotten in the way. So it is with you and me. If we try to run the Christian race with a bunch of baggage, a load of sin, we will get tripped up. Hebrews 12:1 says we are to "lay aside every weight, and the sin which so easily ensnares us, and let us run with endurance the race that is set before us." It is also worth noting that the Proverbs 31 woman is said to gird herself with strength, in verse 17.

Peter does not say we are to gird up the loins of our heart or soul, but our *mind*. It is the mind that needs to be changed in order for us to live a holy life. When we gird up the loins of our mind, we halt all evil thinking, all speculations, and anything really that would hinder our progress as a Christian. It might be things like worry, fear, jealousy, hatred, unforgiveness, and impurity. Most of us have heard the phrase, "What you think is what you are," which is taken from Proverbs 23:7, which says, "For as he thinks in his heart, so is he." The main work of a Christian lies in the right management of his mind. Every sin we commit begins in the mind; and Paul tells us in 2 Corinthians 10:5 that we are to be "casting down arguments and every high thing that exalts itself against the knowledge of God, bringing every thought into captivity to the obedience of Christ." We are to take any thought that is in opposition to God and smash it and then replace it with God's thoughts. The only way you can replace those unbiblical thoughts with God's thoughts is to know what His thoughts are—which means you must know what He says in His Word! If your thought life is out of control, I would first highly recommend that you read Elizabeth George's book, *Loving God with all Your Mind*.[12] In this practical book, Mrs. George gives practical helps for controlling our mind and how to truly love God with all of our heart, all of our soul, and our entire mind. Secondly, I would encourage you to memorize as much of God's Word as you can—because it will truly change the way that you think. *This is the first means to holiness: to gird up the loins of our mind.*

Married with this command to gird up our mind is the command for sobriety. *This is our second means to holiness: Peter says we are to be sober.* *Sober* is a word that refers primarily to abstaining from getting drunk with wine and is used metaphorically to describe moral alertness. But it also means to be discreet, to be watchful, to be self-controlled, to be calm in spirit and mind. The person who is sober minded evaluates things correctly, is not thrown off balance by new ideas, and does not give way to hysterical fears. They're levelheaded. This is how our minds should be: self-controlled and free from worry and fear. I find it interesting that in the King James Version this is the very first character quality mentioned in Titus 2:4 in Paul's description of what an older woman is to teach a younger woman. We are to teach younger women to be sober minded, to have self control in regard to their emotions and passions, which sometimes can become out of control. If we women would gain control of our thoughts alone, life would be a lot less complex.

In 1 Timothy 3:2, Paul lists being sober minded as a qualification for a leader in the church. Peter also brings out the importance of this again later on in this epistle, in 1 Peter 4:7 and 1 Peter 5:8. The repetition of this command would have been a powerful reminder to those believers in Peter's day who were likely tempted on more than one occasion to give into hysterical fears regarding their own persecution and that of their family members. Their minds were probably tempted to be tossed to and fro with fears and anxious thoughts. But Peter says if you want to be holy, then it must begin with a sober mind. And, my friend, this is one of the means to

---

[12] Elizabeth George, *Loving God with All Your Mind* (Eugene: Harvest House Publishers, 2005).

holiness for us, as well. We cannot be holy and at the same time entertain thoughts that are not under the control of the Holy Spirit.

Peter goes on; he says *rest your hope fully upon the grace that is to be brought to you at the revelation of Jesus Christ.* What Peter is saying is that we should live in a state of *hope*, a perfect hope that is complete and will find its culmination when Christ appears to take us home to glory. In the midst of our trials, we are not to become weary or full of doubt; a perfect, complete, steadfast hope is what is called for. *This is the third means to our holiness: hope.* Peter has already referred to this hope as a living hope in 1 Peter 1:3. This isn't a dead hope; it's alive because we have a living Savior. The aged old apostle John says in 1 John 3:1-3,

> Behold what manner of love the Father has bestowed on us, that we should be called children of God! Therefore the world does not know us, because it did not know Him. Beloved, now we are children of God; and it has not yet been revealed what we shall be, but we know that when He is revealed, we shall be like Him, for we shall see Him as He is. And everyone who has this hope in Him purifies himself, just as He is pure.

As we fix our hope on heaven to come, John says, it should be a cause for us to want to live in holiness! Our hope, then, is a means to holiness! That fact that our Lord is returning to judge the living and the dead should motivate all His children to act in a manner that pleases Him. Sadly, it is too often the case that there is no fear of God before our eyes.

Peter is clear that our hope is for *the grace that is to be brought to you at the revelation of Jesus Christ.* Our salvation, which is the grace of our Lord, has in one sense already come to us; in another sense, it will also be completed *at the revelation of Jesus Christ.* Now, this isn't a new truth; Peter has mentioned this reality four other times, in verses 5, 7, 9, and 10. And we need these many reminders to remember the hope we have in Christ's coming! One man helpfully says, "When the *out*look becomes gloomy, try the *up* look!"[13] And Paul says in 1 Corinthians 15:19, "If in this life only we have hope in Christ, we are of all men most miserable" (KJV). Ladies, if we are not hopeful in this life and for the life to come, how can we be holy? This is truly the believer's blessed hope!

So, the means to our holiness include girding up the loins of our mind, being sober, and focusing on the hope of Christ's return. Peter now mentions one last means in verse 14. Of course, these are not all the ways to achieve holy living, but they are the ones mentioned in this text.

> as obedient children, not conforming yourselves to the former lusts, as in your ignorance (1 Peter 1:14)

Peter reminds his readers that they are to be *obedient children*. This literally reads, "children of obedience." This is a reference to those who have been born again, as John mentions in John 1:12, "But as many as received Him, to them He gave the right to become children of God, to those who believe in His name." Peter has already referred to this obedience in verse 2 and he will refer to it again in verses 14 and 22. What does it mean to be *obedient*? It means to be attentive and to listen to what is being said or written and then to submit to it. We often listen to great sermons or read our Bibles attentively, but then do not obey what we've heard or read. This is being a hearer of the Word but not a doer of it, which is dangerous (see James 1:22-25). Obedience to the Word ought to be accompanied by joy. Consider John's words in 1 John 5:3: "For this is the love of God, that we keep His commandments. And His commandments are not burdensome." Obedience to God is not a burden. In fact, it is a delight, as the Psalmist says in Psalm 40:8, "I delight to do Your will, O my God, and Your law is within my heart." This is something we can understand even from our own experiences as parents. When we have a child who is obedient, it brings pleasure and joy. But when that child chooses to disobey, it is disheartening. We as God's children are to be children of obedience, which is contrast to those

---
[13] Warren Wiersbe, Be Hopeful (Colorado Springs: David C. Cook, 1982), 33.

who are children of disobedience, as Paul mentions in Ephesians 2:2. *Obedience, then, is the fourth means to our holiness.*

As obedient children, Peter says, believers should not be *conforming yourselves to the former lusts. Conforming* means to pattern or fashion after. To be conforming ourselves to our former lusts is to be patterning ourselves after what we used to be or what used to characterize us. The same term is used in Romans 12:1-2, when Paul says, "I beseech you therefore, brethren, by the mercies of God, that you present your bodies a living sacrifice, holy, acceptable to God, which is your reasonable service. And do not be conformed to this world, but be transformed by the renewing of your mind, that you may prove what is that good and acceptable and perfect will of God." We are not to pattern ourselves after the world; we are to pattern ourselves after the Word!

The term *lust* means a longing for something that is forbidden, like passions and evil desires. These can be outward expressions like habits, mannerisms, dress, speech, and behavior, but they can also be those inward thoughts and attitudes that no one sees but you and God. My friend, Christ died for these things, and Christ died that we might be obedient and holy daughters. Obedience is a means to your holiness, and without holiness no one will see the Lord (Hebrews 12:14). This is a reality Peter will emphasize again in chapter 2, verse 11, when he says, "Beloved, I beg you as sojourners and pilgrims, abstain from fleshly lusts which war against the soul." Paul even says in Romans 6:12, "Therefore do not let sin reign in your mortal body, that you should obey it in its lusts." A life filled with sinful lusts is who we used to be, but it is not part of the new man who is created in Christ. Peter says this represents who you used to be when you were *ignorant*, which means when you lacked knowledge. This type of ignorance characterizes the unbeliever, as Paul says in 1 Corinthians 2:14, "But the natural man does not receive the things of the Spirit of God, for they are foolishness to him; nor can he know them, because they are spiritually discerned." Paul also describes the unbeliever, in Ephesians 4:18, "having their understanding darkened, being alienated from the life of God, because of the ignorance that is in them, because of the hardening of their heart." Ladies, before we were in Christ, we were ignorant and in darkness—but not now. Paul says in Ephesians 5:8, "For you were once darkness, but now you are light in the Lord. Walk as children of light."

Having explained the means to our holiness, Peter now moves on to explain the mandate for our holiness.

The Mandate for Holiness

1 Peter 1:15

> but as He who called you is holy, you also be holy in all your conduct (1 Peter 1:15)

But is a word of contrast, and here it contrasts those who are living in lust with those who are living in holiness. This phrase *He who called you is holy* can be more literally translated as "the Holy One who called you." So, Peter is essentially saying, "like the Holy One who has called you, so you to are to be holy." The word *holy* has as its root meaning the idea of being different. Holy people are different people, and they are certainly in contrast to unholy people, people who are of the world. Because God is holy, then those who are called His children are to be holy as well. Isaiah says in Isaiah 6:3, "Holy, holy, holy is the LORD of hosts; the whole earth is full of His glory!" We are to pattern ourselves after the Holy One who has called us. We are to be pure and morally blameless. Holy is also the same word as for saint, which means to be set apart. We are to be set apart from sin to righteousness. God should be the standard for our holiness, not our former lusts.

Notice that Peter says this holiness should govern *all your conduct*, our whole manner of living. This would include every aspect of our life. This means holiness should govern our family life, our marriage, our parenting, our work, our entertainment, our sex life, our friendships, our vacations, our everything! We cannot only be holy at church and think that is all that is required of us. Our whole life should be a reflection of Christ. We are to represent Him in all our life. Paul says in 1 Thessalonians 4:7, "For God did not call us to uncleanness, but in holiness." And he says in Ephesians 1:4, that "He chose us in Him before the foundation of the world, that we should be holy and without blame before Him in love." And again in 2 Corinthians 7:1, "Therefore, having these promises, beloved, let us cleanse ourselves from all filthiness of the flesh and spirit, perfecting holiness in the fear of God."

The mandate for holiness is to be holy in all your conduct. You might be saying to yourself, "Well, why are we to be holy anyway?" Peter gives us the motivation for our holiness in verse 16.

The Motivation for Holiness

1 Peter 1:16

>because it is written, "Be holy, for I am holy." (1 Peter 1:16)

The word *because* means on the very account of. In other words, this is exactly what the Scripture teaches; it is on record that we are to be holy. Now, you might be wondering where this is written, since Peter says *it is written*. It is written way back in Leviticus 11:44-45, which says, "For I am the LORD your God. You shall therefore consecrate yourselves, and you shall be holy; for I am holy. Neither shall you defile yourselves with any creeping thing that creeps on the earth. For I am the LORD who brings you up out of the land of Egypt, to be your God. You shall therefore be holy, for I am holy." And in Leviticus 19:2, we read, "Speak to all the congregation of the children of Israel, and say to them: 'You shall be holy, for I the LORD your God am holy.'" Leviticus 20:7 and 26 say similar things, that we are to be holy because God is holy. Jesus reiterates this same truth in His Sermon on the Mount, in Matthew 5:48, where He says "Therefore you shall be perfect, just as your Father in heaven is perfect." When God called the Israelites out of Egypt, He did so in order to become their God. He demanded of them that they would obey Him, and so

He gave them a set of ordinances and commands and laws, which, if followed, would enable them to live holy lives. Now, of course, you and I are not under the Old Testament ceremonial laws, but the moral and spiritual principles are just as applicable for us, who are living under the New Covenant. God has not changed throughout the ages; He remains the same yesterday, today and forever, and He has and always will demand holiness from His children. We are to be holy as He is holy! *The motivation for our holiness, then, is our God, who is Himself holy.* He demands that we follow in His steps. We must remember that we are His image-bearers.

Summary

The means to our holiness are girding up the loins of our mind; being soberminded; holding onto the hope of glory; and obedience. Are you disciplining yourself in these four areas so that you might be holy? Is your thought life under control? What kind of things go through your mind each day? Do you ever stop and take note of what you are thinking? Right thinking leads to right living. And what about living soberly? Is your thinking under the control of the Holy Spirit? Do you rein in all ungodly thinking and replace it with the mind of Christ? Remember, a sober mind will lead to holy living. And, what about hopeful living? Is your mind set on the hope to come? Do you think often on heaven which is our ultimate hope to come? As we meditate on the hope to come, it should motivate us for holy living. Lastly, what about obedient living? Is your obedience full out, or is it partial? Is there any area of disobedience in your life? Our obedience is a means to our holiness.

The mandate for our holiness is to be holy in all our conduct. Holy living is not optional for us as believers in Jesus Christ; it is a commandment. Have you stopped to consider this mandate this week, this day, this hour? How has it changed the way you live?

The motivation for holiness is to be holy because our God is holy. Our motivation for holiness is our God and our Father. We are to walk in His steps and follow His example of holy living. We are to imitate Him in all our manner of living as we are His representatives on earth. Are you endeavoring by God's Spirit to walk in His steps?

Perhaps you're wrestling with the idea of holy living and wondering how it is that this can be possible in this life. You might even deem it impossible. Let me ask you a question: Would a loving Father God give His children a command that is impossible to obey? Do you as a loving mother give your children commands that you know are impossible to obey? Of course, you don't.

I would like to leave you with some thoughts from J.C. Ryle, who wrote a book called *Holiness*. In that book, he lists several ways in which we can practice holiness, which I have here paraphrased for you. If you have never read this book, I would highly encourage you to get your hands on a copy and read it. Ryle says,

1. Holiness is the habit of being of one mind with God. In other words, we are to hate what he hates and love what he loves. Everything should be filtered through what He would think. In order to think like Him, of course, we must know Him through His Word, to know how He thinks.

2. Holiness involves shunning every known sin and keeping every known commandment. We should have a bent to do the will of God. There should not be willful disobedience of even one command.

3. Holiness involves following after meekness, long-suffering, gentleness, patience, kindness, and control of the tongue.

4. Holiness involves self-denial. We should mortify the deeds of our flesh. We should be self-controlled, as we have seen in this lesson.

5. Holiness involves having a spirit of mercy and goodness toward others. We should not be idle, but purpose to be helpful and useful to others. (By the way, this is another character quality that the older women are to teach the younger women.)

6. Holiness involves fearing God. We must live always with the view in mind that our Father is watching us and that one day we will stand before Him and give account of every deed done in our flesh, good or bad, as well as every idle word we speak.

7. Holiness involves humility. We should esteem others better than ourselves. We should see our own hearts as more evil than anyone else's. There should be no room for pride.

8. Holiness involves faithfulness. In all our relationships and duties, we should be faithful and should do things heartily, as unto the Lord and not unto men.

9. Last, but not least, holiness means following after spiritual-mindedness. We ought to set our affections on things above and hold loosely to the things of this world. We ought to ask ourselves these questions: Is there anything or anyone that is occupying the throne of my heart? If God chooses to take that thing, or that person, what would I do?[14]

If you had difficulty with some of these principles, I would urge you to prayerfully consider where you are in your relationship to God. The Bible says in Hebrews 12:14 that without holiness *no man* shall see the Lord. We should not think that if we are not holy now, that we would enjoy heaven in time to come. How could we possibly find any enjoyment there? As J.C. Ryle says,

> Suppose for a moment that you were allowed to enter heaven without holiness. What would you do? What possible enjoyment could you feel there? To which of all the saints would you join yourself, and by whose side would you sit down? Their pleasures are not your pleasures, their tastes are not your tastes, their character not your character. How could you possibly be happy, if you had not been holy on earth?[15]

---

[14] J.C.Ryle, Holiness (Durham, England:Evangelical Press, 1879), 34-37.
15 Ibid, 42-43.

Questions to Consider
A Call to Holy Living
1 Peter 1:13-16

1. (a) What would you say is the theme of 1 Peter 1:13-16? (b) Can you think of any other portions of the Word of God which have the same theme? If so, what are they?

2. Memorize 1 Peter 1:15.

3. (a) How were the Israelites to eat the Passover, according to Exodus 12:11? (b) According to 1 Kings 18:46, what did Elijah have to do before he ran? (c) What did the Lord tell Job to do, in Job 38:3 (KJV)? (d) As you look at these Old Testament examples and then look at Luke 12:35-40; Ephesians 6:14; and 1 Peter 1:13, what do you think Peter means by "girding up the loins of your mind?" (KJV)

4. (a) What happens when "obedient children" become disobedient? See Hebrews 12:3-11. (b) What are the results of one's chastening, according to the same passage? (c) Can you recall a time in your life when the Lord chastened you personally? What lessons did you learn through His discipline?

5. (a) List some of our "former lusts," according to Galatians 5:19-21; Colossians 3:5-9; 1 Peter 4:2-3; and 1 John 2:15-17? (b) In a separate list, list those qualities that our lives should exhibit instead of those former lusts, according to Galatians 5:22-23; Colossians 3:12-17; and 1 Peter 4:7-11? (c) Since your conversion, how would you say that you have seen your life change from the 1st list to the 2nd list?

6. Peter mentions in verse 16 that it is written, "Be holy for I am holy." Read Leviticus 11:44-45; 19:2; and 20:7, 26 to see where this was first written. (a) What is the context (what comes before and after) of each of these verses? (b) Why was it important

that the Israelites be holy? (c) Why is it important that we as believers are holy today? (d) Do you think it is really possible to be holy, as He is holy?

7. How do you think we as believers can practically gird up the loins of our minds?

8. (a) Should holiness be only an inner attitude of the mind, or should it also include our actions? Support your answer with Scripture. (b) How do you teach the importance of holiness to your children, grandchildren, or anyone else over whom you have influence? (c) How important is holiness to you?

9. Does holiness characterize your life? Please write your need in the form of a prayer request.

Chapter 5

The Cost of Eternal Life
1 Peter 1:17-21

It goes without saying that genuine believers who are living for the glory of Christ will one time or another, endure suffering for the sake of the cross of Christ. Some lose friends or family. Some endure mocking and ridicule. Some even lose their marriage or job because of their stand for Christ. But none of us will ever suffer to the extent that our Lord did. He is the only one who has ever endured death on a cross for the sins of the world. When we consider what Christ suffered on our account, it should humble us.

Crucifixion was one of the most horrific ways to die. The suffering was intense, especially in regions where the climate was hot. The one who was to be crucified would first be scourged. The Roman scourge was a dreadful instrument made of sharp bones that were inter-twisted so that every time the lash came down on a body, pieces of bone would make deep lacerations, and every time the scourge was lifted, it would literally tear off chunks of flesh from the victim's body. Severe local inflammation, coupled with significant bleeding, would produce traumatic fever, which would be aggravated by the heat of the sun, the strain of the body, and insufferable thirst. Torn and lacerated tendons and nerves would cause excruciating agony. Victims often experienced terrible headaches, and their minds would be confused and filled with anxiety and dread. It's been said that the victim of crucifixion would die a thousand deaths. Convulsions would tear at the wounds and add to the pain, until at last the body would become completely exhausted and the victim would sink into unconsciousness and, ultimately, death.

Our Lord endured all these things, and not just these things; there was also mocking and insults, being spat upon, a crown of thorns forced upon His head, and the plucking out of His beard. All this took place before the crucifixion even began. And, added to all this terrible suffering our Lord endured was the weight of every single sin of mankind and the separation from His own Father, a separation He had never known. This is what our Lord endured for our redemption. All of this was for me, and for you, and for all the readers of this epistle of Peter. In reminding his readers of what it cost our Lord to secure our redemption, Peter is reminding us all that it was a high price indeed. Perhaps Peter's readers, who were going through tremendous suffering, would read these verses and be reminded that what their Savior endured was far more agonizing than their own persecutions, and perhaps they would be encouraged to persevere to the end in the sufferings to which God had called them. May this lesson be of great encouragement to each of us, whether our sufferings are now or in the future. Let's read what Peter has to say in verses 17-21.

1 Peter 1:17-21

> And if you call on the Father, who without partiality judges according to each one's work, conduct yourselves throughout the time of your stay here in fear; [18]knowing that you were not redeemed with corruptible things, like silver or gold, from your aimless conduct received by tradition from your fathers, [19]but with the precious blood of Christ, as of a lamb without blemish and without spot. [20]He indeed was foreordained before the foundation of the world, but was manifest in these last times for you [21]who through Him believe in God, who raised Him from the dead and gave Him glory, so that your faith and hope are in God.

Our outline for this lesson will include:

The Judgment of the Father (v 17)
The Sacrifice of the Son (vv 18-19)
The Plan of the Father (vv 20-21)

In the last chapter, Peter has challenged us to be holy, and now he gives us another motivation for holiness, the judgment of the Father, in verse 17.

The Judgment of the Father

1 Peter 1:17

> And if you call on the Father, who without partiality judges according to each one's work, conduct yourselves throughout the time of your stay here in fear (1 Peter 1:17)

Peter starts out by writing *and if you call on the Father*, which really is more accurately translated as "since" or "in view of the fact that you call on the Father." The word *call* means to make an appeal, and it indicates a personal ongoing practice of prayer. Peter assumes that his readers are praying, especially in light of the command for holiness that he has just written about. A holy Christian is a praying Christian. In fact, I would seriously doubt the commitment of a professing Christian who doesn't talk to his Maker. Prayer is just one of the natural responses of obedient and holy children. I also imagine that these believers were making numerous appeals to God during their suffering. When we're going through trials, our prayers seem to multiply, don't they? I know in my own life, as my trials increase, my prayers increase as well. These believers would need to call upon their heavenly Father just as a child calls upon his father when he is in need. When we consider just how often a child asks a parent for something, we can relate to what Peter is saying here. In fact, sometimes it seems as if children are constantly in need of something—and that's the idea here. We are to be praying without ceasing, calling out to our Father in heaven. My sister, this is a wonderful and new relationship that New Testament saints have with God because of the shed blood of Jesus. The veil was torn in two at the time of Christ's death, and because of that, we now have full access to the throne of grace.

In writing these words, it may be that Peter is recalling the account recorded in Luke 11:1-4, when one of the disciples (I wonder if it was Peter!) asked the Lord to teach them to pray. Jesus modeled for them how to pray, and one of the things He said was that they were to address their prayers to the *Father.* This Father, Peter says, judges *without partiality,* which means He is not a respecter of persons. The word means to accept or to raise the face of another person. What Peter is saying is that God does not receive anyone's face. It doesn't matter to God what your face looks like. In Deuteronomy 10:17, Moses established very clearly that God is not a respecter of persons: "For the LORD your God is God of gods and Lord of lords, the great God, mighty and awesome, who shows no partiality nor takes a bribe." It doesn't matter to God what race you are, what imperfections you have, or whether you are male or female. God hears the prayers of all of His children.

Peter says that this impartial Father, to whom we can cry out day or night, will not show partiality in judgment. He *judges according to each one's work.* As Paul says in Colossians 3:23-25, "whatever you do, do it heartily, as to the Lord and not to men, knowing that from the Lord you will receive the reward of the inheritance; for you serve the Lord Christ. But he who does wrong will be repaid for what he has done, and there is no partiality." It is interesting to note that Peter uses the terms Father and judge in the same verse, because according to the Old Testament law, reverence was to be given to parents first, before a judge. How much more in the spiritual realm should we give reverence to the One who is not only Father but judge as well? The word judges is encouraging because it means to judge in order to find something good. It also entails distinguishing or separating and then evaluating and making a decision. Most of us look for the worst in others, but not our Lord. He is going to be testing our works to approve the good He can find in us. God expects to find good in the life of His children. Isn't that grand? Most of us think of judgment day as frightening, and I am sure it will be, but isn't it good to know that God will also be looking for the good in us?

These *works* Peter mentions include our motives, our hearts, our works, our words, and our deeds. And God is the only one able to judge us to that degree; Hebrews 4:13 says that "And there is no creature hidden from His sight, but all things are naked and open to the eyes of Him to whom we must give account." No one will be able to escape this judgment; Paul says in 2 Corinthians 5:10 that "we must all appear before the judgment seat of Christ, that each one may receive the things done in the body, according to what he has done, whether good or bad." And the writer to the Hebrews reminds us in Hebrews 9:27 that "it is appointed for men to die once, but after this the judgment." All our works and our words will be judged without partiality by an all-seeing, all-knowing God. On judgment day, it will not matter if you are rich or poor, tall or skinny, famous or unknown, able-bodied or handicapped, educated or uneducated. God's judgment will not be based on these things; His judgment will be according to truth, as Paul says in Romans 2:2.

Because of the judgment to come, Peter says to *conduct yourselves throughout the time of your stay here in fear*. Notice that Peter doesn't refer to this world as his readers' home but instead references their stay here. They were sojourners here, just as you and I are. A sojourner is a person who is a foreign resident living in a foreign land. This was a word used to describe the Israelites as they were sojourners or strangers in the land of Egypt; they were living in a foreign land. We, too, are living in a foreign land far from our eternal home. We learned about this term, sojourners, back in verse one, and Peter will remind us again of this concept in 2:11. He is reminding his readers that they are only here for a little while and this world not their home. Life is too brief to be caught up in sin and disobedience, especially in light of impending judgment. I think one of the most discouraging things for me is people who don't seem to get victory in certain areas in their life. It might be anger, bitterness, fear or worry, complaining, or submission to their husbands. It is grieving to think of the waste of time we spend involved in useless sinning for which we will someday give an account. We must stop and realize how brief life is and what a waste of time sin is in light of eternity. We should also consider the misery sin causes everyone around us now, including ourselves.

What does this mean here when Peter says to pass *the time of your stay here in fear*? Does this mean I should go around fearful of everything and everyone? No, this means that, in view of the judgment to come, we should cultivate a godly fear as we go through this life here. This is not the kind of fear that is like a slave cringing before a master. Rather, it is the loving reverence of a child before his father. It is not a fear of judgment, as John says in 1 John 4:18, "There is no fear in love; but perfect love casts out fear, because fear involves torment. But he who fears has not been made perfect in love." This is a fear of disappointing God or sinning against His love. It is the idea in 2 Corinthians 7:1, where Paul says, "Therefore, having these promises, beloved, let us cleanse ourselves from all filthiness of the flesh and spirit, perfecting holiness in the fear of God." If you have no fear of offending a holy God, then I would say there is a problem. If you look into the Word of God and see that you are not obeying Him in certain areas, and have no concern about that, then you should be very concerned. I would even go so far as to say, with Paul, that you ought to examine yourself to see if you are in the faith (2 Corinthians 13:5). Paul says in Romans 3:18 that it is the unredeemed who have no fear of God before their eyes. I know many of you have heard me say how grateful I am for an earthly father who taught me to fear my heavenly Father. I would urge mothers to work very, very hard at instilling a holy fear of God in your children. He is not "the man upstairs" or your "best bud" or some of the other terms I hear. He is a Holy and Awesome God, and it is a fearful thing to fall into His hands.

Perhaps you are in need of some motivation to fear God or find that you have no proper fear of God or simply don't know how to instill the fear of God in your children. Well, right here in these verses, Peter shows us three powerful motivations for fearing God. First, he tells us that our life here is brief (v 17). Eternity is soon to come, and we must make this life count. That is a sobering thought. Second, he reminds us that our lives will be judged (v 17). One day, every one of us will stand before God and give an account of our lives. This is a reality that should spur us on to godly living. This point right here was one I heard from my dad growing up more than any other. Third, our eternal life cost Christ's precious blood (v 19). The Son of God poured out His blood for you and me. Certainly, that should cause us to bow before Him in fear. This is Peter's next point, as he now reminds us of the sacrifice of the Son, in verses 18 and 19. We turn from the judgment of the Father, which is without partiality, to the sacrifice of the Son.

The Sacrifice of the Son

1 Peter 1:18-19

> knowing that you were not redeemed with corruptible things, like silver or gold, from your aimless conduct received by tradition from your fathers (1 Peter 1:18)

Peter speaks of us *knowing* of our redemption. My friend, the knowledge that we have regarding our redemption and the price that was paid for it should influence our daily living. The consideration of our redemption ought to be a constant and powerful motivation to holiness and to the fear of God. The word *redeemed* means to loose, and it refers to the ransom of a life, like a slave that has been set free by the payment of a ransom. In the biblical world, a slave could obtain freedom a number of ways. One option was for him to purchase his own freedom if he could collect sufficient funds. Another option was for his master to sell him to someone who would pay the price and then set him free. We, too, were once in slavery, slavery to our sin, but Christ came to redeem us from it. He paid the price for our redemption and set us free. But our redemption was not purchased *with corruptible things like silver and gold,* as it was for the slaves. Peter mentions *gold* and *silver* because they were considered two of the best and most valued treasures of the day. But even silver could tarnish and corrode and lose its value, and even gold, though more durable than silver, could still decay. These precious metals cannot redeem mankind. Peter is saying that even the most valued monies cannot purchase the souls of men, or else the sacrifice of Christ would not have been offered. God would not have given up his only begotten Son if all it took was money. These corruptible things, Peter says, are from our *aimless conduct*, which refers to the vain manner or empty behavior of our former life. It is taken from a word that was many times applied to the worship of idols, which we know is vain and worthless and of no help.

Where did this vain life come from? Peter says to his readers that it came from the *tradition* of their *fathers*, which means it was handed down from the fathers. Futile living is handed down from fathers. Traditions were very deeply imbedded in the life of the Jew, and they passed those traditions down to their children. But those traditions often served as a restraint to one fully embracing Christianity. Those considering the claims of Christianity were often reluctant to break these traditions because doing so would cut off ties with their parents and their teachers. We are in great danger when we try to adhere to strict traditions that are not profitable for our new life in Christ; doing so can become a stumbling block, as Paul warns us in Colossians 2:8: "Beware lest anyone cheat you through philosophy and empty deceit, according to the tradition of men, according to the basic principles of the world, and not according to Christ." The traditions Peter is referring to would only bind men to legalism, asceticism, and Gnosticism. Some traditions are fine, certainly, but we must measure them biblically, asking ourselves whether those traditions are consistent with our new life in Christ. The cost to redeem us from that vain way of life was costly, much more costly than silver and gold. Paul says in 1 Corinthians 6:20 that we were bought with a price. What was the price? What was the cost for your soul? Peter tells us in verse 19.

> but with the precious blood of Christ, as of a lamb without blemish and without spot. (1 Peter 1:19)

The price for our redemption was the blood of Christ. Peter says it was *precious blood*, which means it was valuable, it was costly. The word *blood* issued here to describe Christ's bloody death. Paul says in Hebrews 9:12, "Not with the blood of goats and calves, but with His own blood He entered the Most Holy Place once for all, having obtained eternal redemption." And then again in Hebrews 9:22, "And according to the law almost all things are purified with blood, and without shedding of blood there is no remission." Even when we gather in heaven we will sing a song about the blood, according to Revelation 5:9, "And they sang a new song, saying: 'You are worthy to take the scroll, and to open its seals; for You were slain, and have redeemed us to God by Your blood out of every tribe and tongue and people and nation.'"

Peter says this precious blood of Christ is *as of a lamb without blemish and without spot.* Christ was the only One who was without blemish—the perfect sacrificial lamb. He had no defect in Him whatsoever! If you recall, according to Deuteronomy 15:21, God required the Israelites to only sacrifice animals that were free of defects. If they did otherwise, this would be an abomination to Him. Those unblemished animals were a shadow and a type of what was to come, which was the perfect Lamb of God. He was the only One who was without spot from the world, the only One pure in soul, the only One righteous in life. He was faultless. It is recorded in John 1:29 that when the apostle John saw Christ for the first time, he said "Behold! The Lamb of God who takes away the sin of the world!" The blood of animals could not redeem us, but the precious blood of our Perfect Lamb can redeem even the filthiest sinner! My friend, this was the costliest sacrifice, perhaps one we take for granted too often. I think the songwriter put it well when he wrote: "You paid much too high a price for me, your tears, your blood, your pain, to have my soul just stirred at times, yet never truly changed. You deserve a fiery love that won't ignore your sacrifice, because you paid much too high a price."[16]

"Why did Christ have to die?" you might be asking. The shedding of Christ's blood on your behalf was not an accident, my sister. It was part of the divine plan of the Father, as Peter states in verses 20 and 21. Here, we turn from the sacrifice of the Son, His own blood, to the plan of the Father.

---

[16] Words by Larnelle Harris.

The Plan of the Father

1 Peter 1:20-22

> He indeed was foreordained before the foundation of the world, but was manifest in these last times for you (1 Peter 1:20)

Peter lets his readers know that Christ was *foreordained* to die. The word foreordained means to designate beforehand. It was destined or chosen *before the foundation of the world* that Christ would die. The term *foundation* means to throw down, and it speaks of the laying of the foundation of a home. It refers here to the act of God whereby He threw out into space, so to speak, the spoken word. It is the same idea mentioned over and over in Genesis 1, where it says "God said" and it happened. God said,"Let there be light," and there was. He said,"Let there be a firmament," and there was. What Peter is saying here is that Christ's death was destined before the world or before man was created. Just like our salvation was decided before the foundation of the world (Ephesians 1:4), so the death of our Lord was decided before the foundation of the world. Just as we were chosen and elected before the foundation of the world (1 Peter 1:2), so Christ was chosen before the foundation of the world to be the Redeemer for mankind. Redemption was not some after-thought for God, after sin entered the world. The plan was, from before the beginning of time, that God would send Jesus to pay the ransom for depraved man.

Peter goes on to say that this *was manifest in the last times for you.* He uses the word *but,* which is a word of contrast. Christ was chosen in eternity, yes, but was revealed in time! *Manifest* is a word which means to make or become visible, to reveal. This is referring to the time in history when Christ appeared on earth as a man. Before that, He had never been seen, but was hidden in heaven. Like Galatians 4:4-5 says, "But when the fullness of the time had come, God sent forth His Son, born of a woman, born under the law, to redeem those who were under the law, that we might receive the adoption as sons." The *last times* that Peter is referring to here include everything from the birth of Christ until His return. And all this, Peter says, was done *for you*. Peter is saying something profound here, my friend. He is saying that you may view this as if Christ had come for you only! If we would meditate on that truth alone, it would cause us to humble ourselves before Him. This is certainly proof of God's love, and not of our worth. God's plan for the death of His Son was from the beginning, but so too were His resurrection and ascension planned from the beginning. Look at verse 21.

> who through Him believe in God, who raised Him from the dead and gave Him glory, so that your faith and hope are in God. (1 Peter 1:21)

The ones for whom this precious blood has been shed for are those *who believe in God*. *Believe* is translated "do believe," and it has to do with more than just a mental assent to the facts of the gospel. It has to do with repentance and turning to God and faith toward Christ; it is the idea conveyed in Acts 20:21, where it states, "testifying to Jews, and also to Greeks, repentance toward God and faith toward our Lord Jesus Christ." Repentance and faith are joined as one truth; you can't have one without the other. Where repentance is, there faith is.

Another very important element of the gospel is the resurrection. Peter says God *raised* Jesus *from the dead*. The resurrection of Jesus Christ is what makes Christianity different from all other religions. We serve a living God, not an idol or a dead god. As Paul says in 1 Corinthians 15:14, "if Christ is not risen, then our preaching is empty and your faith is also empty."

What took place after the resurrection? Peter says of Christ that God *gave him glory*. Hebrews 10:12 says, "But this Man, after He had offered one sacrifice for sins forever, sat down at the right hand of God." Christ rose from the dead and ascended to heaven and is now in glory. Christ's death, resurrection, and ascension are all three mentioned in these verses. Why did Christ do all of this? Again, for us, for you! Peter says, it is so *that your faith and hope are in God*! Salvation brings faith and hope into our lives. And it is all in God. Here, again, we have Peter, the apostle of hope, pointing us to our hope, which is in God.

Summary

The Judgment of the Father (v 17): without partiality. Does the judgment of the Father motivate you to holy living? Are you under the false notion that you will be judged differently than others that you know? God will not be a respecter of persons when it comes to His judgment of us.

The Sacrifice of the Son (vv 18-19): His precious blood. When is the last time you meditated on the cost of your redemption? Have you recently thanked Christ for shedding His blood for you? Have you thanked the Father for sending His son?

The Plan of The Father (vv 20-21): Christ's death, resurrection, and ascension to glory, all foreordained from the beginning. The plan of salvation was from before all time. What hope and comfort does this give you in sharing the gospel with others? God has determined who will come, but we must go and share and leave the results to Him. What comfort do these verses give you in your current sufferings or trials? God knew you would go through these before you were even born! He is a loving God who is also our Father and who is there any time we want to call upon Him.

What comfort these verses must have been to these sojourners undergoing tremendous persecution for the Name's sake. To think that nothing could happen to them that their loving Father did not know already! Some of them were crucified, as their Lord was, for their faith in God. These words from Peter would have been a great blessing to them. In fact, it is said that the words of verses 18-21 were likely an early Christian hymn. What a song it must have been! And that is what I would like to do—to close out this lesson with a song.

Frances Havergal once saw an artist's rendition of the crucified Christ, and under it was the caption: "I did this for thee. What hast thou done for Me?" She was so deeply moved by the painting and its caption, that she quickly composed a poem about it. But she wasn't satisfied with what she'd written, so she threw it into the fireplace. Miraculously, it floated out of the flames and landed on the floor—the paper came out unharmed! Later, at her father's suggestion, she published that poem, and today many believers in Jesus Christ sing it. Please read this song reflectively as our closing—or sing it if you'd like! As you do, think about the price our Lord paid for you. Think about how you might honor His sacrifice with Holy Living.

"I Gave My Life for Thee"
by Frances R. Havergal, 1836-1879

I gave My life for thee,
My precious blood I shed,
That thou might'st ransomed be
And quickened from the dead.
I gave My life for thee;
What hast thou given for Me?

I spent long years for thee
In weariness and woe
That an eternity
Of joy thou mightest know.
I spent long years for thee;
Hast thou spent one for Me?

My Father's home of light,
My rainbow-circled throne,
I left for earthly night,
For wanderings sad and lone.
I left it all for thee;
Hast thou left aught for Me?

I suffered much for thee,
More than My tongue can tell,
Of bitterest agony,
To rescue thee from hell.
I suffered much for thee;
What canst thou bear for Me?

And I have brought to thee
Down from My home above
Salvation full and free,
My pardon and My love.
Great gifts I brought to thee;
What hast thou brought to Me?

Oh, let thy life be given,
Thy years for Me be spent,
World's fetters all be riven,
And joy with suffering blent!
I gave Myself for thee:
Give thou thyself to Me.

Questions to Consider
The Cost of Eternal Life
1 Peter 1:17-21

1. As you read 1 Peter, chapter 1, what verses do you find that deal with Christ's death? His resurrection? His ascension (or glory)? His second coming?

2. Memorize 1 Peter 1:18-19.

3. Read Matthew 12:31-46; 1 Corinthians 3:12-15; and Revelation 20:11-15 and answer the following questions. (a) What things will we be judged for, according to these passages? (b) What other observations do you notice about the judgment to come? (c) Based on what you have just read, how then should we live?

4. (a) What kind of lamb was to be offered during Passover, according to Exodus 12:1-11? (b) Why did the lamb have to be without blemish, according to Leviticus 22:17-25 (KJV)? (c) What did the Lord say through the prophet Malachi (Malachi 1:6-14) about those who offered imperfect animals for sacrifices?

5. (a) What characteristics of a lamb did our Lord have, according to Isaiah 53:7? (b) Why was Christ the only perfect Lamb worthy to be offered up for our redemption, according to Revelation 5? (c) According to Hebrews 10:1-18, why did Christ have to die? (d) Why couldn't we just continue to offer animal sacrifices as atonement for our sins?

6. (a) What things were foreordained (designated beforehand) by God, according to Jeremiah 1:4-5; Matthew 25:34; John 15:16; Acts 2:22-24; 13:48; 17:26; Romans 8:29-30; Ephesians 1:4-14; 2:10; 2 Thessalonians 2:13; and 1 Peter 1:19-21? (b) What do these verses teach you about the concept of something being foreordained?

7. What does it mean to you personally that Christ would shed His precious blood for you?

8. (a) Would you say that you are walking your pilgrim journey here on earth with a reverential fear of God? (1:17) (b) How do (or did) you instill a fear of God in your children or grandchildren or others you influence?

9. Write a prayer of thanksgiving to the Lord for His gift of salvation to you.

Chapter 6

Genuine Believers Possess Genuine Love for Others

1 Peter 1:22-25

There is a story that is told of a crippled young girl who lived in the slums. She needed an operation that would enable her to walk again. The time came for her operation, and when it was over, she needed a blood transfusion. Her 14-year-old brother, who was a tough boy of the streets, volunteered. He was taken to the hospital and to the bedside of his sister. He stared in silence while the vein in his arm was opened so that his blood might flow out of his body to his unconscious sister. When it was over, the doctor put his hand on the boy's shoulder and told him how brave he had been. After a moment, the boy looked up at the doctor and said, "Doc, how long will it be before I croak?" As far as the boy knew, he had been dying slowly and willingly. He had stoically watched his blood flow from his veins, drop by drop, into his sister's veins. He expected his sister's life to mean his own death. He had been willing to do what few of us would do, even for our own family—to lay down our lives for another. Jesus said in John 15:13, "greater love has no one than this, than to lay down one's life for his friends."[17]

As we end chapter one of Peter's first epistle, Peter will inform his readers that genuine salvation produces a correct understanding of several things, and one of those things is our responsibility to love one another. Let's read the final verses of chapter one and discover what Peter has to say.

---

[17]Donald Grey Barnhouse; *Let Me Illustrate* (Grand Rapids: Flemming H. Revell, 1994),211, paraphrase.

1 Peter 1:22-25

> Since you have purified your souls in obeying the truth through the Spirit in sincere love of the brethren, love one another fervently with a pure heart, ²³having been born again, not of corruptible seed but incorruptible, through the word of God which lives and abides forever, ²⁴because "All flesh is as grass, and all the glory of man as the flower of the grass. The grass withers, and its flower falls away, ²⁵but the word of the Lord endures forever." Now this is the word which by the gospel was preached to you.

Peter mentions in this text that we have been born again by the gospel. Those who are born again will evidence certain fruits. One of those fruits, and the one that Jesus says is the main one (John 13:35), is love for others. With that truth in mind, the following is our outline for this lesson. Our salvation produces a correct understanding of:

> *Our Relationship to Others* (v 22)
> *Our Relationship to the Word* (vv 23 and 25)
> *Our Relationship to Ourselves* (v 24)

As he closes chapter one of his epistle, Peter is still writing about our salvation, and he wants his readers and us to understand that our salvation should produce something, particularly three things. (Of course, these three things aren't the only things that our salvation should produce, but they are the things Peter focuses on in this text.) Peter begins this section by telling his readers that salvation should produce a right understanding of our relationship to others. That relationship should be marked by fervent love for one another, as Peter states in verse 22.

Our Relationship to Others

1 Peter 1:22

> Since you have purified your souls in obeying the truth through the Spirit in sincere love of the brethren, love one another fervently with a pure heart (1 Peter 1:22)

Peter begins his exhortation by appealing to the reality that his readers had *purified their souls*, which indicates a process that is past and complete. In other words, they had already purified their souls; it was a specific past experience with ongoing present results. This purifying of their souls took place at the time of their salvation and they were still in a state of being pure. This word *purified* is a term which describes the purification of the people and the priests. It was a word that was used to describe ceremonial cleansing, separation from wine and strong drink, and even one's virginity. Here, it is used to describe moral purity, as is made clear by the use of the word souls. This purification would include being free from all pollution of sin. Peter is not referring to an outer cleansing of the body, but to an inward cleansing of the heart.

How does one purify the soul? Peter says it is by *obeying the truth*. The *truth* he's referring to is the truth of the gospel, as seen in 1:2. Practically speaking, the truth of the gospel is something we obey at the moment of salvation, but also continue to obey as we go on turning away from any known sin in our lives. In a broader sense, though, obeying the truth would include all that is revealed in the Word of God. Jesus says in John 17:17, "Your word is truth." In Psalm 119:9, David says, "How can a young man cleanse his way? By taking heed according to Your word." In John 15:3, Jesus says to His disciples, "You are already clean because of the word which I have spoken to you." Ephesians 5:26 tells us that Christ sanctifies and cleanses the church by the washing of water by *the word.* Obedience results in, or leads to, purity. It is impossible for one to be pure without obedience to the Word.

The word *obey* is a word we have had before, in verses 2 and 14 of this chapter in 1 Peter. It means attentive hearkening, along with submission. Peter adds that this obeying the truth is *through or by the Spirit*. The Holy Spirit aids us in our obedience. He is the one, we saw in verse 2, who enables us to be obedient to the faith. He enlightens our minds to the truth, as Jesus said in John 16:13. As this truth is engrafted on our hearts, the Spirit empowers us to follow through on what we know to obey.

There are many things that we are called to be obedient to in the Christian life. But one of the central callings on God's children is loving others. John 13:35 tells us that this is how the lost will know we belong to God. Peter calls it *sincere love of the brethren*. The King James translates it "unfeigned love." To feign is to be an actor or to play a part, to be hypocritical. But we are to be sincere in our love, not hypocritical; we are to love without hypocrisy, as Paul says in Romans 12:9. A good example of hypocritical love would be that shown by the coworkers of a young businessman whose wife was expecting a baby. His business associates seemed to take a genuine interest and almost daily one of them would ask, "How's your wife doing?" or "What is the doctor saying?" or "How many more days?" He thought that their questions were because they cared and were genuinely interested in his wife's well-being. Little did he know that their motives were purely greedy; they had a bet going in the office over when the baby would arrive. That is love that is hypocritical. We might tell a friend that it is no trouble to help her out with baby-sitting or a meal, and yet our heart is resentful when we might have to actually make good on our word! That is hypocrisy.

In contrast to hypocrisy, our love should come from a pure heart, as Peter tells us to *love one another fervently with a pure heart*. In this verse, Peter uses two different Greek words for love. The first one, *love of the brethren*, is philadelphia, which is brotherly love. It speaks of liking someone and indicates an affection or fondness. It is the type of love that we as women are commanded to have toward our husband and our children, according to Titus 2. We should be fond of others and have a tender affection for those who are made in the image of God. Philadelphia love, or phileo love, is the easy one for most of us. But the second kind of love is where the challenge is for most of us. The second word for love, *love one another fervently*, is agapao, which is a sacrificial love, like that of our God. It is a love that is self-sacrificing for the benefit of someone else. It's the love that John mentions in John 3:16 that caused God to give His only Son for wretches like us! This is a love that would sacrifice time, energy, sleep, money, for the good of someone else. This love would look like the qualities Paul mentions in 1 Corinthians 13. As believers in God, we can love others with fondness and affection, and that is generally easy for us, but if we are not careful, we can become attached to others in a selfish way and thwart the agape love we should exhibit. We should have both types of love as Christians, phileo love and agape love.

It is interesting that Peter says this agape love we have for another is to come *from a pure heart*, because he's just mentioned that his readers have already purified their souls in obeying the truth. Without a pure soul, one cannot have a pure heart. As we purify our hearts from sinful desires, we are then able to love one another as we should. Our love for one another should flow from pure hearts and not be tainted with hypocrisy. It should be *fervent*. We should love one another intensely, with all of our powers being stretched, with all the energy we have. This word is also used in Luke 22:44 to describe our Lord and the agony He felt in the garden prior to His crucifixion. It states that He prayed more earnestly, fervently. Our Lord's praying stretched Him so much that His sweat was like great drops of blood falling to the ground. So, we can see that this love is work, and it is hard work, and we must constantly work at it all the time, or we will become selfish with our time and our energies and our resources. In fact, we all can measure our love practically in how we respond when quarantines, shutdowns, or natural disasters happen from time to time in our nation. As you look back on those times, did you find yourself becoming more selfish and isolated in your home, or did you look for creative ways to love other believers? Did your love stretch to the max?

Perhaps you're wondering why Peter would have to admonish his readers to love one another. Did their persecution not draw them closer together? There were two circumstances going on which likely would have prompted this exhortation. First, some of these believers were probably tempted to go back to their old way of life, to their old friends (consider 1:14; 2:11; and 4:1-3). The admonition for them, then, is to love the brethren fervently and not to be drawn away by the sinful companions of their past. Second, in the early church, just as today, there were different classes of people: slaves and free, rich and poor, educated and uneducated. Peter reminds these believers that in their new life in Christ there is no room for partiality, but they were to love all the brethren fervently, no matter which class they fell into. Perhaps Peter's readers needed this admonition to love others because the persecution they were experiencing was so great and their spiritual resolve was comparatively weak; the love and preservation of self may have been preeminent on their minds. When we go through suffering it is not always easy to focus on the needs of others; all too often we are absorbed in ourselves, which is why we need to be reminded even more to love others fervently. The best antidote for selfishness is to get our minds off ourselves and on to others. Ladies, that kind of love is impossible apart from our new life in Christ.

Our new life in Christ will produce a correct understanding of our relationship to others, a fervent love for others that is genuine. Our new life in Christ will also produce a right understanding of our relationship to the Word, as we see in verse 23.

Our Relationship to the Word

1 Peter 1:23, 25

> having been born again, not of corruptible seed but incorruptible, through the word of God which lives and abides forever, (1 Peter 1:23)

In writing about our redemption, Peter uses the words *born again*. He reminds us that we were redeemed not of seed that was *corruptible* but seed that was *incorruptible*. These words, corruptible and incorruptible, seem to be favorite words of Peter; he used them back in 1:4 and 1:18. What does Peter mean by the fact that we have been *born again, not of corruptible seed?*

As all gardeners know, one of the characteristics of a seed is that it dies. And, by dying, that seed generates life. Jesus said in John 12:24, "Most assuredly, I say to you, unless a grain of wheat falls into the ground and dies, it remains alone; but if it dies, it produces much grain." That is our natural state; like the seed that dies, we are corruptible and we will die. However, the incorruptible seed is imperishable; instead of dying, it simply gives life. We have been born again by a seed that does not decay; born again *through the word of God*. We were dead but have been given life. In the parable of the sower, in Luke 8, Christ tells His disciples that the seed is the word of God (v 11), and when that seed falls on good ground, it brings forth fruit. In fact, John says in 1 John 3:9 that "whoever has been born of God does not sin, for His seed remains in him; and he cannot sin, because he has been born of God." (John is saying in this context that a genuine believer does not practice sin because he has been born of God.) You and I have been born again by the Word of God, and Peter says it is *the word of God which lives and abides forever*. This Word lives; it is alive! Hebrews 4:12 states, "For the word of God is living and powerful, and sharper than any two-edged sword, piercing even to the division of soul and spirit, and of joints and marrow, and is a discerner of the thoughts and intents of the heart." Matthew Henry who wrote concerning this Word: "[It] is quick; it is very lively and active, in all its efforts, in seizing the conscience of the sinner, in cutting him to the heart, and in comforting him and binding up the wounds of the soul."[18] My friend, the Word of God is alive; it is not dead, and not only does it live, but it *abides forever*, which means that it stands and remains permanent and unchanging. The Psalmist said in Psalm 119:89, "Forever, O LORD, your word is settled in heaven." It is eternal; it is without end. We are born again by the Word of God. It is the Word that changes lives. It was the Word that our Lord used to combat Satan during His hour of temptation. It is the Word that God says will not return to Him void. The Word of God produces results; therefore, it behooves us to love it, read it, study it, and memorize it! It is the means to our spiritual growth, as we will see in our next lesson.

Our new life produces a correct understanding of our relationship to the Word, which lives and abides forever. Our new life also creates

---

[18] Matthew Henry, Matthew Henry's Commentary; PC Study Bible Software.

within us a correct understanding of ourselves, since we are now born again. Peter mentions this in verse 24.

Our Relationship to Ourselves

1 Peter 1:24

> because "All flesh is as grass, and all the glory of man as the flower of the grass. The grass withers, and its flower falls away, (1 Peter 1:24)

There is an interesting contrast here, between the incorruptible seed, the Word of God, in verse 23, and the corruptible seed, pictured here in verse 24 as grass. Peter compares our *flesh* to *grass*, which means vegetation or a blade of grass. He says the *grass withers*, which means it shrivels and dries up. Then he adds that its *flower falls away*, which means to drop off. Peter may have had in mind tulips and poppies, which were among some of the more common flowers of the time. Both these flowers were short lived in their beauty. We've all seen flowers and gazed at their beauty and thought, "Oh, if only I could capture that beauty forever!" And then you look out the window the next day and their beauty is gone. I just recently took some purple irises from my back yard and thought, "How lovely!" But I enjoyed them only a few days and their beauty faded. The glory of man is like that; it is short-lived. Man's glory fades and drops off, just like the flower of the grass. The *glory of man* is all that represents what man centers his attention on: his wealth, social status, talent, beauty, education, religion, friends and family—all of it is short-lived, like the grass.

In Job 14:1-2, Job says, "Man who is born of woman is of few days and full of trouble. He comes forth like a flower and fades away; he flees like a shadow and does not continue." The Psalmist describes man in Psalm 103:15-16 in similar ways. He says, "As for man, his days are like grass; as a flower of the field, so he flourishes. For the wind passes over it, and it is gone, and its place remembers it no more." James 1:10-11 talks about the rich man being like the flower of the grass, which passes away. Ecclesiastes 1:11 says there is no remembrance of former things, and even those yet to come will not remember the things to come. Ecclesiastes 2:16 says that the wise man and the fool will both be forgotten and that both will die. As I was thinking about the placing of this verse here in the context of loving the brethren, I was reminded of how important it is for all of us to take every opportunity to show love to one another, because none of us know what tomorrow may bring forth. Just like the grass, many people are soon gone, some taken young, some old. So many times, people are left with guilt after someone dies because they did not show love to them. We need to not wait till a convenient time, my friend, to love each other. That convenient time may never come!

Our salvation produces a correct understanding of ourselves. We are here today and gone tomorrow. We are like the grass or the flower whose beauty shines only for a moment, and then it withers and is gone. But, is all dismal? No. As Peter ends these thoughts, he goes back to our need to have a correct understanding of our relationship to the Word. The Word is eternal, in contrast to man, who is here today and gone tomorrow. Peter, the apostle of hope, ends this section by giving us hope, in verse 25.

Our Relationship to the Word

1 Peter 1:23, 25

> But the word of the Lord endures forever." Now this is the word which by the gospel was preached to you. (1 Peter 1:25)

The word *but* presents us with a contrast to the previous verse. Man is here today and gone tomorrow, *but the word of the Lord endures forever*. Peter repeats what he has written in verse 23, that the Word endures forever. Jesus said in Matthew 24:35, "Heaven and earth will pass away, but My words will by no means pass away." Perhaps you're thinking that these words sound familiar and, indeed, they are familiar; Peter takes them from Isaiah 40:6-8, which says, "The voice said, 'Cry out!' And he said, 'What shall I cry?' 'All flesh is grass, and all its loveliness is like the flower of the field. The grass withers, the flower fades, because the breath of the LORD blows upon it; surely the people are grass. The grass withers, the flower fades, but the word of our God stands forever." The context here in Isaiah is the glory of the Lord, verse 5, in contrast with the glory of Assyria and Babylon, which would vanish.

Peter has one last thing to say about this Word. He says that it is *this word which by the gospel was preached to them*. This is the third time that Peter reminds his readers of the gospel that has been preached to them (see 1:10-12). Though we are nothing but grass, the gospel is offered to you and to me! It is the living Word which was preached that brought us salvation. It is our sustenance in trials and our guide in how to love others.

As we finish 1 Peter, chapter one, it is pretty amazing to note all the many wonderful things offered to man, who is mere grass: Grace *unto you* (v 2); inheritance *for you* (v 4); grace come *to you* (v 10); prophets ministered for you (v 12); grace to be brought *to you* (v 13); Jesus manifest *for you* (v 20); the gospel preached *to you* (v 25). What a blessed note Peter ends on!

Summary

Our salvation gives us a correct understanding of our relationship to others. We are to love them fervently and sincerely. Our salvation also produces a right understanding of ourselves. We are grass withering away and dying. Our salvation also produces a right understanding of our relationship to the Word. It is alive and it abides forever.

As we close, I want us to emphasize Peter's command to love one another. We know from our text that it is impossible to love others without the help of the Holy Spirit and obedience to the Word of God. I thought I would close by asking you a series of questions based on 1 Corinthians 13, which is the key passage on love in the Word of God, in my opinion.

Are you patient with others? Do you become easily frustrated and irritated? Do you wait patiently on the spiritual progress of others? Are you impatient with a child who is trying to learn a concept that is difficult? **Love is patient.**

Are you kind to others in your tone of voice? Are you kind to your enemies? Are you kind to your children and husband, even when under pressure? Are you kind to your neighbor who is unkind to you? **Love is kind.**

Are you jealous of others, wanting what is not yours to have? Do you secretly wish you had their talents and gifts? Do you want their material possessions? **Love is not jealous.**

Do you boast around others, making your self look good while making others look bad? Do you think you are better than others? Do you think you have arrived? Do you look down on others who do not do things the way you do? **Love is not boastful.**

Do you involve yourself in arrogant, prideful speech? If we had a recording of your conversations this past week, would the focus have been on you or on others and the Lord? **Love is not arrogant.**

Is your behavior unbecoming around others? Are you rude in traffic; on the phone; to your husband or children? Are you courteous to others? Do you treat others the way you would like to be treated? **Love does not act unbecomingly.**

Do you seek your own selfish desires in your relationship with others? Do you hope others will serve you, instead of you serving them? Do you demand your own way, or do you lovingly let others have their way? Do you and your husband bicker about things that do not matter in light of eternity? **Love does not seek its own.**

Do you get easily provoked at others, responding in anger and frustration when you don't get your way? **Love is not provoked.**

Do you keep a record of things that are done wrong to you? Are you unforgiving? Do you hold grudges? **Love does not keep a record of wrongs.**

Do you rejoice in the evil that others do? Or is your heart grieved at the sins of others and the sins of yourself? **Love does not rejoice in evil.**

Do you rejoice in the truth? Do you delight when God's Word is taught and obeyed? **Love rejoices in truth.**

Do you bear with others, seeking to protect and not expose their sin? **Love bears all things.**

Do you expect the best in others? **Love believes all things.**

Do you easily give up on people? **Love hopes all things.**

Can you withstand just about anything, even the most horrible of situations and people? **Love endures all things.**

Does 1 Corinthians 13 characterize how you love others?

As we think of the text from this lesson, consider these questions: Have you been born again by the incorruptible Word of God? Has it made a change in your life? Do you have a correct view of your responsibility to love others and do you love others with purity of heart? Is your love without hypocrisy? Does your love for others show itself with intense energy? What about that man or woman in your church who sits on the other side of the auditorium to whom you never speak? Do you love them? What about that lady that rubs you the wrong way for some reason or another? Do you love her? What about that teenager in the church who has purple hair and a nose ring and who obviously couldn't care less about you? Do you love them? For some of you, it may be your husband who says hurtful things to you or wrongs you in some way. Do you love him? Do you love others, deeply and from your heart?

Has your salvation produced a correct understanding of your relationship to the Word? Are you in it day and night? Is it the delight of your heart, knowing that it reveals the character of the Author, our God and Lord? Do you pant after the eternal, living Word?

Lastly, what about your understanding of yourself? Do you think more highly of yourself than you should? Do you stop and think about the fact that you will one day die? The things you glory in now, will fade away. Only what is done for Christ will last. Peter says we must think less of ourselves, love others more, and love the living, eternal Word of God. These things, my friend, will aid you more than you know as you go through the fiery furnace with your Master!

Questions to Consider
Genuine Believers Possess Genuine Love for Others
1 Peter 1:22-25

1. (a) Read 1 Peter, chapter one, and note all the words or phrases you see that are repeated. (b) Why are these words or phrases important?

2. Memorize 1 Peter 1:22.

3. (a) What did Jesus say would characterize a Christian, according to John 13:34-35? (b) How should we love one another, according to 1 Thessalonians 3:12; 4:9-10; Hebrews 13:1; and 1 John 4:7? (c) What are the characteristics of love, according to Romans 12:10; 1 Peter 3:8-9; 4:8; and 1 John 3:17-18? (d) In 1 John 4:20-21, what does John say about those who do not love their brother?

4. (a) According to 1 Corinthians 13, what are the characteristics of genuine love? (b) How would you define each of these qualities of love in 1 Corinthians? (c) What qualities of love do you find difficult to practice?

5. (a) In 1 John 4:7-10, who does John say is the supreme example of love? (b) How did this example show His love? (c) Because of His example, what should we do, according to 1 John 3:16? (d) How does one practically lay down his or her life for another?

6. (a) Besides our Lord, who else comes to mind in Scripture as one who showed love to the brethren? (b) How was their love shown? (c) What principle(s) do you learn from them?

7. What practical tips can you give others for how to love difficult people that God has placed in one's life?

8. How would you summarize the first chapter of 1 Peter using only three sentences?

Chapter 7

Get Rid of Sin and Grow!
1 Peter 2:1-3

After my husband graduated from seminary many years ago, we moved to Tulsa, Oklahoma, where we planted a new church. I was so excited to start the ministry and especially to begin a ministry for the women. As head of our women's ministry, I thought it would be wise to begin by laying a solid biblical foundation. I wanted the women in our church to be students of God's Word, and so we began our ladies' ministry by going through a video series entitled *Living by the Book*, by Howard Hendricks. This was a wonderful study that taught us how to do inductive Bible study. We felt it was imperative that the foundation of our women's ministries be God's Word. It has always been my desire that God's Word be taught, studied, and memorized, because it is the means to our spiritual growth. Yet, some Christians do not see the importance of God's Word. Why is that? Why is there not an appetite for spiritual things? Howard Henricks answers that question well in one of his opening remarks in the first lesson of his video series; he says, "The Bible will keep you from sin, or sin will keep you from the Bible."[19] The apostle Peter says the same thing in a more detailed way in 1 Peter 2:1-3.

1 Peter 2:1-3

> Therefore, laying aside all malice, all guile, hypocrisy, envy, and all evil speaking, ²as newborn babes, desire the pure milk of the word, that you may grow thereby, ³if indeed you have tasted that the Lord is gracious.

---

[19]Howard Hendricks, *"Session 1: Observation," Living by the Book* (Dallas: Video Ministries).

In this lesson, we will outline the first few verses of 1 Peter 2 this way:
> *Our Grievous Sins* (v 1)
> *Our Need to Grow Up* (v 2)
> *Our Gracious Lord* (v 3)

Peter ended chapter one of his epistle with an emphasis on the Word of God, and he continues that emphasis as he begins chapter two. But before he emphasizes the Word of God, he reminds his readers of the importance of getting rid of sin so that they can grow. Before you and I can receive the Word, we must lay aside the sins that will hinder our receiving of the Word of God. Let's take a look at these grievous sins.

Our Grievous Sins

1 Peter 2:1

> Therefore, laying aside all malice, all deceit, hypocrisy, envy, and all evil speaking, (1 Peter 2:1)

Peter begins by saying *therefore*, which means because of. So, we must ask the question, "Because of what?" Because of what Peter has said in the previous verses: because of the fact that we have been born again with an incorruptible seed; because the Word of God lives forever; because we have purified our souls in obeying the truth; because of these things, we must get rid of these grievous sins. (This is an unfortunate chapter division; really, the flow of thought which began at the end of chapter one is continuing on into chapter two; Peter is still writing about the Word of God and our need to be pure. We must always keep in mind that the chapter and verse numbers were added to the text many, many years after the Scriptures were written and that they are not inspired by God.)

Peter says that we must lay aside certain things in order to grow spiritually. Paul communicates a similar idea in Colossians 3:5-9, where he says, "Therefore put to death your members which are on the earth: fornication, uncleanness, passion, evil desire, and covetousness, which is idolatry. Because of these things the wrath of God is coming upon the sons of disobedience, in which you yourselves once walked when you lived in them. But now you yourselves are to put off all these: anger, wrath, malice, blasphemy, filthy language out of your mouth. Do not lie to one another, since you have put off the old man with his deeds." In Galatians, Paul has yet another list of sins we are to put off: "Now the works of the flesh are evident, which are: adultery, fornication, uncleanness, lewdness, idolatry, sorcery, hatred, contentions, jealousies, outbursts of wrath, selfish ambitions, dissensions, heresies, envy, murders, drunkenness, revelries, and the like; of which I tell you beforehand, just as I also told you in time past, that those who practice such things will not inherit the kingdom of God" (Galatians 5:19-21). In the epistle of James, James has a shorter list than Paul, but he writes, "Therefore lay aside all filthiness and overflow of wickedness, and receive with meekness the implanted word, which is able to save your souls" (James 1:21).

So Peter tells his readers that they are to lay aside these grievous sins. The words *lay aside* mean to put away, to cast or strip off. It is the idea of flinging off a garment that has been stained or infected in some way. It is the idea mentioned in Isaiah 30:22, where Isaiah admonishes the people to cast away their idols like they would cast away a menstrual cloth; he tells them to say to their idols, "Get away!" As women, we can identify with what Isaiah is saying. Most of us would admit that wearing those things is not enjoyable and flinging them off is fabulous. That's what Peter is saying here: get rid of these sins in that same manner! (Peter also reiterates this in chapter 3, verses 10-11.) This is a once for all laying aside that Peter is talking about. Because of our new life in Christ, it is imperative that we put away once and for all any sin. Now, my friend, the scriptures are replete with admonishments regarding the importance of getting rid of sin. Consider Ezekiel 18:31-32; Romans 13:12-14; Ephesians 4:22-25; 2 Corinthians 12:20-21; Hebrews 12:1; and James 1:21, just to name a few.

Before we deal with each one of these sins, I want to point out that these sins are in contrast to what Peter wrote back in 1:22. These sins are the opposite of fervently loving our brother with a pure heart. If we love the brethren with purity of heart and with the intensity that we ought, then these sins of malice, deceit, hypocrisy, envy, and evil speaking will not plague us. If we have purified our souls in obeying the truth, as Peter says in verse 22, then these sins will not be present in our lives. These sins are in opposition to love.

The first grievous sin is *malice*. Malice refers to evil, badness, and even the term naughtiness, which is a word we don't use much anymore. When I was growing up, people would use the term naughty in reference to children who were behaving badly. Malice is also a general term for all sorts of wickedness. Someone who is malicious delights in hurting others and is determined to hurt others. King Saul is a good example of someone who was malicious; he was bent on doing harm to David. Right after I got married, I worked with a girl who was bent on doing evil to me. It was a devastating time in my life, and many times I would come home as a new bride in tears. Paul says in Titus 3:3 that we used to live in malice and envy before we came to Christ. James 1:21 tells us that we are to put away all filthiness or naughtiness. There is no room for this in the life of a believer. Did you notice that little word before malice, the word *all*? Peter says that *all malice*, which means every bit of it, the whole, all manner of malice must be flung off! We cannot hold on to even one little sin and think we are living in obedience to God and practicing holiness. As Paul says in Romans 6:1-2, "What shall we say then? Shall we continue in sin that grace may abound? Certainly not! How shall we who died to sin live any longer in it?"

Secondly, Peter says, we are to lay aside the grievous sin of deceit, and note again it is *all deceit*. The King James Version uses the term guile. What is deceit, or guile? It is trickery, and it comes from a word that means to catch something with bait, like bait you would use for catching fish. The person who practices deceit deceives others for his own means and his motives are never pure in doing so. Deceit takes on the appearance of truth so that the victim is tricked. We are not only to not practice this sin, but we are not to speak deceit, as the Psalmist says in Psalm 34:13: "Keep your tongue from evil, and your lips from speaking deceit." Peter will bring this up later on in this letter, noting that the Lord did not possess this sin; he says, about our Lord in 1 Peter 2:22, "Who committed no sin, nor was deceit found in His mouth." Peter will also tell his readers in 1 Peter 3:10 that if they want to love life and see good days then they need to put off this wicked sin: "He who would love life and see good days, let him refrain his tongue from evil, and his lips from speaking deceit." Deceit is a wicked sin that we should have no part in.

There is a third sin Peter mentions, and that is the sin of *hypocrisy*. Hypocrisy is a word which was used to describe an actor on the Greek stage. The actor or actress pretended to play a part that was not who they truly were. That's what actors are: they put on a mask, so to speak, and pretend to be a person whom they are not. A hypocrite is one who assumes the mannerisms, speech, and character of someone else, thus hiding his or her true identity. A hypocrite speaks words that are different from his or her true heart. Ananias and Sapphira, in Acts 5, are clear examples of hypocrites. They outwardly pretended to be religious by bringing money and laying it at the apostle's feet, claiming that they'd given the full amount, but all the while they inwardly knew they'd kept back part of the money for their own interests. Their hypocrisy cost them their lives. God killed them instantly. That's a pretty high price to pay for hypocrisy. Christians should be themselves; they should be an open book; they should be honest and transparent about who they are and what they do. Pretending to be someone you are not is hypocrisy. God hates hypocrisy. It's clear from His Word that He takes it very seriously. In fact, in our last lesson, we saw in verse 22 that our love for each other is to be without hypocrisy, which means it is to be sincere and without pretending.

Number four on Peter's get-rid-of list is envy. What is envy? Envy is a longing for what someone else has that you do not have. "Envy is the feeling of displeasure produced by witnessing or hearing of the advantage or prosperity of others."[20] Envy is a horrible sin, and it can lead to hatred and murder if not kept under control, as the example of Cain and Abel demonstrates so well. We know from 1 Corinthians 13 that genuine love does not envy. Someone once said that envy is the last sin to die. "As long as self remains active within someone's heart, there will be envy in that person's life."[21] Even among the disciples, envy reared its ugly head; in Luke 22:24, we see them striving with each other over who among them would be the greatest. Jesus reminds them, as He often did, that the greatest one among them would be the one who is a servant (verse 27). James says it well in James 3:14-16: "But if you have bitter envy and self-seeking in your hearts, do not boast and lie against the truth. This wisdom does not descend from above, but is earthly, sensual, demonic. For where envy and self-seeking exist, confusion and every evil thing are there." Proverbs 14:30 says, "A sound heart is life to the body, but envy is rottenness to the bones." Ladies, we who are prone to osteoporosis cannot afford any more rotting of the bones, right? We certainly need to fling off all envy! In fact, I believe that we as women are more prone to this sin than men.

The last sin on Peter's throw-off list is evil *speaking*, and once again he uses the word *all* to emphasize that absolutely no evil speaking is becoming to a child of God. Evil speaking means speaking against or speaking down. It refers to slandering or speaking against another person. This would be manifested in malicious gossip, back-biting, and slander. The term was used in biblical times to speak of a slave who would blab his master's secrets. Evil speaking often is the result of envy. When we are jealous of another's accomplishments or position, we may be tempted to use those opportunities to speak evil of that person to others. By doing so, we defame their character behind their back. Peter will mention in 1 Peter 3:16 that this kind of speech is practiced by evil men. James writes in James 4:11-12, "Do not speak evil of one another, brethren. He who speaks evil of a brother and judges his brother, speaks evil of the law and judges

---

[20] D. Edmond Hiebert, First Peter: An Expositional Commentary (Chicago: Moody Press, 1984), 111.

[21] William Barclay, The Letters of James and Peter (New Daily Study Bible), (Louisville: Westminster John Knox Press, 2003), 220.

the law. But if you judge the law, you are not a doer of the law but a judge. There is one Lawgiver, who is able to save and to destroy. Who are you to judge another?" Once again, I believe this is a special challenge for us as women. I hope none of us here in this room will have written on our tombstone what one lady had: "Beneath this stone a lump of clay, lies Arabella Young, who, on the 24th of May, began to hold her tongue."

We could spend a whole lesson on the tongue alone—and perhaps need to—but we must move on to the next verse. I would encourage you before you speak to ask yourself, "Is what I am about to say true? Is it necessary? Would I say this about that person if they were standing right here?" If not, then don't say it. I would also encourage you to talk less; Proverbs 10:19 says, "In the multitude of words sin is not lacking, but he who restrains his lips is wise." One man's poem puts it well: "If your lips would keep from slips, five things observe with care. To whom you speak, of whom you speak, and how and when and where."[22] We probably have all been the victims of malicious gossip that has cut deep into our hearts, and we know how destructive it can be, and yet as women we almost seem to enjoy it. I would encourage you, if this is difficult for you, to do a study in the Word on the tongue—I guarantee you will be deeply convicted. James 3 is a good place to start! Instead of being involved in such wickedness, in the next verse Peter tells us that we need to grow up! We move from our grievous sins to our need to grow up!

Our Need to Grow Up

1 Peter 2:2

> as newborn babes, desire the pure milk of the word, that you may grow thereby, (1 Peter 2:2)

James writes similar words in James 1:21: "Therefore lay aside all filthiness and overflow of wickedness, and receive with meekness the implanted word, which is able to save your souls." Before we

---
[22]Anonymous

can receive the Word of God and grow by it, we must first get rid of sin.

Peter uses the analogy here in verse 2 of *newborn babes*, which actually means one who has just been born. Luke uses this same word in Luke 2:16 when writing of Jesus in the manger; He had just been born. In classical Greek, this term was used of a baby at the breast. In other words, just like a newborn baby acts like its life depends on the next feeding, so we must have that same longing for the Word. When a baby is born, what is the one thing they continually want to do? Eat! Peter says they desire milk, which means they have an intense craving for it. It not only entails intensity, but it includes the idea of a reoccurring yearning. That is the type of desire that we must have for the Word of God! It is the same word that the Psalmist uses in Psalm 42:1 "As the deer pants for the water brooks, so pants my soul for You, O God." I remember hearing that making a baby wait a few minutes to eat is like making an adult wait three days. Now, I don't know how they know that or even if it's true—but if it is true, do you hunger for the Word like that? Do you hunger and ache for it until you partake and are satisfied? When my two children were infants, I remember that they would wail when they were hungry, but as soon as they were put to the breast they stopped crying; they even made noises indicating they were satisfied! My dear sister, do you kick and scream if you don't get to spend time in God's Word? Do you partake until you're satisfied? We should not be content with just a taste of the Word, a verse here and a verse there; our spiritual appetite should be such that we drink deeply until we're satisfied. I also remember that one feeding did not satisfy my babies for the whole day. It seemed as if I would just get them fed, and 3 hours later, they were hungry again. Does that describe your appetite for the Word? Or are you satisfied with a chapter a day? Do you partake of it until you're satisfied, only to go a few more hours and realize you're hungry again for the Word? Our desire should be like that of the prophet Jeremiah, who said in Jeremiah 15:16, "Your words were found, and I ate them, and Your word was to me the joy and rejoicing of my heart; for I am called by Your name, O LORD God of hosts." Or like the Psalmist who said in 119:103, "How sweet are

Your words to my taste, sweeter than honey to my mouth!" Or even Job, who said even in the midst of tremendous suffering, "I have not departed from the commandment of His lips; I have treasured the words of His mouth more than my necessary food."

The Psalmist tells us in Psalm 1 that it is the godly man (or woman) who meditates on the Word day and night. Does this describe your appetite for God's Word? If not, what do you have an appetite for? Most of us can identify with appetite, or at least those of us who like to eat. I think of how many times I have ruined a perfectly healthy meal, by eating the wrong things before the meal. Many of us will tell our kids, "no snacking" before a meal because we know it will ruin their appetite. Have you ruined your appetite for God's Word? What is ruining your appetite for the Word? Are you putting junk in your mind and heart? Are you wasting time shopping, talking on the phone, surfing the internet, watching television? My friend, anything that takes away your spiritual appetite should be forsaken so that you might desire the pure milk of the Word. Sin will destroy your appetite for Scripture. If you are involved in any of those sins Peter just listed in verse one, or any other sins, then I would imagine you do not have a healthy appetite for the Scriptures. Just like a fat piece of cake will take away your appetite for a healthy dinner in the physical realm, so it is in the spiritual realm. If you are being satisfied with what the world has to offer, then you will have no appetite left for the things of God. Remember Howard Hendricks' words from the beginning of this lesson? Either the Word will keep you from sin, or sin will keep you from the Word. Even in the physical realm, when a person does not have an appetite for food, that clues the doctor in that something isn't right; God made our bodies to desire and enjoy food. So it is in the spiritual realm. If you do not have an appetite for God's Word, that should clue you in that something is wrong. A spiritually healthy Christian should be a hungry Christian. A hungry baby is a sign of a healthy baby. A hungry Christian is a sign of a healthy Christian. One man said, "My rule for Christian living is this: anything that dims my vision of Christ, or takes away my taste for Bible study, or cramps my prayer life, or makes Christian work difficult is wrong for me, and I must, as a Christian, turn away from it."[23] If you do not have an appetite for the Word on a consistent basis, then perhaps there is sin in your life. Your hunger for God's Word will be in direct relation to your obedience to it.

Now, the Word has a certain quality to it. What is the quality of our spiritual food? It is *pure*, which means it is sincere, uncontaminated, unadulterated. It has nothing added to it, no additives or preservatives. It is not watered down, like some other spiritual books are. They tell us that a mother's milk is the best source of nutrition for her newborn baby, even over formulas, because it is pure, it is unadulterated, and it is full of nutrients and natural immune fighters. So it is in the spiritual realm. The *pure milk of the Word* is the best means of spiritual nourishment for you. In fact, one translation of the Greek is pure spiritual milk. It is pure, in contrast to the sins mentioned in verse one, which are impure and unholy. I once discipled a gal who refused to read any other religious books but chose to read only the Bible. Sometimes I have thought that might not be a bad idea, though I am grateful for the writings of others, especially in the spiritual realm. That may seem extreme to you, but on the other hand, I know many more women who substitute devotional literature or religious books for time in the Word. I would encourage you not to let that happen to you. You should be spending more time in the Word than in any other book. If you don't, I can guarantee you will become stunted in your spiritual growth. You will also become spiritually undiscerning of truth and eventually be swept away by man's ideas over God's. And, ladies, I would also lovingly warn you that some so-called religious books are filled with dangerous ideas that are not from God. Jay Adams says, "Watered down teaching, psychologically oriented drinks, superficial Bible study methods and pale preaching fail to give the true taste of pure milk that will make one cry out like a baby for more."[24]

---

[23] Dr. Wilbur Chapman

[24] Jay Adams, The Christian Counselor's Commentary: Hebrews, James, I and II Peter, and Jude (Woodruff, S.C.: Timeless Texts, 1996), 247.

Why should we crave God's Word? What is the result of craving God's Word? Peter says so that we can *grow*! In other words that we might be nourished and *grow thereby*. The original text reads so that you might grow up in your salvation. Some have said that milk may be the most nourishing of all foods and that children who drink milk grow faster than children who do not. The Word is the most nourishing of all spiritual food. Spiritual children, who drink the milk of the Word, grow faster than children who do not. Have you asked yourself lately, am I growing spiritually? Are my spiritual muscles being developed? Have you ever been around someone and wondered why they are not growing spiritually? Maybe it is in direct relation to the Word of God and time spent in it, or the lack thereof. Some of us, as believers, are very anemic spiritually because we do not have proper spiritual nutrition. We don't know where even the simplest things in Scripture are; we don't have power over the sin in our lives; and we are unable to help others because we are still crawling around in spiritual diapers. My friend, if you starve your newborn baby, he or she will die. If you starve yourself as a Christian, you will die out spiritually and become ineffective for the Lord. Peter tells us we need to grow up by desiring the Word of God. He then reminds us of how good the Lord tastes, in verse 3. I mean, why would we want to partake of sin when we can partake of our gracious Lord? Let's consider this fact from verse 3.

Our Gracious Lord

1 Peter 2:3

if indeed you have tasted that the Lord is gracious. (1 Peter 2:3)

The word *if* means for as much, or since, *you have tasted*. Peter is quoting here from Psalm 34:8, which says, "Oh, taste and see that the LORD is good; blessed is the man who trusts in Him!" What does it mean to *taste* the goodness of the Lord? It means to experience that the Lord is excellent. The word *gracious* here comes from a Greek word which is used in Luke 5:39 to speaks of old wine being better; it literally means excellent. Peter is reminding his readers of the fact that they have tasted of the Lord, they have found that He is excellent, and now they are to continue to taste of Him. We can understand what Peter is saying here because even in the physical realm a taste of something excites our appetite for more. A potato chip, a piece of chocolate, a chocolate chip cookie, or something that our palate really enjoys—we want more! So it is with the Word of God; once you have truly tasted of it, your appetite is excited and you want more. Jesus Himself said in John 6:35, "I am the bread of life. He who comes to Me shall never hunger, and he who believes in Me shall never thirst." Jesus Christ is the only thing that satisfies the hungry and thirsty soul. If you are eating something else besides the Living Word, I guarantee that your soul is not satisfied.

Summary

What are our grievous sins from verse 1? They are malice, deceit, hypocrisy, envy, and evil speaking. Are you practicing any of these sins or any others that Peter does not mention? If you are, then I can promise you they are keeping you from growing up.

Peter tells us of our need to grow up in verse 2. Do you desire to grow in your knowledge of God and His Word? Do you desire the Word like a newborn baby desires milk with great intensity? If not, why not?

Why not taste and see that the Lord is gracious, as Peter tells us in verse 3? Have you tasted the Lord to know that He is excellent? Are you craving the Word often and with great intensity? Do you not only taste it but also chew on it, memorize it, and study it? I promise you that once you taste of it, you will develop an appetite for more. This was just recently illustrated to me with a woman I disciple. I have often encouraged her to get into the Word in a deeper way, but she has resisted. Just recently, though, because of some unusual circumstances, her excuses were stripped away. She finally "got into it," and the delight she has experienced has been amazing! Oh, my friend, do not lose your appetite for God and for His word! Taste and see how good it is! It satisfies the deepest longings.

Martin Luther said, "Whoever sits at the table and is hungry relishes everything heartily; but he who has previously been satisfied, relishes nothing, but he can only murmur at the most excellent food."[25] My dear friend, I beg you to repent of any sin you are holding on to. Throw it off like a filthy rag, and do it now, so that it doesn't spoil your appetite for God's Word. And then get into the Word. If you don't know how or where to start or how to study, get with someone who does and who will challenge you and hold you accountable. I encourage you to be like that newborn baby with an always-hungering, never-satisfied desire for God's Word.

---

[25]Martin Luther, Commentary on Peter and Jude (Grand Rapids: Kregel Publications, 1982), 84.

Questions to Consider
Get Rid of Sin and Grow!
1 Peter 2:1-3

(You may want to glance at Question 8 before completing the following questions.)

1. As you read 1 Peter 2:1-3, do you see any connection between these verses and the last several verses from chapter one? If so, what is the connection?

2. (a) What are the characteristics of a hypocrite, according to Matthew 7:1-5; 15:7-9; 23:13-33; and Mark 12:13-17? (b) What is going to happen to hypocrites, according to Job 36:13 (KJV) and Matthew 24:51?

3. Memorize 1 Peter 2:2.

4. Make three columns on your paper. Label the first column *Who was Envious*. Label the second column *Why They were Envious*. Label the third column *The Result of Their Envy* (or *What I Learned about Envy*). Using the following verses, fill in these columns: Genesis 37; 1 Samuel 18:1-16; Psalm 73; Matthew 2.

5. (a) In James 3:1-12, what does James say our tongue is like? (b) According to James, why is the tongue so hard to tame? (c) What does the Word say about women and their speech in Proverbs 6:24; 31:26; 1 Timothy 3:11; 5:11-14; and Titus 2:1-3? (d) What do you find personally challenging about taming your own tongue?

6. (a) King Saul committed each of the five sins listed in 1 Peter 2:1. Read 1 Samuel 18-19 and write down each incident in Saul's life where you see these five sins committed. (b) What does this teach you about the fact that one sin leads to another, which leads to another? (c) What biblical counsel would you

have given King Saul after the incident in 18:7-9 happened? (d) How would you admonish him so that his sin would not produce other sins?

7. (a) Are you guilty of any of the sins listed in 1 Peter 2:1? (b) What have you done in the past to root it out, and what are your current plans for laying it aside?

8. Would you say you have a hearty appetite for God's Word? If not, what are you filling up on? Try this exercise this week: Make two columns. Label one column *Biblical Input*, which would include Bible reading, study, teaching, preaching, etc. Label the other column *Other Input*, which would include all forms of entertainment, phone calls, meetings, internet surfing, etc. Keep a record each day of the time you spend and the types of activities you engage in for each of these columns, and then total up the hours in each column. What did you discover?

9. Reflecting on your answers to Questions 7 and 8, how do you need others to be praying for you?

Chapter 8

Is Jesus Precious or Offensive to You?
1 Peter 2:4-8

There is a song I learned as a child that goes right along with our lesson. The song goes like this:

> The wise man built his house upon the rock
> The wise man built his house upon the rock
> The wise man built his house upon the rock
> And the rain came tumbling down
>
> Oh, the rain came down and the floods came up
> The rain came down and the floods came up
> The rain came down and the floods came up
> And the wise man's house stood firm.
>
> The foolish man built his house upon the sand
> The foolish man built his house upon the sand
> The foolish man built his house upon the sand
> And the rain came tumbling down
>
> Oh, the rain came down and the floods came up
> The rain came down and the floods came up
> The rain came down and the floods came up
> And the foolish man's house went "splat!"
>
> So, build your house on the Lord Jesus Christ
> Build your house on the Lord Jesus Christ
> Build your house on the Lord Jesus Christ
> And the blessings will come down
>
> Oh, the blessings come down as your prayers go up
> The blessings come down as your prayers go up

> The blessings come down as your prayers go up
> So, build your house on the Lord Jesus Christ[26]

The message of this song, which many of us learned as children, is a simple one, and yet its meaning has tremendous implications. It is the exact message of 1 Peter 2:4-8, only Peter uses more grown-up words. Let's read them together.

1 Peter 2:4-8

> Coming to Him as to a living stone, rejected indeed by men, but chosen by God and precious, [5]you also, as living stones, are being built up a spiritual house, a holy priesthood, to offer up spiritual sacrifices acceptable to God through Jesus Christ. [6]Therefore it is also contained in the Scripture, "Behold, I lay in Zion a chief cornerstone, elect, precious, and he who believes on Him will by no means be put to shame." [7]Therefore, to you who believe, He is precious; but to those who are disobedient, "The stone which the builders rejected has become the chief cornerstone," and "A stone of stumbling and a rock of offense." They stumble, being disobedient to the word, to which they also were appointed.

In this lesson, we'll ask and answer two questions:

> *How Do We Recognize a Living Stone?* (vv 4-5)
> *How Do We Recognize the Chief Cornerstone?* (vv 6-8)

Let's consider, first, how to recognize a living stone. What I mean by that is: how do we know that we are a part of God's building, a genuine child of God? In verses 4 and 5, Peter will give us five descriptions of living stones.

---

[26] The Wise Man and the Foolish Man; Words by Ann Omley.

How Do We Recognize a Living Stone?

1 Peter 2:4-5

> Coming to Him as to a living stone, rejected indeed by men, but chosen by God and precious, (1 Peter 2:4)

Peter begins by saying *coming to Him*, and *Him* is a reference back to the Lord in verse 3, who is described as excellent or gracious. The word *coming* means to approach, to draw near, or to worship. This would indicate a close and a habitual presence as well as an intimate association. The person who is coming to the Lord is seeking the Lord with the intention to stay with Him. This is one who has tasted that the Lord is good and whose longing for that taste is never satisfied. This is the one who pants for God like the deer that pants for water. Those who have tasted of the Lord's goodness and continue to taste of His goodness have no dread of coming into His presence. *So, the first description of a living stone, one who belongs to God, is that they come to God habitually for worship and intimacy.*

We not only come to Him for our spiritual food, as we saw in our last lesson, but we also come to Him as our Rock. Peter says we come *as to a living stone*. This *stone* we come to is *living*, not dead. Jesus is alive; He's risen from the dead. He is a living Savior. No other religion can claim a living God—all other gods are dead! Now, we know that stones don't have life, but Peter is speaking figuratively here. He evidently likes the term living; he has already talked about our living hope in 1 Peter 1:3 and the living Word in 1 Peter 1:23. In addition to these references, in John 6:51, Jesus is also called "the living bread." In Hebrews 10:20, He's called "the living way." And in John 4:10, He speaks of Himself as "the living water." Peter even referred to Christ as being "the living God," in Matthew 16:16, where he confesses, "You are the Christ, the Son of the living God." Jesus is alive because He has been raised from the dead and will die no more, as Romans 6:9 says. Jesus said in John 14:6 that He is the way, the truth, and the life! He is the life, and He is living.

Not all have tasted this gracious stone to see that He is good. Some have rejected Him. This stone, Jesus, is *rejected indeed by men.* The word *rejected* is also translated as disallowed. In biblical times, cut stones were examined and either approved or disapproved before they would be used in first class buildings. Those stones which were rejected were thrown out or cast away. Jesus was put to the test for 33 years on earth. He was examined by the Jews for the purpose of approving Him as their Messiah, but they rejected and disapproved Him. He was not the kind of Messiah they were expecting. They wanted an earthly King to rule them, not a man of sorrows who would save them from their sin. Isaiah says it well in Isaiah 53:3, "He is despised and rejected by men, a Man of sorrows and acquainted with grief. And we hid, as it were, our faces from Him; He was despised, and we did not esteem Him." John says in John 1:11, "He came to His own, and His own did not receive Him." And, my friend, men and women are still rejecting Him today. Men and women don't want a God they have to be accountable to, one who will be their authority; they want a God who will provide for them physically and materially, who will make their lives easy and pain-free. They do not want a Savior who confronts their sin and demands complete denial of self. He is still rejected indeed by men today.

Jesus may be despised and rejected by men, but He is *chosen by God* and He is *precious. Chosen* means to be chosen of God or chosen in the sight of God. It means to select and, by implication, to favor. It implies the absolute power of decisive choice, which is with God, as we saw already in 1 Peter 1:20. Isaiah the prophet said in Isaiah 42:1, "Behold! My Servant whom I uphold, *my Elect One* in whom My soul delights! I have put My Spirit upon Him; he will bring forth justice to the Gentiles" (emphasis mine). Peter says this One is not only chosen, but He is also *precious,* which means He is dear, more honorable, more recognized, or held in honor. This must have been a great comfort to Peter's readers, as they too were being rejected by their persecutors. But, praise God, they were precious to Him and chosen by Him, as we have already seen in 1 Peter 1:2. In the same way that both Christ and His followers are spoken of as chosen by

God, so Christ is not the only One referred to as a living stone; His children are also called living stones in verse 5.

> you also, as living stones, are being built up a spiritual house, a holy priesthood, to offer up spiritual sacrifices acceptable to God through Jesus Christ. (1 Peter 2:5)

Peter says *you also*. Even those who once were complete outsiders but have now come to Christ, you also are *living stones. Living* is the same word here as in verse 4. Christians are so closely united with Christ that the life that is in Him is in them. Jesus mentions this several times in His High Priestly Prayer, in John 17 (verses 21 and 23). Paul also spoke of it in Galatians 2:20: "I have been crucified with Christ; it is no longer I who live, but Christ lives in me; and the life which I now live in the flesh I live by faith in the Son of God, who loved me and gave Himself for me." *So, the second way to recognize a living stone is that it has life!* Jesus said in John 10:10, "I have come that they may have life, and that they may have it more abundantly." When we get to 1 Peter 3:10, we are even going to see that Christians ought to love the life we have right now on earth!

Christians not only have life, but we are known as *a spiritual house*, Peter says. The temple was the most honored building to the Jew, so for Peter to refer to it is important. Peter says we are *being built up*, which means to be a house-builder. As living stones, we are being built up into a *spiritual* house, which means to be non-carnal or supernatural; the stones of this building are characterized by belonging to the Spirit. This spiritual house is the body of Christ or the church universal. This would include all saints, past, present, and future. "The Scriptures know nothing of an individual piety that is out of touch with the living body of God's people. Furthermore, a house is not a jumbled pile of stones. The image implies the orderly and purposeful arrangement of the individual stones, each shaped and placed to fulfill its assigned task."[27] New Testament saints should not be isolated from other believers or get their regular diet of spiritual food from the television and on-line teaching, yet I know

---

[27] D. Edmond Hiebert, *First Peter: An Expositional Commentary* (Chicago: Moody Press, 1984), 121.

people now who refuse to go to church because they prefer to get their spiritual food via media. My friend, this is not God's intention for His children. We need each other.

I've heard my husband say that the church is the learning lab of how to love. I mean, how are you going to learn to love and serve others if you isolate yourself at home? The writer to the Hebrews says in Hebrews 10:25 that we should be "not forsaking the assembling of ourselves together, as is the manner of some, but exhorting one another, and so much the more as you see the Day approaching." Paul also speaks of the importance of the body of Christ in 1 Corinthians 12:12-31 and Ephesians 4:11-16; he also speaks to our being built into a spiritual house in Ephesians 2:20-22.

Peter and Paul aren't the only biblical authors who mention the fact that we are a building. The writer to the Hebrews refers to God's children as the house of God in Hebrews 3:6. We are all living stones that make up a spiritual house. We are all sizes and shapes; we all have different gifts and functions. But we still need one another. We are a body; we are a building. When one stone is missing, it puts a strain on the whole building. In fact, when you consider this in the physical realm, it is true there as well. If you take a stone or brick out of the structure of your house, you are eventually going to have problems. My friend, we need one another for strength and stability. One of my great concerns during the Covid-19 quarantine was that people might accustom themselves to staying at home and not see the value of corporate worship and gatherings. *So, a third description of a living stone is that it is a part of a spiritual building that works together.*

Peter goes on to describe these living stones in a fourth way: they are a holy priesthood. Peter will refer to us in verse 9 as a royal priesthood, but here it is a *holy priesthood*. The word priests is also used in Revelation 1:6, where John refers to us as priests: "And has made us kings and priests to His God and Father, to Him be glory and dominion forever and ever. Amen." Peter says here that we are *holy*, which means we are sacred, consecrated. In the Old Testament, priests were chosen by God and their primary responsibilities were to offer sacrifices on the behalf of God's people. They had to be clothed in a certain manner, and they were expected to obey God in everything and to live holy lives. We too have been chosen by God, clothed in His righteousness, for the purpose of offering up spiritual sacrifices, living in holiness, and obeying Him in all things. Priests were the only ones who had access to God. In the same way, you, as holy priests, have access to God because of the shed blood of Jesus Christ.

(Just a side note here: Did you know that we as older women are especially admonished in this area, to have behavior that is like that of a priest or priestess? In Titus 2:3, the older women are called to be reverent in behavior, which means she is to have the behavior of a priest, behavior that is holy. This is a sober calling for those of us who are older women! We must be holy so that we can pass on those good things to the young women we teach.) Living stones are continually coming to Christ, they have life, they are part of a spiritual house, and they are holy as priests.

Peter also describes living stones in one more way. He says that they *offer up spiritual sacrifices acceptable to God through Jesus Christ.* One of the main responsibilities of the Israelite priests was to offer up sacrifices to God, and Peter says that is one of the main things we as priests are to do as well. *This is the fifth sign of a living stone: they offer up sacrifices acceptable to God.* To *offer up* means to bring up to the altar. The word *sacrifice* means to slaughter. This is a reference to what took place in the Old Testament when the priest would offer up a sacrifice; he would carry it four and a half feet up to the altar. These animal sacrifices were offered up in atonement for the people's sins; they were also emblematic of thanksgiving and communion with God. James uses this term, offer up, in James 2:21, in writing about Abraham offering up Isaac, his only son, as a test of his faith. Obviously, we are not expected to offer up literal sacrifices, like lambs, but we are called to offer up our lives in spiritual service.

We are called to deny ourselves daily; we are called to take up our cross daily; we are called to follow Him daily; and we are called to serve others daily. These sacrifices, Peter says, are to be *acceptable to God*, which means to receive to one's self with pleasure, to be well-received or approved. These are offered *to God through Jesus Christ*, which means that Jesus is the channel by which we offer our sacrifices. Hebrews 13:15 states it well: "Therefore by Him let us continually offer the sacrifice of praise to God, that is, the fruit of our lips, giving thanks to His name." That's an amazing truth, because I don't know what you and I could offer to Him that is not tainted with sin. It is a wonderful but often neglected privilege that you and I have, the privilege of being able to give back to the One who gave His life for us.

In summary, we have five ways in which to recognize a living stone, a believer.

1. They come to God habitually.
2. They have life.
3. They are a body working together like a building.
4. They are holy as priests.
5. They offer up daily sacrifices acceptable to God.

Let's move from how we can recognize a living stone to how can we recognize the chief cornerstone. There are three ways to recognize Him.

How Do We Recognize the Chief Cornerstone?

1 Peter 2:6-8

> Therefore it is also contained in the Scripture, "Behold, I lay in Zion a chief cornerstone, elect, precious, and he who believes on Him will by no means be put to shame." (1 Peter 2:6-8)

The first question that comes to mind when reading this verse is: What scripture is Peter referring to? Peter is referring to Isaiah 28:16, which says, "Therefore thus says the Lord GOD: 'Behold, I lay in

Zion a stone for a foundation, a tried stone, a precious cornerstone, a sure foundation; whoever believes will not act hastily.'" The context here in Isaiah is judgment, which was being poured out on the ten tribes for their pride and drunkenness. God's Word went out and they rejected it, yet a remnant was preserved. Those who had entered into the false covenant with Egypt, rather than God's deliverance, the tried stone, would be swept away in judgment. The others, who trusted in the Lord, the precious cornerstone, would not be ashamed. They would not have to flee in panic at the coming judgment. Later on in Peter's epistle, he will write that judgment begins at the house of God (1 Peter 4:17). We know that his readers were undergoing terrible persecution and God's hand of judgment was at work. Peter's words here would be a comfort to them as they see judgment falling. They would not have to panic or be ashamed. They'd have the comfort of the chief cornerstone. My friend, this should be a comfort us, as well, as we see the judgment of God falling around us.

Peter says that *Zion* is the place of this chief cornerstone. What does he mean by that? Zion was a hill in Jerusalem, and here the term is being used figuratively to represent the church. Jerusalem was the place that Christ suffered and where the preaching of the Gospel took place. The writer to the Hebrews says in Hebrews 12:22, "But you have come to Mount Zion and to the city of the living God, the heavenly Jerusalem, to an innumerable company of angels."What does it mean *to lay in Zion a chief cornerstone*? The *cornerstone* was the part of a building which was the support for the rest of the building. It was visible, and without it, the building would not have any strength or stability. Paul says in Ephesians 2:20 that Jesus Christ is the chief cornerstone. Just as a building cannot support itself without the chief cornerstone, so you and I cannot support ourselves without our cornerstone, Jesus Christ. Without Him, we can do nothing. We have no strength or stability without Him. Paul tells us in 1 Corinthians 3:11, "For no other foundation can anyone lay than that which is laid, which is Jesus Christ." And this cornerstone is *elect*, which means the same thing we saw in verse four, chosen by

God. This is not just any stone, but one chosen by God for a purpose. *So, the first way to recognize the chief cornerstone is that He is elect by God.*

Not only is this cornerstone elect, but He is also precious. This is the second way we recognize the chief cornerstone. Precious is another word which we had in verse four; it means that He is dear or held in honor. This must be a favorite word of Peter's; he uses it seven times in his epistles. Peter says that *he who believes on Him,* that is, Jesus, the chief cornerstone, *will by no means be put to shame.* Those who entrust their spiritual well-being to Christ will not be put to shame. The words *no means* come from a strong negative in the Greek that means never, no never will be put to shame. The word *shame* means to be disgraced or put to the blush. Now, the quote from the Isaiah passage says whoever believes will not act hastily, which means they will not flee in panic. What Peter is saying is this: if you are a child of God, when judgment comes, you will not flee away in haste, for no enemy shall ever be able to thwart Him. We will not flee from our faith; we will not be disappointed in Him. We will not flee in confusion and terror from the danger hanging over us. In the hour of crisis, the believer will stand firm. This would have been of great importance to those Peter was writing to; they were undergoing tremendous persecution and these words would have encouraged them to remain steadfast. They would not be disappointed in the living, Chief Cornerstone; He would hold them together; He would not fail them. This is not a promise that we'll never die in judgment or persecution, because we know countless believers have. But even if we do die as a result of persecution or God's judgment on our land, God has not failed us. To live is Christ, and to die is gain.

To those of us who believe in the chief cornerstone, we will never be disappointed. Why? Because to us He is precious, as Peter says in verse 7.

> Therefore, to you who believe, He is precious; but to those who are disobedient, "The stone which the builders rejected has become the chief cornerstone," (1 Peter 2:7)

Those *who believe* and have been selected as living stones have a different attitude toward this chief cornerstone than the attitude of those who don't believe in Him. To us, *He is precious*, He is dear, He is honored. Just as Christ is precious to God, He is precious to us! But *to those who are disobedient*, to those who have not believed in Jesus, which is what the word disobedient means, He has been *rejected* by them. The disobedience that Peter refers to here is a refusal to believe the gospel message. In Titus 3:3, Paul describes us as disobedient before our new life in Christ: "For we ourselves were also once foolish, disobedient, deceived, serving various lusts and pleasures, living in malice and envy, hateful and hating one another."

Peter describes those who are disobedient as *builders*. These were the ones who tested and rejected the living stone. During Passion Week, Jesus quoted this verse directly and applied it to the scribes and Pharisees, in Matthew 21:42-46: "Jesus said to them, 'Have you never read in the Scriptures: 'The stone which the builders rejected has become the chief cornerstone. This was the Lord's doing, and it is marvelous in our eyes'? Therefore I say to you, the kingdom of God will be taken from you and given to a nation bearing the fruits of it. And whoever falls on this stone will be broken; but on whomever it falls, it will grind him to powder. Now when the chief priests and Pharisees heard His parables, they perceived that He was speaking of them. But when they sought to lay hands on Him, they feared the multitudes, because they took Him for a prophet." Peter also talks about this in Acts 4:5-12 and applies it to the persecuting Jewish Sanhedrin. This also is mentioned in Psalm 118:22, which is a Psalm many believe was sung by Christ and the disciples before He went to the cross. *The stone which the builders rejected has become the chief cornerstone.*

According to tradition, during the building of the temple, an unusually shaped stone was rejected by the builders as useless, only later they realized that it was the very stone they needed to complete the building. This is probably what Peter was saying here: You builders examined this Stone, this living Head of the Corner, and you disapproved Him, you rejected Him, you regarded Him as useless, and little did you know that it was exactly what you needed so desperately! *This is the third way to recognize the Chief cornerstone: He is rejected by some.* Peter goes on to say,

> and "A stone of stumbling and a rock of offense." They stumble, being disobedient to the word, to which they also were appointed. (1 Peter 2:8)

Christ was not only rejected by them, but He was *a stone of stumbling*. A stone of stumbling would be a stone on which one would trip while walking on the road. Paul says in 1 Corinthians 1:23, "but we preach Christ crucified, to the Jews a stumbling block and to the Greeks foolishness."

One man helps us here: "The picture is of a stone cast aside in the process of building. On the construction site where it has been left after throwing it aside, grass has grown up on all sides. As they work, the builders continually find themselves stumbling over this stone which they cast aside and now lies in their way. Christ is like that—as they go on attempting to build for God in their own way, they stumble over the One who should be the very cornerstone of the building. They find, to their dismay, that they can never quite rid themselves of this Stone that they have rejected. He has become a Stone of stumbling (see Paul's discussion of Israel's stumbling so as to be rejected by God: Romans 11:9-11)."[28]

But Jesus was not only a stone of stumbling; He was also *a rock of offense*. What is a rock of offense? The terms rock and stone in this verse come from two different Greek words. A *rock* refers to a mass of rock large enough to crush a person. The word *offense* refers to a deadly trap intended for an animal. The point Peter is making is that rejecting Christ brings spiritual devastation. *They stumble*, and they are *disobedient to the word*. This, again, is a quote taken from Isaiah, this time from Isaiah 8:14. The context in that passage is more or less the same as what we saw in Isaiah 28. The people were following Ahaz and Assyria, rather than God. They followed

---

[28] Jay Adams, The Christian Counselor's Commentary: Hebrews, James I and II Peter, and Jude (Woodruff: Timeless Texts, 1996), 249.

worldly wisdom and rejected the Word. They would be smashed by this rock of divine judgment. Both these quotes from Isaiah are really proclaiming the same message. Mankind has two choices: Obey Jesus, who is the Cornerstone, and He will be precious to you and never give you cause to be ashamed; or disobey Jesus, and you will be crushed in judgment by this Chief Cornerstone. That's what Peter is saying here. This stone of stumbling causes the unbeliever's destruction. It not only causes them to stumble but also to be crushed or destroyed for all eternity.

Peter says they are *disobedient to the word*, which means to disbelieve willfully and perversely. A heart of unbelief will soon find itself deliberately disobedient, and this judgment that will come because of willful unbelief will be for all eternity in hell, as Peter ends with very sobering words, *to which they also were appointed*. To this doom they were also appointed. *Appointed* means to destine someone to or for something. God does not accept responsibility for man going to hell; man's sin does the appointing. God appoints them, that is true, but man is still responsible for the choices that bring about that appointment. My dear friend, this is a scary and awful truth, but when you look at this passage, along with the Romans 9 passage, there is no other conclusion to which we can come. And yet, what do we do with 2 Peter 3:9, which says, "The Lord is not slack concerning His promise, as some count slackness, but is long suffering toward us, not willing that any should perish but that all should come to repentance"? I asked my husband this question. His reply was, "I don't know; both are true." Some illustrate it like this: As you enter into the gates of heaven, you read "Whosoever will may come." But after you enter in, the other side of the gate reads, "Chosen before the foundation of the world."

We know God is not willing that any should perish, and yet obviously not all will repent; some will willfully disobey. Sin does not go unpunished; these disobedient unbelievers have rebelled against God and will pay the penalty. John MacArthur helps us here. He says, "I once read about a conversation in the Louvre Museum in Paris. One of the curators of the museum, a man with great appreciation for art, overheard two men discussing a masterpiece. One man said to the other, 'I don't think much of that painting.' The curator, feeling obliged to reply to the man's statement, said to him, 'Dear sir, if I may interrupt, that painting is not on trial; you are. The quality of that painting has already been established. Your disapproval simply demonstrates the frailty of your measuring capability.' Similarly, Jesus is not on trial before men, men are on trial before Him. He has already been approved by the Father. Those who arrogantly dismiss Him as unworthy of their devotion simply demonstrate their inability to recognize the most precious treasure of all."[29]

Summary

How do we recognize a living stone?

1. They come to Christ habitually for worship and intimacy.

    Do you read a verse a day and pray? Is your life one of habitually coming to Him and drawing near to Him moment by moment through His Word and communion?

2. They have life.

    Do you have life? Do you have abundant life? How do you know? Do you love the life that He has given you here?

3. They are a body working together like a building.

    Do you work as a living stone with others in the body, or are you a stone that is isolated from others? Are you doing your part in the church by serving?

---

[29] John MacArthur, Drawing Near (Wheaton: Crossway Books, 1993), July 4.

4. They are holy as priests.

   Is your life characterized by holiness? Are you separated from the world? What things did you do this week that would not have been holy or pleasing to God?

5. They offer up daily sacrifices acceptable to God.

   What sacrifices have you offered up to God today? Are you dying daily? Are you willing to do whatever the Lord asks you to do?

How do we recognize the chief cornerstone?

1. He is elect.

2. He is precious.

3. He is rejected by some.

Are you being willfully disobedient or is Jesus precious to you? Is Christ a stumbling block to you, or is He precious to you? Have you rejected the Head, the Chief Cornerstone that can hold your life together, or is He precious to you? I pray He is, oh, so precious to you and never an offense! My dear friends, in these days of increased evil and uncertainty, we need stability. We need Jesus Christ our Chief Cornerstone, the one who will hold us together in life and in death!

Questions to Consider
Is Jesus Precious or Offensive to You?
1 Peter 2:4-8

1. (a) Read 1 Peter 2:4-8. List the names or characteristics that Peter uses for believers and for unbelievers. (b) Also read over Acts 4:1-13 and note how Peter applies these same characteristics to the Jewish leaders.

2. Memorize 1 Peter 2:7-8.

3. (a) What kind of garments were the priests to wear, according to Exodus 28:1-2 and Psalm 132:9? (b) What kinds of restrictions were put on their personal lives, according to Leviticus 21? (c) What was a priest to do, according to Numbers 18:7; Malachi 2:7; Hebrews 9:6-7? (Also skim Leviticus 8 and 9 to answer this question.) (d) Taking what you have just learned, how does this help you to understand what Peter says in 1 Peter 2:5?

4. (a) What are some of the spiritual sacrifices we, as believers, should be offering to the Lord, according to Psalm 4:5; 50:14, 23; 51:17-19; 141:2; Micah 6:6-8; John 4:24; Romans 12:1-2; 15:16; Ephesians 5:2; Philippians 2:17; 4:17-18; Hebrews 13:15-16; and Revelation 8:3? (b) Which of these sacrifices do you need to be offering to the Lord?

5. Isaiah 8:14-15 and Isaiah 28:16 are two of the quotes Peter uses in 1 Peter 2:6-8. Read both of these chapters in Isaiah. (a) What was happening in Isaiah's time that caused him to write these things? (b) How does this help you to understand better what Peter was saying in 1 Peter 2:6-8?

6. Read Romans 9, and especially note verses 14-24. (a) How does this reiterate what Peter says in 1 Peter 2:8, "being disobedient to the word to which they were also appointed"? (b) What do you

think this means? (c) How do you rectify this with what Peter says in his 2 Peter 3:9?

7. In what ways is the Lord Jesus precious to you?

8. In looking over question 4, where could you improve in your service to God? Please put this in the form of a prayer request.

Chapter 9

Priests, Pilgrims and Peculiar People Giving Praises to God!

1 Peter 2:9-12

Since its inception, one of the most discouraging things to mark the church has been the presence of hypocrites in its midst. Repeatedly, the claim is made that the reason people won't come to church is because there are too many hypocrites in it. Unfortunately, there *are* hypocrites in the church, and, to those who make this claim, I would lovingly remind them that by staying home and not obeying the command to assemble with God's people, they too are manifesting a form of hypocrisy!

I doubt that there is a single church on our planet without some hypocrites in it. There always have been professing Christians who claim to be one thing and yet live another. But the Scriptures do not lack clarity regarding those who live as hypocrites. Matthew 24:51 tells us that there will not be a place in heaven for hypocrites. In Matthew 6:2, Jesus describes hypocrites as performing their works for others to see; in Matthew 6:5, He says they pray to be seen of men; in Matthew 15:8, He says they draw near to God with their mouths, but their hearts are far from Him. In Matthew 23:14, He says they devour widow's houses and for a pretense make long prayers; in Matthew 23:23, He says they pay their tithes but omit justice, mercy, and faith; in Matthew 23:27, He says they are outwardly beautiful yet inwardly full of dead men's bones and all uncleanness.

But for the genuine believer, hypocrisy is unthinkable. In this lesson, Peter will remind us that we have the wonderful privilege and responsibility of winning the lost by our lips and by our lives. If, however, we live a life of hypocrisy, we may not only find ourselves one day eternally judged but find that we have taken a multitude of people with us as well. Jesus makes this abundantly clear in Matthew 15:14, when He says of the Pharisees that they are the blind leading the blind, and in Matthew 23:15, when He says that the one who follows them will be made more of a child of hell then they are. Let's read together verses 9-12 of 1 Peter 2.

1 Peter 2:9-12

> But you are a chosen generation, a royal priesthood, a holy nation, His own special people, that you may proclaim the praises of Him who called you out of darkness into His marvelous light; [10]who once were not a people but are now the people of God, who had not obtained mercy but now have obtained mercy. [11]Beloved, I beg you as sojourners and pilgrims, abstain from fleshly lusts which war against the soul, [12]having your conduct honorable among the Gentiles, that when they speak against you as evildoers, they may, by your good works which they observe, glorify God in the day of visitation.

In this lesson, Peter will show us four ways to discern genuine believers, those who are not hypocrites. Genuine believers are:

> *Priests Giving Praises to God* (v 9)
> *People Who Have Obtained Mercy from God* (v 10)
> *Pilgrims Abstaining from Sin because of New Life in God* (v 11)
> *Peculiar People Receiving Accusations because of their Attachment to God* (v 12)

Let's begin by looking at verse 9 and consider the first characteristic of those who are genuinely born again of the incorruptible seed.

Priests Giving Praises to God

1 Peter 2:9

> But you are a chosen generation, a royal priesthood, a holy nation, His own special people, that you may proclaim the praises of Him who called you out of darkness into His marvelous light; (1 Peter 2:9)

The word *but* presents a contrast to what is found in verse 8, a contrast to those who are disobedient and have been appointed to eternal damnation. But *you*, Peter says, you are different. Instead of being appointed to disobedience and eternal wrath, believers in Christ have a different calling. Peter calls those who are believers in Christ by four names. Almost all of these titles were at one time used to describe Israel; now, Peter applies them to Christians who have been born again. What an encouragement this must have been to these persecuted believers!

First, Peter calls these believers *a chosen generation*. This means they are an elect race, and this title really goes back to Deuteronomy 7:6, which says, "For you are a holy people to the LORD your God; the LORD your God has chosen you to be a people for Himself, a special treasure above all the peoples on the face of the earth." Just as Israel was chosen as God's people in the Old Testament, so we too as New Testament saints have been chosen by God. A chosen generation is often defined as a body of individuals with a common life and descent. Peter already mentioned the fact that these believers were elect, in 1 Peter 1:2. Jesus made it very clear in John 15:16, "You did not choose Me, but I chose you and appointed you that you should go and bear fruit, and that your fruit should remain, that whatever you ask the Father in My name He may give you." All Christians are a part of this chosen generation in the sense that we are chosen, we are distinct from the world, and we are a family. And persecution seems to highlight the importance of our Christian family as we suffer together for a common cause.

Second, Peter calls these believers *a royal priesthood*. This refers to a kingly kind of priesthood. If you recall from our last lesson, in 1 Peter 2:5, Peter referred to believers as a holy priesthood; here, he calls us a royal priesthood. What is a royal priesthood? *Royal* is a word that was used to describe a royal palace, sovereignty, a crown, or a monarchy. The *priesthood* included those specifically called to offer sacrifices unto God and represent the people in so doing. But Peter is saying here that we are all priests serving together the same High Priest. We are priests in the sense that we have the right to intercede with God as the Old Testament priests did on behalf of others. God uses this terminology in Exodus 19:5-6, right before Moses was about to receive the 10 commandments. Listen to what God says, "Now therefore, if you will indeed obey My voice and keep My covenant, then you shall be a special treasure to Me above all people; for all the earth is Mine. And you shall be to Me a kingdom of priests and a holy nation. These are the words which you shall speak to the children of Israel." Isaiah also uses this term in Isaiah 61:6, "But you shall be named the priests of the LORD, they shall call you the servants of our God. You shall eat the riches of the Gentiles, and in their glory you shall boast."

Third, Peter calls these Christians *a holy nation*. The word *holy* means to be set apart for service. The word *nation* means a multitude of people held together by the same laws, customs, and mutual interests. We just saw that God used that word in Exodus 19:6. The Israelites were a holy nation in the sense that they were separated from all the peoples of the earth and their sinful practices in order that they might worship the one and only true God. In the same way, we New Testament saints are also a holy nation in the sense that we have been set apart to serve the one true God and avoid the sinful ways of the world. Holiness is imperative for any believer of Jesus Christ, and this isn't the first time Peter has mentioned the importance of holiness. He has already written about it in 1 Peter 1:15 and 16 and 1 Peter 2:5, and he will mention it again in 1 Peter 3:5 when talking about holy women.

Fourth, Peter calls these children of God *His own special people*, or a people of His own, as your translation might say. This is a term that means peculiar people. Now, when you and I think of a person who is peculiar we think of someone who is odd or strange, but that is not what this word means in the Greek. The word peculiar means "to make around, that is to make something and then to surround it with a circle, thus indicating ownership."[30] So we might say that those who are His own special people are purchased people. He has

---

[30]Kenneth Wuest, Wuest's Word Studies From the Greek New Testament (Grand Rapids:Wm. B. Eerdmans Publishing Company, 1973), pg. 56, 57.

acquired us for a price and, of course, Peter has already told us that that price was Christ's precious blood (1 Peter 1:19). Again, these are words that were used to describe the Israelites in the Old Testament. In fact, the very same verb is used in Isaiah 43:21: "This people I have formed for Myself; they shall declare My praise." Titus 2:14 says that Christ "gave Himself for us, that He might redeem us from every lawless deed and purify for Himself His own special people, zealous for good works." "The Christian may be a very ordinary person but he acquires a new value because he belongs to God."[31]

There is a reason that Christ has chosen us from before the foundation of the world, a reason that He has purchased us with so high a price, and that reason is so *that we may proclaim the praises of Him who called us out of darkness into His marvelous light*. Isaiah 43:21 mentioned that, as we just saw. What does it mean to *proclaim* praises? It means to publish, to show forth, to advertise. Did you know, my friend, that every believer is an advertisement for the Lord? You and I, so to speak, are advertisements for the Lord; hopefully, we are convincing others by our lives and by our lips that Christianity is a great product. Have you ever asked yourself, "What kind of advertisement am I for the Lord?" Would others be sold on Him based on what they see in your life? One of the ways we advertise Him is by *praises*. This means we must open our mouths and give glory to the One who saved us! We have not been chosen and redeemed for our own personal satisfaction, as some Christians think and teach—our purpose is to glorify God! We are to tell others how excellent He is.

The fact that we have been *called out of darkness into His marvelous light* is reason to praise Him. *Darkness* symbolizes ignorance, sin, and misery. This, my sister, was our condition before Christ. But Peter says we didn't stay there—praise God! Instead, we have been called *into His marvelous light*. What is *marvelous light*? *Light* is the opposite of darkness, and Peter calls it *marvelous*, which means that it is wonderful. It has been said that the Christian conversion is often so great that the transition seems like that from midnight

---

[31] William Barclay, The Letters of James and Peter (Louisville: Westminster John Knox Press), pg. 199.

to noon. I have heard people testify that, after coming to the Lord, it seemed as if the lights went on, all of a sudden, they realized the birds were singing, or the grass appeared greener—all the results of having been transformed to marvelous light. (Some verses that speak to this reality include Acts 26:18; Ephesians 5:8; Colossians 1:13; and 1 Thessalonians 5:5.)

Now, you might be wondering how we are to proclaim God's praises. It begins by opening our mouths. We should be ready at all times to give praise for what He has done or is doing in our lives, whether it be publicly, or privately, or with our family or friends. We should also be giving forth praises, even to the unbeliever; we should be telling them of God's mercy and goodness in our lives. I've sat in countless church services or gatherings of believers where the church leaders will ask for someone to share praises or testimonies of what God is doing in individual lives, and many times there is silence. It is grieving to my heart to think that we cannot open our mouths and give glory to the One who gave His life for us. If nothing else, we can praise Him for our salvation, right?!

So, the first description of a genuine Christian, found in verse 9, is that of priests giving praises to God. Peter goes on in verse 10 to remind his readers again of their condition before Christ and to describe a second characteristic of a genuine believer.

People Who Have Obtained Mercy from God

1 Peter 2:10

> who once were not a people but are now the people of God, who had not obtained mercy but now have obtained mercy. (1 Peter 2:10)

What does Peter mean when he says *who once were not a people but are now the people of God*? We can understand this phrase when we go to the place from where Peter is borrowing this terminology. These are words taken from the Old Testament, specifically Hosea 1 and 2. Hosea was a prophet who wrote of God's unchanging love for Israel, and Hosea was told by the Lord to take a prostitute named Gomer as his wife. The first three chapters of the book of Hosea report their stormy relationship as husband and wife. Soon after they were united in marriage, Gomer bore three children. Hosea gave his children symbolic names—Jezreel (meaning "God scatters"), Lo-Ruhamah (meaning "Not Pitied"), and Lo-Ammi (meaning "Not My People")—in order to show that God was about to bring His judgment upon the nation of Israel because the people had fallen into the worship of false gods. Just as the nation had rejected God, Gomer eventually left Hosea and her children to return to her life of prostitution. But Hosea's love for his wife refused to die. He searched for her until he found her at the slave market, and once he had found her, he bought her back and restored her as his wife. This tender picture clearly demonstrated that God had not given up on Israel, though the people had played the harlot repeatedly by returning to their old life of pagan worship and enslavement to sin. In Hosea 2:19-23, we are given a beautiful picture of God's incredible love and mercy for His people: "'I will betroth you to Me forever; yes, I will betroth you to Me in righteousness and justice, in loving kindness and mercy; I will betroth you to Me in faithfulness, and you shall know the LORD. It shall come to pass in that day that I will answer,' says the LORD; 'I will answer the heavens, and they shall answer the earth. The earth shall answer with grain, with new wine, and with oil; they shall answer Jezreel. Then I will sow her for Myself in the earth, and I will have mercy on her who had not obtained mercy; then I will say to those who were not My people, "You are My people!" And they shall say, "You are my God!"'"

Paul picks up on this same terminology and applies it to the Gentiles in Romans 9:25: "As He says also in Hosea: 'I will call them My people, who were not My people, and her beloved, who was not beloved.'" Peter, too, picks up on this incredible fact and reminds these persecuted Christians of God's wonderful mercy on their lives, that they were once not a people but are now the people of God, that they once *had not obtained mercy but now have obtained mercy*! Peter has already mentioned in the beginning of his letter that these dear ones had been begotten by God's abundant mercy (1 Peter

1:3). And Paul mentions this in Titus 3:5, as well: "Not by works of righteousness which we have done, but according to His mercy He saved us, through the washing of regeneration and renewing of the Holy Spirit." It is always God's mercy that saves any of us.

The second mark of a Christian is that they are a people who have obtained mercy from God, and because of this great mercy that has been bestowed upon believers, Peter shifts in verse 11 to plead concerning the believer's personal holiness.

Pilgrims Abstaining from Sin because of New Life in God

1 Peter 2:11

> Beloved, I beg you as sojourners and pilgrims, abstain from fleshly lusts which war against the soul, (1 Peter 2:11)

Peter calls his readers *beloved*, which is a term of endearment. It actually means dearly loved ones. This is the only time Peter uses this term in either of his epistles. I think you can sense the urgency of Peter's heart here as he uses this term. Peter's example here is a good model for us to apply when exhorting others; using terms of endearment helps those receiving our message to understand the love behind our exhortations. Galatians 6:1 reminds us that our exhortations ought to be presented with gentleness and humility.

Peter says to his fellow believers *I beg you*, which means I entreat you, or I exhort you, or I urge you, please, and then he calls them *sojourners and pilgrims*. A *sojourner* describes one who has no rights or legal status in the place where they dwell; they're just staying where they are for a temporary time. A *pilgrim* refers to one who is only a temporary resident of a place and not a citizen of it; they're here today and gone tomorrow. For the Christian, it could be said that this refers to one who settles down alongside the pagans. Hebrews 11:13 refers to all those heroes of the faith in that chapter as strangers and pilgrims on the earth. Paul reminds us in Philippians 3:20 that our citizenship is in heaven. If you have ever traveled to a foreign country, then you know exactly what Peter means; you don't speak the language, you don't eat the same food, the time is different, the customs and the clothes are different, everything is different, and you feel like you don't belong. You're a stranger. So it is with believers living in this world—or, it should be. We don't speak the same language the world does, we don't have the same desires they do, our goals and ambitions in life ought to be different, and we should look and act differently from them. (Consider the words of 1 John 2:15-17 concerning the danger one is in as a lover of this world!) As strangers and pilgrims in this world, we should hold loosely to the things of this world because when we leave here, we will not be pulling U-Hauls behind our hearses. A question I have asked myself from time to time to see if I am really a stranger here is this: "Is there any material possession or person that I am holding on to so tightly that I would be devastated if God took it?" If I can answer yes to that question, then perhaps it is an indication that I'm too attached to this world and not really the stranger or pilgrim I am called to be. And I have found many times that if I hold on to something or someone too tightly, God will loosen that thing or that person from my hand.

If we are strangers and pilgrims living in this world, then we should act differently from the world. That's why Peter begs us to *abstain from fleshly lusts which war against the soul*. The word *abstain* means to hold oneself off, to constantly refrain, and it should be a continual abstaining. What are *fleshly lusts*? They are unregenerate longings for what is forbidden. This doesn't only include sexual temptations, but it includes anything that is sinful. These fleshly lusts, Peter says, war against our soul. What does it mean to *war against the soul*? The word *war* means to serve in a military campaign. The war that goes on in our souls when we fight against sin is like two nations who are constantly at war with one another.

Paul speaks of this struggle in Romans 7:15-25. It is grievous when we consider that our souls, for which Christ shed His precious blood, can at times be engaging in sinful lusts. My dear sister, if you choose to engage in sin, you rob your soul of joy. It weakens your soul and destroys your moral resolve to do what is right. It also renders you useless to God. The fight against sin is a war, but it is not one in which we should surrender to the enemy. There have been countless times in my own life that I have had to wrestle and fight and pray until the victory has been won, and I know each of you have had similar experiences. But to give in to our flesh is a grief to the Spirit and eventually can dull our conscience to the voice of God! In fact, 1 John 3:9 is very clear that if we continue to practice sin we cannot be born of God.

The third mark of a Christian is that they are pilgrims abstaining from sin because of new life in God. Now, there are many reasons that we are to behave differently than the rest of the world; there are many reasons that we should not engage in fleshly lusts. Peter has mentioned some of these reasons already in this epistle: because God is holy, because we are born again with incorruptible seed, and because it cost God the precious blood of His Son. But there is another reason for us to behave righteously and that is because the world is watching us, as we read in verse 12.

Peculiar Ones Receiving Accusations because of Their Attachment to God

1 Peter 2:12

> having your conduct honorable among the Gentiles, that when they speak against you as evildoers, they may, by your good works which they observe, glorify God in the day of visitation. (1 Peter 2:12)

Peter tells us that our *conduct* should be *honorable among the Gentiles*. For our conduct to be *honorable* means that our behavior is honest and virtuous. This speaks of an outer goodness that strikes the eye or a goodness that can be seen by others. Our conduct includes not just our conversation, but our whole manner of life, the activities that take place in our life on a daily basis. Our whole manner of life should be honorable *among the Gentiles*, which is a reference to the unsaved world. You might ask, "Why?" Peter says because even though they might *speak against you as evildoers*, it's possible that they will see the *good works* you do and *glorify God* as a result. Unbelievers (and, sadly, even believers sometimes) will at times speak evil against us, they will slander us, they will gossip about us—this is a fact. In fact, these believers Peter was originally writing to, as we learned in our introductory lesson, were going through a lot of persecution and slander. This is the fourth way Peter describes a child of God: peculiar ones receiving accusations because of their attachment to God.

But Peter says even though they have slandered you, let them see your good works, and by this they may come to glorify God. Even though these believers were being slandered and misunderstood, Peter calls them to live their lives in such a way that no one would ultimately believe what was being said about them and that all such accusations would be recognized as unfounded. There have been many times I have wanted to defend myself when falsely accused, and then my husband has reminded me that God will vindicate me, and I have watched Him do that many times—in His timing, not mine.

Peter says the unbelieving world *observes your good works*, which means they watch and view carefully. The Greek indicates that this is a watching that occurs over a period of time. Perhaps Peter was reminded of what our Lord said in His Sermon on the Mount, in Matthew 5:16: "Let your light so shine before men, that they may see your good works and glorify your Father in heaven." If your faith is not producing good works, then, my friend, there is reason to be very concerned about your faith because James says faith without works is dead (James 2:26). The unbelieving world should be able to see the believer's life so full of good works that there is sufficient compelling proof of who Christ is and of the Gospel; the believer's life should be so compelling that it has the potential to lead unbelievers to embrace Christ and thus glorify Him. Unfortunately, though, we often hear from the unbeliever, "I won't embrace Christ because I know Christians and they are nothing but a bunch of hypocrites!" Indeed, there are hypocrites—but God forbid that it should be so!

Peter writes that as the unbelievers around you see your good works, they will glorify God *in the day of visitation*. What is Peter referring to in this verse? *Visitation* is a term that means to observe or inspect. So, *the day of visitation* is another way of saying the day of looking on. In other words, when unbelievers fully investigate our lives, they will see that Christ is indeed real, they will embrace the gospel, and they will therefore bring glory to God on the day of visitation, the day of their salvation! (See also 1 Peter 3:15-17.) What a sobering and yet wonderful opportunity and responsibility we have toward a lost world as they watch our lives. That's why I said in my opening remarks that if we don't glorify God by our works we may find on that day that our lack of being holy will have caused others to stumble by making the doctrine of God unattractive. Perhaps, they will have watched our lives and said, "If that is the behavior of a believer, then I want no part of it." If we continue to live lives of hypocrisy, then we may find that not only have we caused others to stumble in this life, but we too will be doomed to eternal hell with them, because Jesus is very clear that no hypocrite will enter into heaven! (See Matthew 24:51.)

Summary

What is a Christian? And does your life match the descriptions Peter gives of a Christian?

- Priests giving praises to God. Are you known as a woman who gives continual praises to God for what He has done? What praises have you given to God this week? What praises have you given to Him today?

- People who have obtained mercy from God. Have you obtained mercy from God? Are you thankful for God's mercy in saving you?

- Pilgrims abstaining from sin because of new life in God. Are you fighting hard against those sins that war against your soul? What weapons of warfare do you use in your battle against sin?

- Peculiar ones receiving accusations because of attachment to God. What persecution have you received because of your attachment to Christ?

What does the world see as they watch you? Do they see Christ? Do they hear your mouth pouring forth praises to God for what He has done in your life? Do they see God's mercy manifest in your life? Or do they watch your life and see your religious jewelry, while you're screaming at your kids at the checkout stand? Do you have religious bumper stickers on your car while you honk impatiently at other drivers or speed down the highway going 85 miles an hour when the speed limit is 65 miles an hour? If you were the only representation of Jesus Christ to this lost world we live in, what kind of Jesus would they see?

Not too long ago, a song was written that stirred my soul, and I want to close with its words in the hopes that it will also stir yours.

> If not you, I wonder where will they ever find the One who really cares.
>
> If not you, how will they find the One who heals the broken heart, gives sight to the blind.
>
> Cause you're the only Jesus some will ever see,
>
> You're the only Words of Life some will ever read.
>
> So let them see in you the One in whom is all they'll ever need.
>
> You're the only Jesus some will ever see.[32]

---

[32] Words by Kathleen Harris.

Questions to Consider
Priests, Pilgrims and Peculiar People
Giving Praises to God!
1 Peter 2:9-12

1. (a) Read 1 Peter 2:9-12 and write down the different names that Peter uses for believers. (You should find at least eight.) (b) What do you think these names mean?

2. Memorize 1 Peter 2:11.

3. Hosea 1 and 2 are the background for Peter's words in 1 Peter 2:10. (a) Read Hosea 1 and 2 and write down the context of what is going on. (b) Did Israel deserve God's mercy? Why or why not? (c) Did she receive God's mercy? Why?

4. In 1 Peter 2:11, Peter speaks of sin warring against our soul. (a) In the following verses, what does the Psalmist say happened to his soul when he gave up the fight against sin? See Psalm 6:3-4; 31:9-10; 38:3; 41:4; 51:8, 12. (b) What happens to your soul when you give up the fight against sin? (c) How would you explain to a struggling believer that giving up the fight against sin is not worth it?

5. (a) According to Romans 8:13, what happens to those who live after the flesh? (b) What are some of the works of the flesh, according to Galatians 5:16-21? (c) Do you think that someone can practice these things and still rightly be called a "Christian"? See Galatians 5:19-24; 1 Corinthians 6:9-11; and Revelation 21:8. (d) If you know a professing Christian who is practicing sin, how would you compel them to be reconciled to God?

6. (a) In Titus 2:3-5, what is the command given to women? (b) What is the reason for this command, according to verse 5? (c) What is the command given to young men, in Titus 2:6-8? (d) In

Titus 2:9-10, what is the command to servants? (e) Again, what are the reasons for these commands, according to verses 8 and 10? (f) How does this go along with what Peter says in 1 Peter 2:12?

7. (a) When was the last time you gave praise to God in the presence of others? (b) Why do you think we as Christians are reluctant to praise God in the presence of others? (If you have difficulty in knowing what to praise God for, read Psalm 103.)

8. (a) Look back over the list of character qualities in Titus 2:3-5 (question 6) that should be present in us as women. How would you say you are faring in each of these characteristics? (If you really want to deal with this honestly, ask your husband or a close friend.) (b) Do you think the unbelieving world sees these things as evident in your life? (c) How would you help another woman who is struggling with one or more of these areas?

9. Write praise to God expressing your gratitude for the fact that you have been chosen by Him!

Chapter 10

The Christian's Response to Government
1 Peter 2:13-17

In March of 2020, most of our world went into a "lock-down" or what our local government called a "stay at home order." This was because of the now well-known Covid-19 virus which spread rapidly from China throughout most of the world during the early months of 2020. One part of this lock-down was the shutting down of churches, a rather unusual move in the United States. This caused many Christians to wonder what was happening and to question the wisdom of our government. There were godly men and women who had opposing views on what the church should do in response to these orders. Should we obey the government and close our church? Doesn't the Bible say in Hebrews 10:25 that we are not to forsake the assembling together of ourselves? Approaching the situation from a different perspective, many were pleading with their neighbors to obey the command to love our neighbor as ourselves, arguing that leaving our homes could mean infecting the vulnerable. But the passages of Scripture I heard most during the pandemic were Romans 13:1-5 and 1 Peter 2:13-17, the passage we are going to study in this lesson.

What should be our response to our government, evil as it may be? Are we always to obey the government? What if it infringes on our liberties as Americans or our duty to God? Should we open our businesses and churches even though the government tells us to shut them down? Should we buy a gun to protect ourselves against those in authority over us? Should Christians become political activists? Is it permissible to slander those in authority and tell dirty jokes about them? For the true Christian, our response to government—even if it is evil—is a little different than one might guess. Let's read what our brother Peter has to say to a group of persecuted Christians, suffering under the hand of an evil government.

1 Peter 2:13-17

> Therefore submit yourselves to every ordinance of man for the Lord's sake, whether to the king as supreme, ¹⁴or to governors, as to those who are sent by him for the punishment of evildoers and for the praise of those who do good. ¹⁵For this is the will of God, that by doing good you may put to silence the ignorance of foolish men—¹⁶as free, yet not using liberty as a cloak for vice, but as bond servants of God. ¹⁷Honor all people. Love the brotherhood. Fear God. Honor the king.

As we think about the Christian's proper response to government, we will ask and answer the following questions:

> *Who Do We Submit To?* (vv 13-14)
> *Why Do We Submit?* (v 15)
> *How Do We Submit?* (vv 16-17)

Peter has just mentioned in the previous verses that it is imperative that we behave ourselves wisely toward unbelievers, and one of the ways we let our good works shine before those who do not know Christ is by our response to the governing authorities. So, let's answer this first question from verses 13 and 14 about who we are to submit to.

Who Do We Submit To?

1 Peter 2:13-14

> Therefore submit yourselves to every ordinance of man for the Lord's sake, whether to the king as supreme, (1 Peter 2:13)

Peter begins with the term *therefore*. In other words, because we are to let the world see that we live a life that is in obedience to God's will, because we are to let our good works shine forth to a lost world, then we must submit to government. This is not the only reason we submit to government; Peter will go on in the coming verses to elaborate on the reasons why we should submit. (By the way, this is not the only area of submission Peter will write about. He will write at the end of this chapter about servants being submissive to masters, even if they are harsh. Then, at the beginning of chapter three, he will tell wives married to unbelievers that they need to be submissive in order to show their unbelieving husbands what Christianity looks like. And, in chapter five, he will tell the younger members of the church to submit to the elders, and then he'll even write that we are all to be submissive to each other! Submission is certainly a foreign concept to an ungodly world; no one wants anyone telling them what to do!)

Since we are going to talk about submission, it's important that we understand what it actually means. To *submit* means to arrange in military fashion under the command of a leader. The Greek tense here is in the aorist imperative, which conveys a sense of urgency. It is not a submission that cringes at authority but that freely submits to it and sees that submission as one's duty (see also 2:18; 3:1, 5, 22; and 5:5 for Peter's repetition of this word).

Now, Peter says they are to *submit to every ordinance of man*, which means to every institution of man. This would include every person who is in authority, kings, governors, etc.; in the United States, we would say presidents, vice-presidents, senators, governors, policemen, etc. But this would also include all the laws of the land, which have been set up by those in positions of authority. Notice that Peter says our submission is to be to *every* one of them. We are not permitted to simply obey what we want to obey. We don't get to pick and choose, like a spiritual smorgasbord. Some of us are sticklers about obeying the speed limit, but then we might take a handicap parking space to keep from having to walk so far, and justify it because we think we won't be in the store but five minutes. We really cannot pick and choose the laws we want to obey. Now, I will say that during the Covid-19 pandemic it was often difficult to know what or who to obey because the governing authorities were often not on the same page and were often contradicting one another. It was at times confusing to know what ordinance of man to obey.

We also must keep in mind that the New Testament believers were not under a democratic type of government, as most of us are today. Their government was authoritarian. The ruler or king was an absolute authority, and those under his authority were required to be absolutely obedient. Now, this does not mean that you and I can't make appeals to those in authority over us, because the laws of our land permit us to and we certainly have Scriptural precedent for doing so. Daniel is a good example of one who appealed to those in authority over him. There may also be times when we cannot obey those in authority over us because their commands contradict the commands of God. We have an example of that when the Hebrew midwives were asked to kill all the male babies, yet they chose to obey God over Pharaoh and God blessed them (Exodus 1:15-22). We also have the example of the apostles, who were forbidden to share the gospel and yet they chose to obey God over man and were beaten for it (Acts 5:27-42). There may come a time in our future when some will be asked to worship the false prophet and to receive the mark of the beast on their right hands or their foreheads—that would definitely be a time when one would not want to obey the earthly authorities over them. It might cost them their head to disobey the government, as Revelation 20:4 says, but it will be worth it. There may be instances where we have to disobey the government in order to obey God. But let me just say this before we go on: be certain you have biblical precedent for disobeying the government in your situation, and, if possible, seek counsel from someone who is wiser in the faith, before you refuse to submit to any authority, whether it is the government, your husband, your employer, or anyone else.

Peter continues by giving us a reason for our submission to authority, and it is not just so that we won't get a ticket or go to jail. It is a much more noble and godly motivation. It is *for the Lord's sake*. Submission to governmental authorities is clearly God's will for the believer. Even Jesus Himself was in submission to the government; when He was challenged by the Pharisees regarding whether one should give taxes to Caesar or not, in Matthew 22:15-22, Jesus clearly tells them to give to Caesar what is Caesar's and to give to God what is God's!

I know many believers who have issues with our government because it is corrupt and evil. But, my friend, we do not have the right to rebel against the rulers of our land. The Bible is clear in Daniel 2:21, "And He changes the times and the seasons; he removes kings and raises up kings; he gives wisdom to the wise and knowledge to those who have understanding." I know we have difficulty with this, but many times God gives a nation what they deserve because of their rebellion against His commands. Paul tells us in Titus 3:1-2, "Remind them to be subject to rulers and authorities, to obey, to be ready for every good work, to speak evil of no one, to be peaceable, gentle, showing all humility to all men." This should give us pause before slandering our rulers or telling jokes about them. Paul also has some strong words about our response to governmental authority, in case Peter's abbreviated version isn't convincing enough for us. Consider Paul's words in Romans 13:1-8.

> Let every soul be subject to the governing authorities. For there is no authority except from God, and the authorities that exist are appointed by God. Therefore whoever resists the authority resists the ordinance of God, and those who resist will bring judgment on themselves. For rulers are not a terror to good works, but to evil. Do you want to be unafraid of the authority? Do what is good, and you will have praise from the same. For he is God's minister to you for good. But if you do evil, be afraid; for he does not bear the sword in vain; for he is God's minister, an avenger to execute wrath on him who practices evil. Therefore you must be subject, not only because of wrath but also for conscience' sake. For because of this you also pay taxes, for they are God's ministers attending continually to this very thing. Render therefore to all their due: taxes to whom taxes are due, customs to whom customs, fear to whom fear, honor to whom honor. Owe no one anything except to love one another, for he who loves another has fulfilled the law.

Here, in 1 Peter, he lists two types of authorities to whom we are to submit. The first, he says, is *the king as supreme*. Now, my sister, may I remind you who *the king* was at the time Peter wrote this? It was Nero! The one who was burning Christians at the stake; the one who was having Christians sewn up in the skins of animals so wild beasts could tear them from limb to limb; the one who was blaming Christians for the burning of Rome, which he actually did himself. He came to rule at the age of 17, and so crazed was he that he committed suicide just 14 years later. Nero wasn't exactly kind toward believers, and yet both Peter and Paul—who would both be martyred under his reign—remind their fellow believers that they are commanded to submit to him!

Peter mentions here the king *as supreme*. This obviously does not mean that the king is supreme over God, but that he is supreme over all the other rulers of the land. Peter also mentions another governmental authority believers must submit to, this particular authority falling under the authority of the king.

> or to governors, as to those who are sent by him for the punishment of evildoers and for the praise of those who do good. (1 Peter 2:14)

The *governor* is the second type of ruler we are to submit to. A governor was a deputy or ruler of a province. The New Testament lists three men as governors: Pilate, Felix, and Festus. These governors, Peter says, *are sent by him for the punishment of evildoers*. In other words, governors are sent by the king as representatives of his supreme power. In our land, while our form of government differs greatly from that of Nero's rule, we have a President and we have Governors and Senators and Representatives and Mayors and various kinds of county and city councils and law enforcement officers, each of whom represent and carry out delegated authority in various states, districts, counties, and cities. In biblical times, the governor was responsible for *the punishment of evildoers*. It was the governor's duty to make sure the province he ruled over was peaceable and quiet. He had the highest authority next to the emperor. The governor not only had authority to inflict punishment on criminals but also to *praise those who do good*. This would include rewarding those who were upright in their conduct as citizens, their property and rights being protected. In many ways, our governing authorities carry out these same duties. As Romans 13:3 says, "For rulers are not a terror to good works, but to evil. Do you want to be unafraid of the authority? Do what is good, and you will have praise from the same."

Who are we to submit to? Every ruler that is set up to rule us! In case some of these readers were having a hard time accepting Peter's words of having to submit to authority—and in case some of you are having a hard time accepting what Peter is saying regarding submitting to our government—Peter gives us all a reason why we are to submit, in verse 15.

Why Do We Submit?

1 Peter 2:15

> For this is the will of God, that by doing good you may put to silence the ignorance of foolish men— (1 Peter 2:15)

We already saw in verse 12 that we are to keep our conduct honorable so that others will see our good works, and submission to governing authorities is one of those good works. But Peter adds another reason here, and that is because it *is the will of God*. There are many instances in which we don't know what the will of God is for us, but it is crystal clear in this verse that it is God's will for us to submit to the government. Peter answers the why question by saying *that by doing good you may put to silence the ignorance of foolish men*. It is the will of God that you live a life of righteousness by submitting to the government, and as you do so, ignorant men will be put to silence. The idea here is that of silencing those who were claiming that Christians were rebellious toward the government. *Put to silence* means to close the mouth with a muzzle. A muzzle was a leather or wire covering for the mouth of an animal that prevented it from eating or biting. The term is used in Matthew 22:34 of Christ putting the Sadducees to silence; His answer to their question silenced them. It is also used in Mark 4:39 when Christ calmed the storm by saying,

"Peace, be still," and in Mark 1:25, when He silenced an unclean spirit in a man and said, "Be quiet, and come out of him!"

Peter says that *by doing good*, that is, by your good works, by your submission to authority, you will muzzle or quiet *the ignorance of foolish men. Ignorance* is a Greek word which means obstinate unwillingness to learn or accept the truth; it is the same Greek word used in 1 Corinthians 15:34 to speak of those who have no knowledge of God. Paul talks about being ignorant before he was a believer, in 1 Timothy 1:13. Peter also calls these unbelievers *foolish*, which means that they lack reason, reflection, and intelligence, especially as it relates to Christianity. Titus 3:3 refers to this when it speaks of our life prior to salvation: "For we ourselves were also once foolish, disobedient, deceived, serving various lusts and pleasures, living in malice and envy, hateful and hating one another." The fact of the matter is that many times unbelievers mock Christianity without reason or knowledge; they ignorantly blame believers. The idea here is that by the quiet, peaceable, good works of believers these mocking, ignorant unbelievers will be put to silence. As they view our good works, it will muzzle their mouths.

So why do we submit? It is a three-fold answer: others looking on will see our good works; it is the will of God; and it stops the mouths of foolish men. Perhaps one might argue, "I'm free in Christ, so I don't have to submit to anyone but God." Peter seems to anticipate this very argument and the apprehension his readers might have to this admonition, so he lets them know that there is a way in which they are to submit and perhaps this will be of help to them and to us.

How Do We Submit?

1 Peter 2:16-17

> as free, yet not using liberty as a cloak for vice, but as bond servants of God. (1 Peter 2:16)

Peter says, essentially, do not use your freedom as a cover-up for evil. The Jews often boasted of their freedom; in fact, they did so in a dialogue with Jesus in John 8:31-36. And, my friend, you and I are free in the sense of being free from enslavement to sin, free from the guilt of our sin, and free from trying to earn favor with God, but we are not free to be rebellious and to insist upon our own rights. Paul puts it well in Galatians 5:13: "For you, brethren, have been called to liberty; only do not use liberty as an opportunity for the flesh, but through love serve one another." Peter tells us that we are not to use our freedom *as a cloak for vice* or maliciousness, which literally means a veil for badness. We should never use our Christian freedom as a mask for disobeying the government. Believers should not abuse the freedom they have in Christ. True freedom in Christ would not be involved in harming or injuring anyone else.

Peter says yes, you are free, free from sin and Satan, but you are still *bond servants of God*. Paul puts it well in 1 Corinthians 7:22: "For he who is called in the Lord while a slave is the Lord's freedman. Likewise he who is called while free is Christ's slave." You are bound to obey God and, as He has said, you should obey the earthly authorities. Service to God includes submitting to every ordinance of man! We totally belong to God as His servants, and it is His will that we be in submission to government.

How do we submit? We submit as free servants of God, but not abusing our freedom in Christ. Peter goes on to wrap up this section regarding submission to government with four specific commands.

> Honor all people. Love the brotherhood. Fear God. Honor the king.
> (1 Peter 2:17)

The verb tense in all these commands is one of constantly possessing these attitudes. That is, we are to keep on honoring all people; keep on loving the brotherhood; keep on fearing God; keep on honoring the king. In that sense, it is clear that we are never to stop obeying any of God's commands. For example, the command for wives to submit would be very literally rendered keep on submitting; for children to obey your parents would literally read keep on obeying. These are not one-time acts we do but continual patterns of obedience.

The first command given here is to *honor all people*, which means to esteem them highly. *All people* would include those in authority over us, even wicked leaders, even Nero, even all our current authority figures. But, in addition to those in authority, this command would include all those not in positions of authority, like slaves. At the time of this letter's writing, there were 60 million slaves in the Roman Empire. Slaves were considered things, not people with rights. But Peter says we are to show honor to every human being; regardless of their social status, they are created in the image of God. Paul says something similar in Romans 12:10: "Be kindly affectionate to one another with brotherly love, in honor giving preference to one another." Philippians 2:3 says, "let each esteem others better than himself." This command in Philippians is certainly the mindset that ought to motivate our showing of honor to others. This means honoring those who are rude to us in traffic. It means being respectful to those in long grocery lines who forgot to purchase items with price tags on them. It means honoring our husbands who don't treat us the way we think we ought to be treated. This is a command we would do well to instill in our children too, by our instruction and by our example. I'm appalled at the lack of respect in our society, especially from our youth toward their teachers and from children toward their parents. We are raising a generation of people who do not understand what it means to respect and honor those who are in authority over them.

The second command Peter gives is to *love the brotherhood*. This is <u>agape</u> *love* Peter is calling for, which is a love that is self-sacrificing, which goes right along with honoring them too. The *brotherhood* refers to the Christian fraternity, the family of Christ, the collective body of believers (see 1:22, 3:8, 4:8; 5:14). It really goes without saying that we are to love our brothers and sisters in Christ. Jesus said in John 13:35, "By this all will know that you are My disciples, if you have love for one another." The aged apostle John says in 1 John 3:14, "We know that we have passed from death to life, because we love the brethren. He who does not love his brother abides in death."

The third commandment is to *fear God*. The word for *fear* means reverence, not terror. Proverbs 1:7 states, "The fear of the LORD is the beginning of knowledge, but fools despise wisdom and instruction." I love the book of Ecclesiastes and especially the last part of the book where Solomon is summing up all of life and his vain pursuits and he says, "Let us hear the conclusion of the whole matter: fear God and keep His commandments, for this is man's all" (Ecclesiastes 12:13). I remember one time doing a word study in the Bible on the word fear and discovering that every reference to fear in the Bible is to God, with the exception of one reference to parents and one reference to the king. Ladies, we are to revere God, and this is something we as mothers and grandmothers need to be instilling in our children and grandchildren. I am thankful for an earthly father who instilled in me the importance of fearing my heavenly Father.

The fourth and final commandment Peter gives is to *honor the king*. It is interesting that Solomon also gives his son this same advice in Proverbs 24:21: "My son, fear the LORD and the king; do not associate with those given to change." The word *honor* means to prize, and let us remind ourselves of who the king was at the time Peter was writing this command. It was Nero. Many believers have a hard time giving honor to our current president, and yet think how those Christians were challenged. We may not admire the person who holds the office of president, but we must show respect to the office. We must respect the position God has given to those in authority over us. This holds true for any who are in authority over us: leaders in the church, parents, employers, teachers, even husbands. You may not admire the person in that position or think of them as respectable, but you must show respect toward them because of the position God has given them. We have already been told to submit to the king, now we are told to honor the king. We are to honor all men, and especially we must honor the king."What can even ignorant men say against us if we follow these injunctions? What charge can they bring against us before any magistrate if we live thus: honoring all men, in particular loving our brethren, fearing God in holy reverence, honoring the king?"[33]

Summary

Who are we to submit to? Every ruler that is set up to rule us! Are you submitting to every governing authority?

Why do we submit? Because others look on and see this as one of our good works; it is the will of God; and it has the potential to stop the mouths of foolish men. Are you obeying God by your submission to authority? What foolish man or woman have you muzzled lately by your submission to authority? Do others look on and see that your submission to government is one of the ways you have shown that you are a Christian?

How do we submit? As free servants of God, but not abusing our freedom in Christ. Are you allowing your freedom in Christ to be an excuse for disobeying the government?

We have several examples in the Scriptures of those who appealed to their governing authorities: Daniel, Esther, Nehemiah, Paul, and Abigail, just to name a few. In fact, during the Covid-19 pandemic, I even wrote a gracious appeal to President Trump. We have this freedom and this responsibility as believers. But we also have precedent in Scripture to not obey the government when doing so would require us to disobey God. The Hebrew midwives and the apostles are good examples of this kind of gracious disobedience to civil authorities. We need much wisdom when choosing to do so, and we must make sure that it is specifically a sin issue, rather than simply a preference.

I would like to encourage you to show honor to the government of our land by *not* telling jokes about them or even listening to those who do, but by praying for them, as Paul instructs us to do in

---

[33] R.C.H. Lenski, *Commentary on the New Testament: 1-2 Peter, 1-3 John, Jude* (Minneapolis: Augsburg Publishing House, 1966), 114.

1 Timothy 2:1-4: "Therefore I exhort first of all that supplications, prayers, intercessions, and giving of thanks be made for all men, for kings and all who are in authority, that we may lead a quiet and peaceable life in all godliness and reverence. For this is good and acceptable in the sight of God our Savior, who desires all men to be saved and to come to the knowledge of the truth." I would like to close with a prayer of Daniel's, a prayer that focuses not only on governmental authorities but also on our need for confession. Will you join me in praying Daniel's prayer, in Daniel 9:4-19?

> And I prayed to the LORD my God, and made confession, and said, "O Lord, great and awesome God, who keeps His covenant and mercy with those who love Him, and with those who keep His commandments, we have sinned and committed iniquity, we have done wickedly and rebelled, even by departing from Your precepts and Your judgments. Neither have we heeded Your servants the prophets, who spoke in Your name to our kings and our princes, to our fathers and all the people of the land. O Lord, righteousness belongs to You, but to us shame of face, as it is this day—to the men of Judah, to the inhabitants of Jerusalem and all Israel, those near and those far off in all the countries to which You have driven them, because of the unfaithfulness which they have committed against You.
>
> "O Lord, to us belongs shame of face, to our kings, our princes, and our fathers, because we have sinned against You. To the Lord our God belong mercy and forgiveness, though we have rebelled against Him. We have not obeyed the voice of the LORD our God, to walk in His laws, which He set before us by His servants the prophets. Yes, all Israel has transgressed Your law, and has departed so as not to obey Your voice; therefore the curse and the oath written in the Law of Moses the servant of God have been poured out on us, because we have sinned against Him. And He has confirmed His words, which He spoke against us and against our judges who judged us, by bringing upon us a great disaster; for under the whole heaven such has never been done as what has been done to Jerusalem.
>
> "As it is written in the Law of Moses, all this disaster has come upon us; yet we have not made our prayer before the LORD our God, that we might turn from our iniquities and understand Your truth. Therefore the LORD has kept the disaster in mind, and brought it upon us; for the LORD our God is righteous in all the works which He does, though we have not obeyed His voice. And now, O Lord

our God, who brought Your people out of the land of Egypt with a mighty hand, and made Yourself a name, as it is this day—we have sinned, we have done wickedly!

"O Lord, according to all Your righteousness, I pray, let Your anger and Your fury be turned away from Your city Jerusalem, Your holy mountain; because for our sins, and for the iniquities of our fathers, Jerusalem and Your people are a reproach to all those around us. Now therefore, our God, hear the prayer of Your servant, and his supplications, and for the Lord's sake cause Your face to shine on Your sanctuary, which is desolate. O my God, incline Your ear and hear; open Your eyes and see our desolations, and the city which is called by Your name; for we do not present our supplications before You because of our righteous deeds, but because of Your great mercies. O Lord, hear! O Lord, forgive! O Lord, listen and act! Do not delay for Your own sake, my God, for Your city and Your people are called by Your name."

Questions to Consider
The Christian's Response to Government
1 Peter 2:13-17

1. Compare Romans 13 and 1 Peter 2. (a) What things do you find that are similar? (b) Why do you think Paul and Peter write similar admonitions?

2. Memorize 1 Peter 2:17.

3. (a) Read Daniel 1. How did Daniel make his appeal to earthly authority (the king)? (b) What was the result? (c) What principles do you learn about making appeals to governmental authorities when you don't agree with them?

4. (a) Now read Daniel 3. What happened that caused Daniel's three friends to defy the king's command? (b) Did God protect them? If so, how? (c) Do you think God will always protect His own when they have to disobey earthly authorities? Why or why not?

5. (a) In Acts 5, what were Peter and the apostles doing that caused them to be thrown into prison? (b) How did Peter justify disobeying the high priest, according to verse 29? (c) What was the apostles' response to suffering because of their loyalty to Christ, according to verses 40-42? (d) Recall a time when you suffered because of your loyalty to Christ.

6. (a) How do you think we as believers should respond to jokes about our president and others in authority? (b) What does the Bible say in 1 Timothy 2:1-2?

7. (a) Do you think it is okay for a believer to exceed the speed limit? (b) To cheat on their income taxes? (c) To tell jokes about

their governmental authorities? (d) To not participate in voting in the elections? Come with some thoughts to share!

8. Are you living in submission to authority? (Governmental? Church? Husband? Employer?) If not, write a prayer request asking God to help you in this area, or write a prayer request for those in authority over you.

Chapter 11

Our Supreme Example in Suffering, Christ our Lord!

1 Peter 2:18-25

Many years ago, a very precious friend of mine passed away from a rapidly growing cancer. In fact, the cancer was discovered in December of 1996, and she died just a month later. After Cheryl's death, I received a most heartbreaking letter from a dear friend of hers, basically blaming me and our church for Cheryl's death. In this woman's letter, she said that God did not need my friend to die in order that He would be glorified, and that it was not God's will for Cheryl to suffer. She said, "God would have healed Cheryl. God wanted to heal Cheryl. Jesus paid the price. He overcame the works of the enemy, because God was with him."

Are those true statements? Is that what Peter means in 1 Peter 2:24 when he states, "by whose stripes you were healed"? Are we to just throw out verse 21, which says that we are called to suffer? Just what does this passage of Scripture mean? Let's read it and together discover the meaning of what Peter wrote.

1 Peter 2:18-25

> Servants, be submissive to your masters with all fear, not only to the good and gentle, but also to the harsh. [19]For this is commendable, if because of conscience toward God one endures grief, suffering wrongfully. [20]For what credit is it if, when you are beaten for your faults, you take it patiently? But when you do good and suffer, if you take it patiently, this is commendable before God. [21] For to this you were called, because Christ also suffered for us, leaving us an example, that you should follow His steps: [22]"Who committed no sin, nor was deceit found in His mouth"; [23]who, when He was reviled, did not revile in return; when He suffered, He did not threaten, but

> committed Himself to Him who judges righteously; ²⁴who Himself bore our sins in His own body on the tree, that we, having died to sins, might live for righteousness—by whose stripes you were healed. ²⁵For you were like sheep going astray, but have now returned to the Shepherd and Overseer of your souls.

Our outline for this lesson will be simple. We'll consider our supreme example in suffering, our Lord Jesus, and, as we consider this, we will note two important things:

> *The Servant's Call to Patient Suffering* (vv 18-20)
> *The Savior's Example of Patient Suffering* (vv 21-25)

In the verses we'll consider in this lesson, Peter continues to write about submission, but this time he focuses in on the submission of the servant to his or her master.

The Servant's Call to Patient Suffering

1 Peter 2:18-20

> Servants, be submissive to your masters with all fear, not only to the good and gentle, but also to the harsh. (1 Peter 2:18)

The Greek word here for servants is not doulos, the term that is most often used for slaves in the New Testament. Rather, the Greek word here is ouketace, which indicates a slave who has a close personal relationship with the family. As we mentioned in our previous lesson, there were about 60 million slaves in the Roman Empire at the time that Peter wrote this epistle. Slavery in the Roman Empire was in some ways quite like and quite different from what we typically think of as slavery. Slaves didn't only do mundane tasks and grueling labor; they served as doctors, teachers, musicians, actors, and many other types of professional work. Generally speaking, all of the work of Rome was performed by slaves. In many instances, slaves were not allowed to marry, and if they were allowed to marry, any children born to those slaves were considered the property of the master, not of the slave who bore the child. Slaves had no legal rights and were considered no more than tools. Slave masters possessed unlimited power and absolute ownership over their slaves. In fact, the prevailing thinking among Roman slave owners regarding the value of slaves was that the only difference between a slave and an animal was that the slave happened to be able to speak.

Peter writes that these slaves, who would have been intimately acquainted with the daily family life of their masters, were to be *submissive* to those masters, which means they were to obey those masters. He even goes on to write that they should obey *with all fear*, which has the same meaning as we saw in verse 17, where we are commanded to fear God. Peter is saying that a Christian slave should obey his or her earthly master out of reverence for the Lord and the fear of dishonoring Him. The word *all* tells us that there should be no half-hearted attitude in this submission. This is a command which is repeated numerous times in the New Testament. Ephesians 6:5-8; Colossians 3:22-4:1; 1 Timothy 6:1-2; and Titus 2:9-10 have much to say regarding the master-slave relationship.

The command for servants to submit is followed by a harder command, in my opinion. Peter says these servants are to submit *not only to the good and gentle masters but also to the harsh* masters. The word for good means good at heart, and the word for gentle means gentle in disposition, mild or yielding. This would be a master who was reasonable and considerate toward their slave; those kinds of masters are easy to submit to.

But Peter doesn't stop there; he goes on tells these slaves that they have to submit even to the masters who are harsh! The word harsh comes from the Greek word skolios, where we get our medical term scoliosis, which refers to the curvature of the spine. These masters would be bent or crooked, so to speak. They certainly wouldn't be favorable toward Christian slaves and would treat them unfairly. Now, you might be wondering why these pagan masters would be so harsh toward such submissive Christian slaves. Some of you who work outside the home might be asking this same question about your own boss who is harsh with you. These Christian slaves, if they were living as they ought to, would have been pure, meek, honest, willing to serve, and obedient. This would, of course, have been both a powerful testimony and a tremendous conviction to their masters. And this would have the potential to irritate these masters, who would then resort to punishing their servants unmercifully.

Ladies, when we live our lives as salt and light, our lives serve as both a restraint to evil as well as a constant conviction to those who do evil, to those who are lost. We should remember that salt can serve not only as a preservative but also as an irritant. Godly behavior can be irritating to an unbeliever, which is what was happening here. Such godly behavior would cause the masters to treat their slaves harshly. It was well known in the early days of the church that masters often preferred not to purchase pagan slaves because they knew the Christian slaves would serve them better. But the Christian slave would have to be subservient even in the most difficult of circumstances.

The slaves reading this letter from Peter might have been asking the same question you and I would be asking: "Why do I have to do that?" You and I might even ask, "What about my rights?" Peter anticipates those questions in verse 19.

> For this is commendable, if because of conscience toward God one endures grief, suffering wrongfully. (1 Peter 2:19)

Peter says something absolutely amazing: that a slave's submission to his or her master is *commendable*. This means it is an action that is beyond what is to be expected and is therefore worthy of commendation. It is a word used in the New Testament to describe God's grace, which certainly is an action beyond what you and I should expect from a just and sin-hating God. A slave reacting in a godly manner toward his or her cruel master would, of course, be an unexpected response. Yet, this is the attitude our Lord expects of us, as it was also His attitude.

The motive driving such a godly attitude is the slave's conscience before God. Peter puts it this way: *if because of conscience toward God one endures grief, suffering wrongfully*. This statement is a reference to the slaves being conscious of their relationship to God, to His presence, and to His will. Slaves should perform all their duties as unto God, not unto their masters. God's ongoing presence in their lives should cause them to willingly endure suffering. Paul makes this point very clear in Colossians 3:22-24, where he commands slaves to submit to their masters and says in verses 23 and 24, "And whatever you do, do it heartily, as to the Lord and not to men, knowing that from the Lord you will receive the reward of the inheritance; for you serve the Lord Christ." My dear sister, that should be the attitude for each of us in all that we do: we should always remember that the presence of our Lord is with us, that He is watching, and it is He to whom we will give an account someday. This makes our suffering here endurable and worthwhile.

Often, I speak to women who are in very difficult situations, and I encourage them to do the hard thing as unto the Lord. Sometimes, we do not understand why we have to endure such difficulty, but it's such a comfort to know that we know the One who does understand.

Peter goes on to say that even if these slaves must *endure grief, suffering wrongfully*, even this is commendable. To endure grief is to undergo hardship, to bear up under sadness. It conveys the idea of something sustaining a weight that has been placed upon it. The Greek tense here indicates one who constantly bears up under the load and does not give in at all, even if what is done is unjust or wrongful, as Peter puts it. This is the idea that our Lord speaks about in the Sermon on the Mount, in Matthew 5:39, "But I tell you not to resist an evil person. But whoever slaps you on your right cheek, turn the other to him also." My friend, this is indeed commendable for any of us, whether we are slave or free! To suffer for doing what is right is a righteous thing before our God. Peter will write later in this same letter, in 1 Peter 3:17, "it is better, if it is the will of God, to suffer for doing good than for doing evil." Peter goes on with more encouragement in verse 20.

> what credit is it if, when you are beaten for your faults, you take it patiently? But when you do good and suffer, if you take it patiently, this is commendable before God. (1 Peter 2:20)

Peter encourages these slaves that there is no glory or *credit* when they get what they deserve by not obeying their masters, but when they *do good* and they still *suffer* for it, this is *commendable before God*. Servants were often struck in anger by their masters, either with a hand or an object. Peter tells them that they should not retaliate if they are beaten for their faults, but they should *take* the beating *patiently*. The meaning for *beaten* here is the same one mentioned in Matthew 26:67 where it speaks of our Lord's beating, "Then they spat in His face and beat Him; and others struck Him with the palms of their hands." It is the same idea as in Isaiah 52:14 where it tells us that Christ's visage was marred more than any man. Christ was beaten so much that He did not even look like a man. Peter, of course, would have memories of that awful night, and so he exhorts these slaves to remember the Lord Jesus and His sufferings and to react the way He did, as we will see in following verses. We know Christ did not deserve the punishment He received and neither did some of the slaves to whom Peter is writing. But they still must accept such unjust punishment with patience. If they were beaten for their faults, that was what they deserved, and they should take that patiently too.

But, Peter says, when *you do good and suffer, if you take it patiently, this is commendable before God*. Peter is saying that patient endurance on the part of these Christian slaves is an action beyond what is expected and is therefore commendable. God is pleased when one accepts unjust behavior from his or her master or employer in a godly way. Peter encourages his readers with much the same things, when he writes in 1 Peter 4:14, "If you are reproached for the name of Christ, blessed are you, for the Spirit of glory and of God rests upon you. On their part He is blasphemed, but on your part He is glorified."

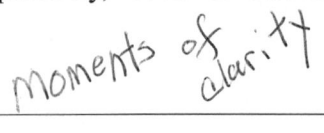

So, the servant is called to submit with all reverence, to suffer patiently, even if suffering wrongfully, knowing that this is commendable in God's sight. We now move from the servant's call to patient suffering to the Savior's example of patient suffering, in verses 21-25. Peter reminds us of our supreme example of suffering in the remaining verses.

The Savior's Example of Patient Suffering

1 Peter 2:21-25

> For to this you were called, because Christ also suffered for us, leaving us an example, that you should follow His steps: (1 Peter 2:21)

In this verse, we have a fairly clear-cut rebuttal to the woman who claimed that it was not God's will for my friend Cheryl to suffer. Peter says clearly that we are *called* to suffer. In 2 Timothy 3:12, Paul clearly states, "Yes, and all who desire to live godly in Christ Jesus will suffer persecution." He also writes in Philippians 1:29, "For to you it has been granted on behalf of Christ, not only to believe in Him, but also to suffer for His sake." And even in Acts 14:22, he states, "We must through many tribulations enter the kingdom of God." We are clearly called to suffer. Why? Peter says *because Christ also suffered for us, leaving us an example, that you should follow His steps*. The word *suffered* means to experience a painful sensation. My friend, He suffered *for us*! He suffered for many reasons, but here Peter says that He suffered in order to leave us an example to follow. The word *example* means a copy for imitation. It is an interesting word which describes the way children would learn to write. They would have a book which contained letters that they would trace over again and again until their own letters were patterned exactly like their teacher's. The word *follow* means to take the same road as someone else takes. The idea is that we are to follow the same steps Christ took, the same footprints He left for us, the same path of suffering. This would not be a new concept to Peter's readers; Jesus made this clear to the disciples in the upper room, in John 15:20: "Remember the word that I said to you, 'A servant is not greater than his master.' If they persecuted Me, they will also persecute you. If they kept My word, they will keep yours also." This reference to following Christ must have had special significance to Peter, as these were both Christ's first words to Peter (Matthew 4:19, "Follow me and I will make you fishers of men") and Christ's last words to Peter (John 21:22, "You follow Me").

What example did Christ leave for us to follow? The example He left is difficult, especially for twenty-first century American Christians, but it is certainly not impossible. In the coming verses, Peter gives us five specific steps we ought to follow. He says,

> "Who committed no sin, nor was deceit found in His mouth."
> (1 Peter 2:22)

In these verses, Peter gives us four steps concerning what not to do when we're going through suffering, and then one step concerning what we are to do. He says of Jesus that He *committed no sin*. It literally reads, "Who never in a single instance committed sin." Peter already said back in 1 Peter 1:19 that Jesus' blood was as of a lamb without blemish and without spot. John the apostle says in 1 John 3:5, "And you know that He was manifested to take away our sins, and in Him there is no sin." *This is the first step we are to emulate when going through suffering: we are not to sin.* I know this can seem difficult at times—but, my friend, it is possible! I often tell women going through hardships or difficult marriages that they can live above their circumstances and the difficult people in their life. They can be holy regardless of what is going on around them.

Not only was there no sin in Christ, but Peter also says *nor was deceit found in His mouth*. There was no trickery or guile in His mouth. Peter is probably alluding to Isaiah 53:9, where Isaiah says the same thing about our suffering Savior. Peter said no deceit could be found in Christ's mouth. *Found* is a word which speaks of finding something after careful scrutiny. But it wasn't just that deceit wasn't there—it was never to be found! My sister, when we're going through suffering, we should not use our mouths for deceit. *This is the second way we follow our Master when going through suffering: we do not practice deceit.* Remember that Peter has already mentioned in 1 Peter 2:1 that deceit, or guile, is a sin we are to put off in order that we can receive the Word. It certainly should be put off not only then but also when we're going though suffering. Peter goes on to say of Christ,

> who, when He was reviled, did not revile in return; when He suffered, He did not threaten, but committed Himself to Him who judges righteously; (1 Peter 2:23)

When Christ *was reviled*, He *did not revile in return. Revile* means to be reproached like a harsh railing, which not only serves to rebuke a man but also sharply bites him. Jesus endured such reviling: "Hail King of the Jews"; "You who destroy the temple and build it in three days, save Yourself! If You are the Son of God, come down from the cross"; "He trusted in God; let Him deliver Him now if He will have Him; for He said, 'I am the Son of God'" (Matthew 27:29, 40, 43). How did Jesus respond? He did not revile back; He showed no anger; He did not use abusive speech; He did not take vengeance, even though He had the power to do so. Instead of reviling back, Jesus endured the suffering patiently and He prayed for His abusers to be forgiven. My dear friend, He did this to set an example for us, and we are to follow His pattern. *As you and I go through suffering, we must follow our Lord in this third step: we must not revile back when we are reviled.* I know that goes against our fleshly rationale, but nonetheless, it is what we will do if we want to be like our Savior.

I just recently had a difficult situation in my own life where I was sorely tried, and I tell you it can be done with much prayer and self-control. It doesn't relieve the hurt from the one who does the reviling, but it does prevent us from sinning. When we are being reviled, we should remember that a soft answer turns away wrath (Proverbs 15:1).

Peter goes on to say of Christ that *when He suffered, He did not threaten.* Peter certainly could have testified that this was true about Christ; Peter was in the courtyard when Jesus was being tried. Peter also saw Christ hang and suffer on the cross without threatening.

And, though Peter did sin with his mouth by denying his Lord, and Peter did threaten and take vengeance by cutting off the ear of the high priest's servant, Christ did not. *When you and I suffer, it is imperative that we follow our Savior in this fourth way: that we do not threaten people.* We must not try to bully or intimidate people, even if they are doing that to us. That never does anyone any good.

Christ set an example for us of what not to do in four specific areas, now Peter tells us of Christ's example of what we should do. Christ did something that I think everyone of us needs to practice when we're suffering: He *committed Himself to Him who judges righteously.* The word for *commit* means to surrender or to hand over something. The idea is that as we hand it over, we hand it to someone to take care of it and manage it for us. Oh, my friend, what a blessed, comforting thought! We do not have to retaliate, and we do not have to react in anger, but we do have to commit it to the One who cares about it. Peter will say in 1 Peter 5:7, "casting all your care upon Him, for He cares for you." Christ committed all of His suffering to the Father. You and I might entrust some of our cares to Him, but often we hold back on a few things that we think we can handle ourselves, but not our Supreme Example—He cast the whole thing over to His Father. One writer says, "Our Lord kept on delivering over to God the Father both the revilers and their revilings as both kept on wounding His loving heart."[34] There are people in our lives who wound us over and over and over again, and we must keep on committing and committing and committing it to the Lord, the Righteous Judge. Peter will say in 1 Peter 4:19, "Therefore let those who suffer according to the will of God commit their souls to Him in doing good, as to a faithful Creator."

Peter says Christ committed these things *to the One who judges righteously.* God is the one who judges or determines what is right or just. He decides—not us! These verses are not only some of my favorites, but they are verses that I often share with women who are in difficult marriages or in difficult situations. Of course, we

---

[34] *Kenneth S. Wuest, Wuest's Word Studies from the Greek New Testament* (Grand Rapids: Wm. B. Eerdmans Publishing Company, 1973), 68.

must remember that some of our suffering we bring on ourselves by our sin. I have found that as I commit my cause to the One who judges righteously, many times I am convicted of my own sin which has brought on the suffering. However, even when we're innocent, we must commit our situations to Him. We must live blamelessly regardless of what others might say or do. *The fifth and final step we follow our Lord in as we go through suffering is to commit it to the One who judges righteously.*

Peter goes on to mention our Lord's greatest suffering of all, one that you and I will never have to go through. The writer to the Hebrews puts it this way, "You have not yet resisted to bloodshed, striving against sin" (Hebrews 12:4). Or, as Peter says,

> who Himself bore our sins in His own body on the tree, that we, having died to sins, might live for righteousness—by whose stripes you were healed. (1 Peter 2:24)

The word *bore* is a word which was used to describe the priests as they carried the sacrifice up to the altar. The altar was 4½ feet high, and the priest had to make the incline up the altar, carrying the sacrifice which was to be slain. Christ Himself, by His own personal suffering, *bore our sins* as a burden of guilt up to the cross. I would like for you to pause here for a minute and think about all the sins that just you and you alone have committed in a lifetime. If you only sinned three times a day (I wish!), that would be 1095 sins in one year. And, if you lived to be at least 70, that is 76,650 sins. Imagine Christ bearing the load of just your sin on the cross! When you multiply that number with all the sins of the world, for all time, it is truly mind-boggling and humbling.

Why did Christ do that? Why would He carry such a load of sin? Peter says it was so *that we, having died to sins, might live for righteousness*. Christ did this so that the power of sin would be dead in our lives, so that we might live holy lives. Paul says in Romans 6:18, "And having been set free from sin, you became slaves of righteousness."

Peter adds a phrase: *by whose stripes you were healed*. This is a phrase that the slaves of Peter's day would have easily identified with, because many of them would have received stripes as well. A stripe simply means a blow mark. This would refer to the bloody lacerated marks Christ received as a result of the scourging He endured at the hands of the Roman soldiers. They would take a scourge of cords, which had pieces of lead or bone attached to it. And the victim, who would be Christ in this case, would be stripped down to the waist, hands tied behind his back, and strapped to a post. He would then be whipped intensely. "Thus we have the portrait of the suffering Servant of Jehovah. His blessed face so pummeled by the hard fists of the mob that it did not look like a human face anymore, His back lacerated by the Roman scourge so that it was one mass of open, raw, quivering flesh trickling with blood, His heart torn with anguish because of the bitter words hurled at Him. On that bleeding, lacerated back was laid the Cross."[35] As Isaiah 52:14 says, "His visage was marred more than any man." It was not a pretty sight, my friend. Peter says it is by these *stripes* that *you were healed*, which is a quote from Isaiah 53:5.

So we must ask ourselves, "What is the healing that Peter is referring to? Is it physical, spiritual, or what?" Many people today claim this as a promise of physical healing, but illness isn't even mentioned in this context. This passage cannot be used to teach that healing of our body is promised in the atonement of Christ. To do so is to teach error. The word for *healed* means to make whole. Peter is referring to the healing of the soul. Christ died to save our souls! Sin in the scripture is often referred to as a disease. The Psalmist says in Psalm 41:4, "heal my soul, for I have sinned against You." Jeremiah, when referring to the sins of the nation, says, "Is there no balm in Gilead, is there no physician there? Why then is there no recovery for the health of the daughter of my people?" (Jeremiah 8:22). Jeremiah is talking about disease, but it is not physical; it is spiritual, and it is because of sin. Also, we must consider the verb tense, which is in the past. Peter says you *were healed*, not you are healed. It is not a present tense or even a future tense. It is not you are healed or will be healed. Remember, Peter is writing to those who have been

---
[35] Ibid, 69.

born again. Christ's death on the cross resulted in a once for all healing, salvation, for all who believe. You too, perhaps, have heard the erroneous teaching that Christians will not suffer or get sick if they are in the will of God. I am not sure where that teaching comes from, but it certainly is not biblical! That is why it is essential that we always consider the context of a passage. Also, the next verse gives us even more proof that this is not physical healing.

> For you were like sheep going astray, but have now returned to the Shepherd and Overseer of your souls. (1 Peter 2:25)

The word *for* is a conjunction which connects the current sentence with the previous one, thereby explaining the previous sentence—in this case, explaining this spiritual healing. They were *like sheep going astray*, which is a picture of their spiritual depravity; nothing physical is even hinted at here. In Matthew 9:36, we read of Christ, "But when He saw the multitudes, He was moved with compassion for them, because they were weary and scattered, like sheep having no shepherd." We were like sheep who once went astray, which means we once roamed and wandered out of the way. Sheep are known for straying and getting lost. I don't live in an area where there are too many sheep, but the first readers of this epistle would have completely understood this analogy. It would have been unthinkable to leave the sheep alone without the shepherd, as there were no fences, the paths were rough, and often there were wild beasts that would try to destroy the sheep. The shepherd had to continually watch his flock or else harm would come to them.

We were like those dumb sheep going astray, but praise God, Peter says we *have now returned to the Shepherd and Overseer of your souls*. Like you and me, they were headed in the wrong direction, away from the Good Shepherd, but they have now completely turned around, they have turned toward the Shepherd. This is a reference to our repentance, to our turning around, and embracing Christ as the Overseer of our souls. Does this mean that we come to Christ on our own power? No, Peter has already made this clear in previous verses that we were chosen, that Christ chose some because of His mercy.

The Shepherd seeks the lost sheep. They don't turn back on their own. Ezekiel 34:11-12 reads the following: "I Myself will search for My sheep and seek them out. As a shepherd seeks out his flock on the day he is among his scattered sheep, so will I seek out My sheep and deliver them from all the places where they were scattered." There is no reference to the sheep seeking the Shepherd. He seeks them. If we as dumb sheep were left to ourselves, we would wander around and fall off some cliff to our eternal destruction. But, because of His kindness, we have returned to the Shepherd and Overseer of our souls.

An *overseer* is one that has the oversight. "Episkopos is a word with great history behind it."[36] "It is a word which has many meanings. It means the protector of public safety; the guardian of honor and honesty; the overseer of right education and of public morals; and the administrator of public law and order. So, then, to call God the episkopos of our souls, is to call him our Guardian, our Protector, our Guide and our Director."[37] So then, let the suffering come, because our souls are watched over and entrusted to the great Shepherd and Overseer. Jesus Christ is the Overseer of souls; He has us continually under his eye; He knows our wants and wishes, the dangers we might encounter, and provides for us as well. As our Shepherd, He leads us to the best pastures, defends us from our enemies, and guides us by His watchful eye. Jesus is the good Shepherd that laid down his life for His sheep.

Our supreme example of suffering is Christ, who did not sin even when He was threatened and reviled. He is also our example in committing our souls to the One who judges righteously. Do you commit your suffering to the Good Shepherd, or do you react carnally by threatening those who are causing you pain? Servants are called to be submissive even to perverse masters, as Christ is their supreme example, having suffered too at the hand of unjust men. Has your suffering been brought on by you being sinful, or is your suffering brought on by you being salt?

---

[36]William Barclay, *The Letters of James and Peter* (Louisville: Westminster John Knox Press, 1976), 216.
[37]Ibid, 217.

Summary

One of the last nights that Cheryl was alive we were rehearsing all God was doing through her suffering and illness and how no suffering is ever wasted. I remember saying to her, "I am just so sorry it has to be you, Cheryl, who is afflicted." She simply replied, "I'm not."

Is that your attitude toward suffering? Do you make the most of suffering as my friend did? My friend, Cheryl, reminded me of our Lord in her sufferings as she followed His steps. She prayed much in her affliction, just as Christ did in His. She would take every opportunity to share the gospel on her deathbed, as our Lord did by compelling the rulers and even the thief on the cross to repent and turn to Christ. She poured out gracious words from her lips when she was in immense pain, even as her Lord also did. Do you embrace suffering? Have you, my friend, embraced the cross? Are you following the Master in the fiery furnace of suffering?

Embrace the Cross, by Steve Green

> I am crucified with Christ
> Therefore I no longer live
> Jesus Christ now lives in me
>
> Embrace the cross
> Where Jesus suffered
> Though it will cost
> All you claim as yours
> Your sacrifice will seem small
> Beside the treasure
> Eternity can't measure
> What Jesus holds in store
>
> Embrace the love
> The cross requires
> Cling to the one

Whose heart knew every pain
Receive from Jesus
Fountains of compassion
Only He can fashion
Your heart to move as His

Oh, wondrous cross, our desires rest in you
Lord Jesus make us bolder
To face with courage the shame and disgrace
You bore upon Your shoulder

Embrace the life
That comes from dying
Come trace the steps
The Savior walked for you
An empty tomb
Concludes Golgotha's sorrow
Endure then till tomorrow
Your cross of suffering

Embrace the cross
Embrace the cross
The cross of Jesus[38]

---

[38]Words by Steve Green

Questions to Consider

Our Supreme Example in Suffering: Christ our Lord!
1 Peter 2:18-25

1. (a) What are the names for Jesus that Peter uses in 1 Peter 2? (b) Summarize chapter two in three sentences or less.

2. Memorize 1 Peter 2:21-23.

3. (a) What should be our response to those who treat us unjustly, according to Matthew 5:11-12, 39-48 and Luke 6:32-36? (b) Are these your responses when treated unfairly?

4. (a) Contrast Peter's responses to persecution with our Lord's responses in Matthew 26:57-74 and John 18:1-11. (b) After His Lord's death, how do you think Peter felt about his failures to respond righteously?

5. (a) Peter says in 1 Peter 2:23 that in Christ's sufferings, He did not retaliate but committed Himself to the One who judges righteously. As you read the following accounts of His sufferings, how do you see our Lord committing Himself to the Father? Matthew 26:47-67; 27:45-50; Mark 14:32-38; 15:1-5; Luke 23:26-46; John 19:9-12. (b) How do these verses help you to commit yourself to the Lord during suffering?

6. (a) In what ways are we to follow the example of our Lord, according to John 13:12-15; Ephesians 5:2; Philippians 2:5-8; 1 Peter 2:21; 1 John 2:6 and 3:16? (b) Can you think of any example that Christ left for us while on earth that we should not emulate?

7. (a) In looking at Psalm 23; Ezekiel 34:11-31; and John 10:1-18, 27-29, what things do you notice to be the roles of our Good Shepherd toward His sheep? (b) In what ways have you experienced the role of the Good Shepherd in your own life?

8. (a) What do you think Peter means in 1 Peter 2:24 when he says, "by whose stripes you were healed"? (b) Is this physical, spiritual, or both? Support your answer from the Scriptures.

9. (a) Is suffering for the cause of Christ difficult for you? If so, in what way? (b) What principles have you learned from your own sufferings that you could pass on to others to encourage them in their sufferings?

10. What is the most difficult attitude for you to have when undergoing unjust treatment? Please put your needs in the form of a prayer request.

Phillip Keller
Psalm 23

Chapter 12

What Does a Beautiful Woman Look Like?
1 Peter 3:1-6

One of the most difficult things I have to do when I am counseling women is to give help and hope to those who have unsaved husbands. It requires wisdom from above to know when to counsel them to submit, when to not submit, what to say, what not to say, when to say it, and how to say it. This would also include the wisdom needed in how to counsel them regarding their children. The unbelieving husband many times wants to raise the children according to the world's wisdom, and yet the believing wife wants to rear them according to God's Word. Many women I have counseled got married thinking that they were marrying a believer, only to find out later in the marriage that he is not. What are these wives to do? Theirs is a very difficult situation, and one that requires much wisdom, much compassion, and a lot of prayer. Many of you may be living with an unsaved husband or know someone who is. It is not an easy road, but it is possible to travel on this road with the help of Christ and other believers.

How does a believing wife win her unbelieving husband to Christ? Is it by her outward beauty and worldly compromises? Many women have believed a lie, whether we have unsaved husbands or saved husbands. Do you want to know what that lie is? Here it is: "If I could just be thin enough, and beautiful enough, I would find true happiness and contentment, and a husband who is attracted to me." Unfortunately, our culture today has told that lie (and many others, I might add) to the female gender, and many of us actually believe it. We think that if we could just wear a size 8, have a peachy-cream complexion, and wear the latest fashions, then all would be well with us, with our marriages, and with the world. But is that godly thinking? Is that what Scripture teaches us as women? What should we, as Christian women, be focusing our attention on? How can we truly be attractive to our husbands, saved or unsaved? Will we win them over by being beautiful, skinny, and sexy?

We will see from our text that it is not outward beauty, but inward beauty, that is to be the goal of the godly woman. There are six attitudes that should characterize a godly woman, whether she is married to a believer or an unbeliever. And, by the way, if you are single, you should consider this passage as well, because you might very well get married one day! And even if you don't get married, you will still need to hold married friends and family accountable to heed to this passage! Let's read the beginning of chapter three of Peter's first epistle and see what these six attitudes are.

1 Peter 3:1-6

> Wives, likewise, be submissive to your own husbands, that even if some do not obey the word, they, without a word, may be won by the conduct of their wives, [2]when they observe your chaste conduct accompanied by fear. [3]Do not let your adornment be merely outward—arranging the hair, wearing gold, or putting on fine apparel—[4]rather let it be the hidden person of the heart, with the incorruptible beauty of a gentle and quiet spirit, which is very precious in the sight of God. [5]For in this manner, in former times, the holy women who trusted in God also adorned themselves, being submissive to their own husbands, [6]as Sarah obeyed Abraham, calling him lord, whose daughters you are if you do good and are not afraid with any terror.

In this third chapter of 1 Peter, Peter continues on with his theme of submission, but now he turns to the role of the wife.

> Wives, likewise, be submissive to your own husbands, that even if some do not obey the word, they, without a word, may be won by the conduct of their wives, (1 Peter 3:1)

Before we begin to unpack the meaning of verse 1, we need to understand the culture of Peter's day because it was very different from ours. In the New Testament times, a wife was expected to adopt the same religion as her husband. To change religions would be unthinkable. A wife had no rights, and her husband could divorce her for almost any reason; he could divorce her for being unfaithful, appearing in the streets without a veil, drinking wine, going to the public games, and just about anything else you might imagine, even burning his dinner! She was to be seen and not heard. It is almost impossible for us to understand how brave these women were to become believers under this kind of persecution. If the husband became a Christian, then the culture demanded that the wife must become a Christian as well. But if the wife became a Christian and her husband did not, then her husband could declare her to be unfaithful to him and to his pagan religion. Because her bold stand would undoubtedly incur significant persecution, she would need specific instructions on what to do. This is probably why Peter devotes more space to the role of the wife than to the role of the husband in 1 Peter 3:1-7.

When a wife embraced Christianity and her husband did not, it obviously created great tension in the home. These women were often be beaten by their husbands because of their faith in Christ. But, notice that Peter doesn't tell these wives to get a divorce. Instead, Peter tells these wives to do something much different than divorce; he tells them to submit. And, ladies, Peter means for wives to do this even if their husbands are making their lives miserable! (Now, I want to clarify that if a husband is beating his wife, the wife should make use of the protection provided by the civil authorities and call the local police. If her husband is a believer, she should also begin the process of Matthew 18 regarding church discipline.)

Peters starts out with an interesting word here in verse 1, and the word is *likewise*. This means similar or like. What is Peter referring to? Wives are to be submissive to their husbands, as like everyone is commanded to be submissive to the governing authorities in 2:13; as like the slaves are commanded to be submissive to their masters in 2:18; as our Lord was submissive to unjust men, as Peter explains in 2:21-23; and as all of us are to be submissive to one another, as Peter will mention in 5:5 (and even husbands to wives in 3:7, as we will see in our next lesson). In the same way that all Christians must be submissive to wicked governments, that slaves must be submissive to perverse masters, and Christ was submissive to cruel men, so wives must be submissive to obstinate, unbelieving husbands. *So, the first attitude that we as wives should have toward our husbands is an attitude of submission.*

What does *submission* mean? It is the same Greek term that is used in 2:18, hupatasso, which means to place under rank, or to place under in an orderly fashion. I have heard submission explained this way: the husband is like the president and the wife is like the vice president, or the husband is like a five-star general and the wife is like a four-star general. This is not a spineless submission, as someone once said, but a voluntary selflessness. This also does not mean that a wife is to be passive or can never express an opinion. Submission does not mean wives are inferior, just as slaves are not inferior to their masters, Christ was not inferior to unjust men, and none of us are inferior to our governing authorities. Galatians 3:28 says, "There is neither Jew nor Greek, there is neither slave nor free, there is neither male nor female; for you are all one in Christ Jesus."

My dear sister, there is a reason we are to submit, and the reason is that submission is part of God's sovereign plan for your life to sanctify you. My husband often says a woman's submission is a huge part of her sanctification. (The only exception to a wife's obligation to submit to her husband would be if her husband were to ask her to sin, and in the situation of a believing wife being married to an unbelieving husband, the likelihood of that happening would be greater. (See Acts 5:29.) A wife's loyalty to her Lord must be above her loyalty to her husband.)

This submission is to be to *your own husband*, which emphasizes the bond of marriage. It is *your own* husband, not someone else's, that you're to be submissive to. Now, this particular command to submit is somewhat different than the other New Testament passages regarding submission, in that these husbands are not believers. Peter puts it this way: *even if some do not obey the word*. Peter is referring to husbands who do not obey the gospel. The word for *do not obey* indicates a state of unbelieving disobedience; it is someone who will not allow themselves to be persuaded. These husbands were obstinate and would not listen to the claims of the gospel. They did not obey *the word*, the gospel. Peter has already mentioned these types of individuals in 1 Peter 2:8, and he will mention them again in 1 Peter 4:17.

What is a Christian woman to do in this circumstance? Get a divorce? I would caution you to be very wise about giving that kind of advice. The Word of God provides only two allowable reasons for divorce and being married to an unbeliever is not one of them! Instead of a divorce, Peter, the apostle of hope, encourages these wives in how they could win their husbands to Christ without preaching to them. He says *they, without a word, may be won by the conduct of their wives*. Contrary to what some will teach, Peter is not saying that an unbelieving husband is won to Christ without the gospel, because that is impossible. Peter has already clearly stated in 1 Peter 1:23 that salvation comes through "having been born again, not of corruptible seed but incorruptible, through the word of God which lives and abides forever." Also, Paul says in Romans 10:14, "How then shall they call on Him in whom they have not believed? And how shall they believe in Him of whom they have not heard? And how shall they hear without a preacher?" So, when Peter says the wife may be able to win her husband over *without a word*, he means that these wives win over their husbands without talk, without a lot of speaking, without preaching at them. I've met Christian wives who, quite frankly, preach so much at their husbands that all it does is drive them further away. I am sure that this would also be the temptation for these wives Peter is writing to. Think of it: they had given their lives to the Lord and had been transformed and, of course, they would want desperately for their husbands to embrace Christ as well. It would be only natural that they would want to encourage them in that way. If you are married to an unbeliever, you would be a wise woman not to turn Christian radio on every time your husband is home, so that he's forced to hear it, or to leave Bible verses on the refrigerator or the mirror, hoping that he will read them. This is probably not the smartest way to win your husband. I am not saying you should never share the gospel with your unsaved husband or never confront him with his sin, as you do have those responsibilities. But Peter has a better solution for wives who are married to unbelievers. Do you want to know how to win your lost husband to Christ? It is not by what you say; it is by how you behave. Peter calls it your *conduct* or your behavior, which means your manner of life. (See also 1 Peter 1:15, 18; 2:12; 3:1, 2, 16; 2 Peter 2:7; 3:11, for other instances in which Peter uses this same term. This is a favorite word of Peter, having used it 8 times in his epistles.) I know there are some of you who are married to unbelievers, and I know it is very, very difficult. But I want to say to you that the best way you can win your husband to the Lord is not by nagging him into the kingdom, but by being loving and by being graciously submissive. You should treat him with the greatest respect, love, kindness, and patience possible. Let your lost husband see Christ in you. The purpose clause here, *may be*, or in order that, indicates that a wife's submissive attitude is intended to have an evangelistic function.

We must stop and think about what Peter is saying here. A believing wife has a wonderful opportunity to evangelize her husband by her conduct! Even a harsh, unbelieving, antagonistic husband's heart can be won by watching his wife live out her Christianity. This also does not mean those of us who are married to believers can be as free as a bird with our speech and say whatever we please. Proverbs 21:19 states, "Better to dwell in the wilderness, than with a contentious and angry woman." If you find your husband working late hours and not coming around much, you might ask yourself, "Just what kind of wife, am I? Am I nagging or encouraging? Am I gentle and quiet, or mean and loud?" Peter says by your good conduct you may *win*, or gain, your husband. It is the same word Christ uses in Matthew 18:15, where Christ says we are to confront sin in our brother, and if he receives what we share, then we have gained or won our brother. Here, in 1 Peter, it means we gain him by winning him over to the kingdom of God. So, a wife doesn't preach her faith, but she lives it, which is the harder thing to do, right? Peter goes on with another attitude that should characterize these wives.

when they observe your chaste conduct accompanied by fear. (1 Peter 3:2)

This is similar to what Peter has already written in 1 Peter 2:12, where he said that believers' conduct should be honorable among unbelievers. Peter says in this verse that the unsaved husband is observing the wife's chaste conduct. The word *observe* means to watch attentively, to see for oneself. *So, the second attitude that should characterize us as believing wives is that of chaste conduct.* Now, the words *chaste conduct* might seem odd to us, but it basically means sacred behavior, free from all impurity. It is the behavior that Peter has already admonished all believers to do, in 1 Peter 1:15, "but as He who called you is holy, you also be holy in all your conduct." The husband should observe his Christian wife and see that she lives out what she professes, that is, her Christian faith. So, if you are married, your husband should be able to see that you live out at home the faith that you profess.

This chaste conduct is to be *accompanied by fear*. What does this mean? It means that wives are to not only live in holiness, but they are to do so along with *fear*, or reverence, of their husbands. It is the same word that is used in Ephesians 5:33 where it says that wives are to revere or respect their husbands. It means to notice him, regard him, honor him, prefer him, esteem him, defer to him, praise him, and love and admire him exceedingly! Ladies, respecting your husbands is probably the thing your husbands desire most—I know mine does! Some people also think this command could be referring to a reverence for God, and that certainly is a possibility. Really, both are true—we are to honor our husbands, and we should do so out of honor for God. Peter is saying we should have pure behavior that is married with an attitude of reverence as it relates to our husbands. *Reverence is the third attitude that we should have as women.*

Now, it's possible that these women were thinking, "If I just dress differently or make his favorite lamb stew, then my husband might embrace Christ." But Peter shares something that is much harder than doing our hair and makeup and wearing pretty clothes. Instead of focusing on wearing fine clothing on the outer woman, Peter says we need to focus on wearing meekness on the inner woman.

> Do not let your adornment be merely outward—arranging the hair, wearing gold, or putting on fine apparel— (1 Peter 3:3)

Peter says our adornment should not be merely outward. The word for *adornment* is the Greek word <u>kosmos</u>, which refers to a system in which order prevails. We get our English word cosmetic from this word. Peter is *not saying* to never fix your hair, to never wear jewelry, or to do away with clothes. But he is saying that our adornment should not be *merely* outward. To neglect the outer woman would likely be offensive to our husbands. You and I shouldn't look like we just crawled out of bed when our husbands arrive home from work; we should dress in a manner that pleases our individual husbands. But Peter is saying that we should not look at our outward adorning as being the measure of our true beauty. No matter how beautiful our faces are, how expensive our clothes are, or how skinny our bodies are, we all are going to end up in a grave! Doesn't it seem silly to put so much time into something that is going to burn up?!

Peter goes on to give us some examples of this ordered adornment. The first is *arranging the hair* or braiding the hair. Is Peter saying we can never braid or fix our hair? No! The braiding of the hair refers to an elaborate gathering of the hair into knots. Women in that day were addicted to ridiculous extravagance when it came to adorning their hair. They would take great trouble at building their hair up with many tiers, so much so that their hair looked like a tall building. One man says, "Hair was waxed and dyed, sometimes black, more often auburn. Wigs were worn, especially blond wigs, which are found even in the Christian catacombs; and hair to manufacture them was imported from Germany, and even from as far away as India. Hairbands, pins and combs were made of ivory, and boxwood, and tortoiseshell; and sometimes of gold, studded with gems."[39]

---

[39] William Barclay, *The Letters of James and Peter* (Revised Edition) (Louisville: Westminster John Knox Press, 1976), 221.

The second adornment that was overdone was the *wearing* of *gold*. They would actually put it all around their necks, ankles, arms and fingers. It was a very gaudy display of jewelry. Once again, Peter is not forbidding wearing jewelry, but he is forbidding a lavish, gaudy, elaborate display, intended to draw attention to oneself. In fact, it was said that one woman in that time had a dress covered with so many pearls and emeralds that it cost the equivalent of $450,000 today.[40]

The third adornment that Peter addresses is clothes, or as he puts it, *putting on fine apparel*. Obviously, Peter is not saying don't wear clothes, because God clothed Adam and Eve in the garden after they had sinned. The words *putting on* actually mean investment of clothing. The word for *fine apparel* means expensive garments. Paul says in 1 Timothy 2:9 that we should adorn ourselves in modest apparel, not expensive garments. By the way, the word modest in 1 Timothy means that which is becoming."Every ornament of the body, however beautiful, is soon to be laid aside; the adorning of the soul will endure forever."[41] My dear sisters, we should be spending the majority of our time adorning our hearts, which will be in eternity forever with God, rather than adorning our bodies, which will in a moment be in the ground and turned to dust. These things are what John calls in 1 John 2:15-16 the lust of the flesh, the lust of the eyes, and the pride of life. These are not of the Father, but are of the world, and John reminds us that the world will pass away. In contrast to the outer woman, we are to concentrate on the inner woman. God is always interested in our heart. Often women will dress to please a man, and some will dress to deliberately attract the attention of men. But Peter says don't dress the outer woman to attract attention to yourself, rather, dress the inner woman to please God. Man looks on our outward appearance, but God looks on the heart. Peter puts it this way:

> rather let it be the hidden person of the heart, with the incorruptible beauty of a gentle and quiet spirit, which is very precious in the sight of God. (1 Peter 3:4)

---

[40]Ibid, 221.
[41]Albert Barnes, *Barnes' Notes on the New Testament: Hebrews to Jude* (Grand Rapids: Baker Book House, reprinted from the 1884-55 edition), 159.

Peter says we should be concerned about *the hidden person of the heart*. *Hidden* means concealed or private, and *the heart* refers to our thoughts and feelings. My friend, this is and always will be the issue: the heart. It is not your clothes, your hair, or your jewelry that is the issue with God; it is your heart. The things mentioned in verse 3 are going to burn up, because they are corruptible. But the *beauty of a gentle and quiet spirit,* Peter says, is *incorruptible,* is free from the decay that your jewelry, clothes, and makeup are going to experience. So why do we spend so much time on the outer woman? Our pursuit of beauty and the latest fashions can easily lead to sins of vanity and pride, as well as the misuse of money. It is really a shame that our young girls see us older women put so much emphasis on outer beauty over inner beauty. Yet, that inner beauty is what we really desire in our children, is it not? *The fourth attitude that should characterize us is a meek and quiet spirit.*

What is a meek and quiet spirit? Meek, or *gentle,* as the NKJV translates it, means mild or humble. This is a quality of our Lord mentioned in Matthew 11:29, where it says that He is meek and lowly of heart. Meekness is not weakness; meekness is strength under control. We can learn a lot about meekness from racehorses. They say that the horse that wins the race is the meekest on the track. The reason is that this horse is the most under control, and the one that responds most quickly to the jockey's guidance. The horse that is self-willed is frequently left at the post, and when he does finally get started, he may run faster than some of the others, but he does not finish with the leaders who were meek. We know also that Moses was the meekest man in all the earth at the time the book of Numbers was written. Why would he be considered the meekest man? Well, it took a man who had strength under control to confront Pharaoh numerous times and to lead the rebellious Israelites out of Egypt. Moses was a man who had strength under control!

The word *quiet* means keeping one's seat, or an undisturbed peace. A woman with a *quiet spirit* is a woman who has a calm temper, who is not irritable. Now, quietness is not dullness. "It is 'a spirit which calmly bears disturbances created by others, and which itself does not create disturbances.'"[42] For example, if your husband comes home and says he is considering a job change to New York City, the meek woman doesn't say, "New York City! Are you crazy?! What has gotten into your head?!" She says, in a peaceable tone of voice and demeanor, "Really, honey? What made you consider New York City? Are you not happy here?" And they graciously talk about it. And, of course, the wife can offer her gracious opinion with a submissive attitude.

Peter says meekness and quietness is valuable—in fact, so valuable that it is *very precious in the sight of God*. The King James Version translates it as "of very great price in the sight of God," which means it is extremely expensive. It is not your jewelry or your clothes, but your meek and quiet spirit that is expensive in God's eyes. The first readers of this letter, as well as many of us now, probably read these words and think, "No way! This is too hard!" Peter, perhaps, anticipates that very struggle, and so gives us a godly example to consider in verses 5 and 6.

> For in this manner, in former times, the holy women who trusted in God also adorned themselves, being submissive to their own husbands, (1 Peter 3:5)

Peter lets us know about *the holy women in former times*. He is speaking of the women his audience would be familiar with from the Old Testament Scriptures. What made these women *holy* or set apart? Was it their clothes, their makeup, their jewelry? No, in fact you can search all throughout the Old Testament and you will hardly find mention of these things. Their hope, their *trust* was in God, not in material possessions. *This is the fifth attitude that we should have as wives, that is, hope or trust in God.* It makes sense, doesn't it, that the apostle of hope, Peter, would remind his readers of the importance of trusting in God? Hope is a common word with Peter, as seen in 1:3, 13, 21, 3:15. It is hope that would enable these wives to be submissive under the most difficult of circumstances.

---

[42] D. Edmond Hiebert, *First Peter: An Expositional Commentary* (Chicago: Moody Press, 1984), 188.

Notice what these women of old did: they *adorned themselves, being submissive to their own husbands*. *Adorned* is in the imperfect tense, which means these women had a habit of adorning themselves with a meek and quiet spirit, and with an attitude of submission. Peter gives us a real-life example to follow—and it is not women who are celebrities in the acting or music industries, which so many have followed after in great error. Peter puts forward Sarah as our example, in verse 6.

> as Sarah obeyed Abraham, calling him lord, whose daughters you are if you do good and are not afraid with any terror. (1 Peter 3:6)

Peter calls our attention to *Sarah*, not *Abraham*. He realized that some of these men were difficult to live with, and so he doesn't draw the attention to the man's role for the women to focus on, but the woman's role. This is where I see many, many, wives get into trouble when there are problems in the marriage. Do you know where their attention is focused? It is on their husband and all his faults. "He doesn't do this! He doesn't do that!" A holy woman will focus on herself and purpose to walk in her marriage blamelessly, looking at her own sin first, and she will learn to live above any difficulties that her marriage might bring. She will have the Lord and He will be enough.

Peter says Sarah *obeyed Abraham, calling him lord*. Now, don't start calling your husband "lord"; he would probably faint. Peter is not saying we ought to call our husbands "lord," even though that was the custom of Sarah's day. In fact, when I told my husband I was studying this passage, he asked, "So, are you going to start calling me lord?" which I answered with an emphatic "No!" Of course, he was kidding me. *Lord* is much like calling a man "Mister." It means controller, or supreme in authority. The word has the idea of ruling, and that is what Peter is communicating. Sarah acknowledged that Abraham had a right to direct the affairs of his household and that it was her duty to be in submission to him as the head of the family. It was that attitude of respect that she showed.

Peter goes on to say *whose daughters you are if you do good and are not afraid with any terror*. Sarah is the mother of all women who fear God, just as Abraham is mentioned several times in Scripture as the Father of us all, as well. We are Sarah's daughters *if* we *do good*, which means to be a well-doer, and if we *are not afraid with any terror*. *The sixth and final attitude Peter mentions in this passage that should characterize us as women is that we should be free from fear.* This means we should not be alarmed, scared, or nervously excited. A Christian wife will not allow any threats her husband might make to scare her out of her Christian faith. God will watch over you even if your unsaved husband creates problems for you. And even if you are married to a believer, you should not allow his sinful threats or manipulations to frighten you. "These women's husbands surely did not like their going to Christian meetings and refusing to worship the family gods. All types of intimidation—physical, emotional, social—would be used to force them back in line with the husband's religious beliefs. While calling for gentleness and inner tranquility overall and subordination to their husbands in all areas indifferent to their Christian faith, he encourages them to stand firm in the light of their hope in the coming Christ and quietly refuse to bow to the threats and punishments of their husbands."[43]

---

[43] Peter H. Davids, *The New International Commentary on the New Testament: The First Epistle of Peter* (Grand Rapids: Eerdman Publishing Co., 1990), 121.

Summary

Do these six qualities characterize you? (1) Submission, (2) holy behavior, (3) reverence, (4) a meek and quiet spirit, (5) hope in God, and (6) freedom from fear? Have you asked your husband lately, "Do you think I am attractive, honey?" I don't mean for you to ask him if he thinks you're skinny, stylish, or outwardly breathtaking. Rather, ask him, "Honey, do you think I honor you and show an attitude of submission toward you? Do I have an attitude of a meek and quiet spirit? Do you think I am holy in my behavior? Does my life characterize hope in God, or do I give way to hysterical fears?" We would all do well to have ever before our hearts and minds the wise words of Solomon's mother in Proverbs 31:30, where she says: "Charm is deceitful and beauty is passing, but a woman who fears the LORD, she shall be praised."

Questions to Consider

What Does a Beautiful Woman Look Like?
1 Peter 3:1-6

(You may want to glance at question five first)

1. The major passages in Scripture regarding submission of wives to their husbands are Ephesians 5:22-24; Colossians 3:18; Titus 2:3-5; and 1 Timothy 2:9-15. Read each of these passages and answer the following questions: (a) Why are wives to be submissive? (b) What should be our attitude as we submit? (c) What is the difference between these four passages and the one in 1 Peter 3:1-6?

2. Memorize 1 Peter 3:3-4.

3. (a) Should a believing wife divorce her unbelieving husband? Why or why not? See 1 Corinthians 7:12-16. (b) What if her unbelieving husband initiates divorce, what should she do? (c) What is the only other allowance for divorce, according to Matthew 5:27-32?

4. (a) What are the spiritual benefits of having a meek (KJV) or gentle spirit, according to Psalm 25:9; 147:6; Isaiah 29:19; 57:15; Matthew 5:5; 1 Peter 3:4. (b) For those who are up to it, ask your husband (or if you are unmarried, ask a good friend) if he thinks you have a meek and quiet spirit.

5. (a) What should women be doing with their time, according to 1 Timothy 5:10, 14 and Titus 2:3-5? (b) Would you say that this is how you spend your time? (c) How much time do you think you spend on the outer woman (makeup, doing your hair, exercise, etc.) in contrast to the time you spend on the inner woman (time in the Word, prayer, fellowship with the saints, those things

mentioned in the above verses, etc.)? You might want to keep a journal this week to evaluate how you spend your time.

6. (a) From what you read in Genesis 12 and 18:1-15, in what ways was Sarah submissive to Abraham? (b) What were her attitudes? (c) Do you think she should have been submissive in each of these areas? Why or why not?

7. If you are married, ask your husband this week if you are submissive or not. If he says "no," ask him in what way(s) you could improve, so that with God's help you might change. (If you are single, ask a family member, your employer, or your pastor if your life is characterized by humble submission to authority.)

8. Based on what you have learned, how would you counsel a Christian friend whose unsaved husband is (a) asking her not to attend church anymore, (b) asking her to participate in pornography, (c) asking her not to discipline the children, and/or (d) yells at her and uses verbal and physical abuse?

9. Look over 1 Peter 3:1-6 and ask God what *He* desires for you to work on in your life. Then write a prayer request based on what the Holy Spirit brings to your mind.

Chapter 13

The Rest of the Story!

1 Peter 3:7-9

According to a recent statistic, wives initiate divorce more often than husbands do. In fact, women initiate 69 percent of all divorces, which leaves men initiating only 31 percent.[44] These statistics are disturbing when you consider that, at one time, for every woman who left her home, there were 600 men who did the same. If you ever look at the divorce section in the daily newspaper, you will see that this is true: the woman is now more likely to ask for the divorce than the man. So, we ask ourselves, "Why is that happening? Why have so many women become so frustrated in their marriages that they are leaving their husbands?" I believe most of the time the answer lies with the husband. Ephesians 5:25-28 says that the husband is to love the wife in the way that Christ loved the church and gave Himself for her, and that the husband is to love his wife as he loves his own body. I don't know of too many women who wouldn't love a man who loved her that way, do you? Most women I know—especially godly women—would have no problem submitting to a husband like that. Most women I know would also find it delightfully easy to have that attitude of a meek and quiet spirit with such a husband. It isn't only Paul who gives some helpful counsel to husbands; so does the apostle Peter. Let's read what he has to say on this topic.

1 Peter 3:7-9

> Husbands, likewise, dwell with them with understanding, giving honor to the wife, as to the weaker vessel, and as being heirs together of the grace of life, that your prayers may not be hindered. ⁸Finally, all of you be of one mind, having compassion for one another; love as brothers, be tenderhearted, be courteous; ⁹not returning evil for

---

[44]https://www.asanet.org/press-center/press-releases/women-more-likely-men-initiate-divorces-not-non-marital-breakups

evil or reviling for reviling, but on the contrary blessing, knowing that you were called to this, that you may inherit a blessing.

In this lesson, we will study the "rest of the story," if you will. We will unfold:

> *The Responsibilities of the Husband (v 7)*
> *The Responsibilities of Every Believer (vv 8-9)*

Peter does not end his writing about marriage with the responsibility of the wife; he ends it with the responsibility of the husband. It may seem, at first, as though Peter gives less time and attention to the men here. In fact, the wife does have instruction here that is six times as long as that given to the husband. Maybe you're thinking, "That is not fair! I want my husband to get equal time!" Well, again, let's remember the context and the culture. As we brought out in our last lesson, the culture of the day was such that if the wife became a believer and her husband did not, her newfound faith would undoubtedly bring much tension to the marriage and she would endure serious persecution by her husband. Many of these wives were enduring physical beatings from their husbands. But if, on the other hand, the husband became a believer, it would then be expected that his wife would automatically follow his faith. So Peter, who is the apostle of hope, is doing these wives a great service by encouraging their faith and expounding on how they should deal with such a difficult situation. Let's now look to verse 7 and consider the responsibilities of the believing husband to his wife.

The Responsibilities of the Husband

1 Peter 3:7

Husbands, likewise, dwell with them with understanding, giving honor to the wife, as to the weaker vessel, and as being heirs together of the grace of life, that your prayers may not be hindered. (1 Peter 3:7)

Peter starts out his instruction to the husbands by telling them *likewise*, or in the same manner, they are to do something. The word likewise means to be similar in appearance or character. What is Peter referring to? Is Peter saying that husbands are likewise or in the same manner to be submissive to their wives? Husbands are to be submissive in the sense that they submit to their wives' needs, but husbands are not to submit to their wives in the sense that they allow their wives to take over the leadership of the home. Peter uses this terminology later on in 1 Peter 5:5 when addressing elders in the church; he says, "Likewise you younger people, submit yourselves to your elders. Yes, all of you be submissive to one another, and be clothed with humility, for 'God resists the proud, but gives grace to the humble.'" The idea is that we all in humility think of others as better and more important than ourselves and we submit to one another by being obedient to the roles that God has called us to. Also, Ephesians 5:21 addresses both husbands and wives, saying, "submitting to one another in the fear of God."

Peter goes on to admonish *husbands* to dwell with their wives with understanding. The word *dwell* means to reside or live with, to live together as husband and wife, to cohabitate. Dwelling *with them* implies more than sharing an address. I know of marriages where the husband and wife are no more than two strangers living in the same house; all they have in common is where they live. But, in order for the husband to dwell *with* his wife, the husband must be at home. One survey revealed that the average husband and wife had just 37 minutes a week together in which they actually communicated! It is no wonder that, after the kids leave home, so many marriages end in divorce. They do not know one another, because they have nothing more in common than a shared roof over their heads. It can be a frightening time for many a wife and a husband. I would encourage you, if this is the type of marriage that you live in, to do your part in working hard at your marriage to make it what God would have it be.

This is the first responsibility of the husband: to dwell with his wife with understanding. To dwell *with understanding* means to do it according to knowledge. What does Peter mean by this? The word knowledge means gnosis, a science. Husbands are commanded here to study their wives as a science. The husband should know and understand the Christian principles of marriage and he should know and understand his wife. He should know her inside and out—how she feels about things; what her needs are; her fears; her aspirations; her goals in life. These are just some of the things he should study when it comes to his wife. My son used to say, "I just don't understand women!" And his father would usually reply with something like, "And son, you never will." Women are a science, aren't they? I heard about one counselor who, in his premarital counseling sessions, would usually ask the couple to write down three things that each thought the other enjoyed doing the most. The counselor said that usually the woman could list three things immediately, while the man would sit there and ponder. And usually, she would be right about what he liked to do, and he would be wrong about what she liked to do. What a beginning to a marriage! Now, I am not sharing this with you so you'll complain to your husband, but just to illustrate the differences between us, and that God made men and women different. That's why our husbands have to work at figuring us out—we can be pretty mysterious at times!

Peter gives a second responsibility of the husband to his wife and that is that he gives honor to her. What does it mean to *give honor to her*? It does not mean that the husband gives in to her every whim and temper tantrum. I have seen husbands who do that, and it is not a good testimony before God and others as to what a Christian marriage should be. The word *giving* means to portion out, and the word *honor* means to esteem, especially of the highest degree. It is the same word translated as precious in 1:19, where Peter mentions the precious blood of Christ that took away our sins. One man says, "The husband should treat his wife like an expensive, beautiful, fragile vase, in which is a precious treasure."[45] He should not bully her, or growl and speak to her with intimidating and harsh speech. He should not use the "submission club" as a tool to remind her of the fact that she is supposed to be submissive. This command from

---

[45] Warren Weirsbe, *The Weirsbe Bible Commentary: New Testament* (Colorado Springs: David C. Cook Publishing, 2007), 910.

Peter would certainly be in opposition to the culture of his day, a culture that did not honor women at all. Women were not respected; wives were considered slaves to their husbands and objects for their sexual gratification. It was common to see a man riding on his donkey while his wife walked by his side. Women also did not share in worship at the synagogue; they were segregated from the men. Many years ago, my husband traveled to Myanmar, and he shared with me that the women would not only walk behind the men, but they also would carry their books. He told me that he spoke with the missionaries there and shared how Christ comes in and changes even culture, and that even though that might be the cultural norm, they were not fulfilling God's role for the Christian husband. That really is what Peter is saying here: Christ comes into one's life and changes even our practice of cultural customs so that our way of life matches His Word. Even if the husband and wife disagree on an issue, he can still show her honor, and she can still show him respect. Many times, I will tell my husband that I don't agree with a decision he might be making and explain to him my reasons for it, but that doesn't mean I am allowed to be disrespectful to him, nor does it mean that he should no longer honor me or treat me as precious. Peter has already mentioned in 1 Peter 2:17 that we are to honor all men, and this would include husbands honoring their wives. Also, the husband in Proverbs 31 is seen giving honor to his wife in verse 28, where he rises up to call her blessed and praises her.

Notice, that Peter gives the husband three motivating factors for honoring his wife. First, Peter says the husband is to honor her because she is *the weaker vessel*. The word *vessel* is used in Mark 11:16 in reference to a vessel which was used in the service at the temple. It is also used to describe a household utensil. In Acts 9:15, Paul is called a chosen vessel. Now, maybe you don't like being likened to a vessel, but a vessel is something that is useful. Both the husband and the wife are here called vessels, and both are weak; both are frail. But the wife is the *weaker* vessel, for sure. We are both, you might say, pieces of furniture in God's house, but the wife is weaker than the husband. The husband could be likened to a table, and the wife to a chair. Paul uses this same terminology in 2

Timothy 2:20-21, where he says, "But in a great house there are not only vessels of gold and silver, but also of wood and clay, some for honor and some for dishonor. Therefore if anyone cleanses himself from the latter, he will be a vessel for honor, sanctified and useful for the Master, prepared for every good work." The husband is to treat his wife as a vessel that God has chosen for Him to be used for His glory. And the husband must remember that she is weaker.

Maybe you are wondering how the wife is weaker than the husband. In what way is that so? Is it physical, mental, spiritual, or emotional, or all of these, or some combination? The word weaker refers to physical stamina, not to intellectual ability, or moral or spiritual strength. I know some women think that they are physically stronger than men and try to build their muscles to prove it, but the reality is that women, on the whole, are not physically stronger than men. Try and arm-wrestle your husband, if you think you're physically stronger than him. I know I'm not. There might be some wives who have greater physical strength than their husbands, but in most cases, that isn't true. Now, before we go on, I do want to say that I do think there is also a sense in which the wife at times is emotionally and intellectually weaker, as well. I think about what Paul says in 2 Timothy 3:6 about those silly women who are led astray by false teachers: "For of this sort are those who creep into households and make captives of gullible women loaded down with sins, led away by various lusts." I think there is a sense in which women can be more vulnerable to false teaching because they are more gullible. Paul says in 2 Corinthians 11:3, "But I fear, lest somehow, as the serpent deceived Eve by his craftiness, so your minds may be corrupted from the simplicity that is in Christ." And in 1 Timothy 2:14, we read, "And Adam was not deceived, but the woman being deceived, fell into transgression." These verses lend great weight to the idea of women being more easily deceived than men. I also think that God has made women more emotional than men, and often we are weaker in this area. This may be why Paul tells Titus that the older women are to teach the young women how to be sober-minded, to be self-controlled with their emotions and passions. I know, over the years, I have grown to appreciate my husband more in those areas, as I've come to recognize my own weaknesses.

The second motivating factor for a husband to honor his wife is that they are *heirs together of the grace of life*. This is talking about the fact that they are partners in life here on earth as well as co-heirs of the grace of life. As we've already mentioned, in New Testament times, the women were not allowed to worship together with the men in the synagogue but were segregated behind a screen. Women had no part in the service because they were not held in high esteem. Peter is telling the husband that Christ changes culture and that the husband is to remember that Christ died for her too, and her soul is just as valuable to God as the husband's. She will receive the same inheritance that he will, as we learned when we were looking at 1 Peter 1:3-4. Also, in Galatians 3:28-29, Paul says, "There is neither Jew nor Greek, there is neither slave nor free, there is neither male nor female; for you are all one in Christ Jesus. And if you are Christ's, then you are Abraham's seed, and heirs according to the promise."

Peter gives the husband a third reason why he must honor his wife, and that is so that *your prayers will not be hindered*. The pronoun *your* is in the second person which would indicate a reference back to the husband. What does it mean to have one's *prayers hindered*? The word *hindered* means to make an incision into, to cut into, to interrupt. All of us who have spent any time on the phone on hold can identify with this. Your conversation gets interrupted when the person on the other end says, "Will you hold?" That is the idea here, the husband's prayers are cut into and communication with the Father is hindered. The Lord puts him on hold, so to speak, and potentially for a long time, if he doesn't straighten up.

The husband has three pretty good motivating factors for honoring his wife. We now turn from the responsibilities of the husband toward his wife to the responsibilities we all have toward one another. There are eight of them.

The Responsibilities of Every Believer

1 Peter 3:8-9

> Finally, all of you be of one mind, having compassion for one another; love as brothers, be tenderhearted, be courteous. (1 Peter 3:8)

Peter starts this new section by saying *finally*. Maybe you're thinking he's about done with the letter, but he isn't—we're only midway through his epistle. The word finally means to sum it all up. These are Peter's concluding remarks regarding the attitude of submission for all the people groups that he has mentioned; whether they be citizens, governmental authorities, slaves, masters, wives, or husbands, *all of you*, Peter says, are to be submissive in your attitudes and interactions with one another. (See Philippians 3:1 and 1 Thessalonians 4:1 for similar terminology.) Peter then proceeds to list eight specific responsibilities that all these believers have toward one another. And each of these Peter would have seen modeled in our Lord.

The first responsibility we have toward one another, Peter says, is to be of one mind. We are to be like-minded, to have unity of thought and feeling. This does not mean that we should have uniformity; Christians will always differ on how things are to be done, but we should all agree on what is to be done and why. We should all desire to serve and love both God and one another. We should not seek selfish gain. We should work together and not alone in isolation. We should not neglect to follow the example Christ and the apostles set for us. One writer said, "I must resist the temptation to think that my specific calling from God is so important that I must not allow concern for other people's needs to deter me from pursuing it."[46] Even Christ prayed for unity four times in the High Priestly Prayer in John 17, so you know it is important to Him! Peter would have heard our Lord pray this prayer before He went to the cross, so Peter would have understood that this is our Lord's desire for His children. It would also have been of utmost importance to Peter's readers in

---

[46] I. Howard Marshall, *1 Peter: The IVP New Testament Commentary Series* (Downers Grove: IVP Academic, 2011), 105-106.

the midst of facing terrible persecution. They would have needed to cling to one another to find strength and support, and in order to do that, they needed to be unified in thought and not be divided.

Next, Peter tells his readers to have compassion for one another. This is our second responsibility toward one another. Compassion means "to have a fellow-feeling." We get our English word sympathy from this word, which means to experience pain jointly. The compassionate person is the one who enters into the feelings of another as if those feelings were his own. Compassion is thinking: To the extent that one member suffers, we all suffer, and when one of us rejoices, we all rejoice, as Paul says in 1 Corinthians 12:26. It is illustrated well in Luke 10 in the parable of the Good Samaritan, who had compassion on the man who had been beaten by thieves and left for dead. The Good Samaritan's compassion led him to pour oil on the injured man's wounds and make sure he was well cared for. Peter would have seen such compassion modeled in our Lord. The Scriptures say often that Christ had compassion on the crowds because they were like sheep having no Shepherd. His compassion manifested itself in healing and extending mercy. In Matthew 15:32, Jesus even told His disciples, which would have included Peter, that He had compassion on the people because they had been with Him three days and had nothing to eat; then His compassion was put into action by the miraculous feeding of the 4000! James 2:13 is a sobering verse for those who show no compassion; James says that those who show no mercy will be shown no mercy in the Day of Judgment!

Third, Peter says we are responsible to love as brothers. This is not a new admonition in 1 Peter; Peter has already mentioned this in 1:22 and 2:17, and he will mention it again in 4:8 and 5:14. But this is not the sacrificial, serving, <u>agape</u> kind of love that God produces in our hearts by His Spirit. Rather, it is that human affection and fondness we should have for each other; it is a <u>phileo</u> love, which is a tender affection for others. I admit, some of us are harder to phileo love than others, but that does not negate our responsibility to pursue this type of love. Romans 12:10 tells us, "Be kindly affectionate to one another with brotherly love, in honor giving preference to one another." We are not to stop loving one another in this way; Hebrews 13:1 tells us to "let brotherly love continue." It really goes without saying that Peter saw this character quality manifested in our Lord each and every day, culminating in His death on the cross, the greatest act of phileo and agape love ever.

The fourth responsibility we have to one another is to be tenderhearted. This means to have an inward affection. It was a word that would describe the feelings that come from our inner parts, especially when we observe the sufferings of others. This would clearly be a contrast to the heart of Nero, who was treating Christians with cruelty. Some of us have become immune to the pain and suffering of others; there is so much tragedy in our world and we have so many means of communication from which we hear of these tragedies daily, even hourly. We can become hardened to the sufferings of others. But for the life of the believer, that should not be the case. One of the most powerful illustrations of Christ's tenderheartedness would have been witnessed by Peter himself; in John 11, where we read of Lazarus' death, we also read of Jesus' response. Jesus comes upon the scene and sees the grief of his dear friends, and it says in verse 35 that He wept, and the Jews said, "See how he loved him." Christ was moved by the sufferings of others.

Peter says our fifth responsibility to one another is to be courteous. This word is only found here in this verse, and it does not mean what we might think. We think of courteous as not being rude. But the word actually means to have humility of mind, to have a modest opinion of oneself. This would certainly not be a quality that the Greeks appreciated or even cultivated in their lives, and it is a virtue that Americans don't seek either! We live in a very egotistical, arrogant society, and we are breeding children after our likeness! Our Lord exhibited this quality toward the 12 disciples before He went to the cross; in John 13, it states that He humbled Himself and got up from the dinner table and washed the 12 disciples' dirty feet. Peter was the one, if you remember, with all the questions and objections during this ordeal, and yet, now, remembering back to that time, he can recall the humility of His Lord in such an act.

Having told us what we are to do, Peter moves on to what we should not do, in verse 9.

> not returning evil for evil or reviling for reviling, but on the contrary blessing, knowing that you were called to this, that you may inherit a blessing. (1 Peter 3:9)

Peter says we are not to return evil for evil. This is our sixth responsibility to each other. The word *not* actually means God forbid, never are we to return evil for evil. Peter has already given us the Supreme example to follow in our Lord, in 2:21-23. Peter would have witnessed firsthand our Lord not reviling or threatening back when He was reviled and threatened. Proverbs 17:13 is a very sobering verse to consider in light of Peter's admonition here: "Whoever rewards evil for good, evil will not depart from his house." Proverbs 24:17-18 also says something very sobering: "Do not rejoice when your enemy falls, and do not let your heart be glad when he stumbles; lest the LORD see it, and it displease Him, and He turn away His wrath from him." Instead of repaying evil for evil, our response should be what Proverbs 20:22 says: "Do not say, 'I will recompense evil'; wait for the LORD, and He will save you." Peter did repay evil for evil by cutting off the ear of the high priest's servant, but we see in him in Acts as a changed man. In fact, he has already reminded his readers that their Lord did not behave this way; he wrote of our Lord in 1 Peter 2:23-24, "who, when He was reviled, did not revile in return; when He suffered, He did not threaten, but committed Himself to Him who judges righteously." *Like our Lord, we are also not to return reviling for reviling. This is our seventh responsibility to each other.* This means we are not to slander someone when they slander us. One man says, "to render railing for railing, is to think to wash off dirt with dirt."[47]

---

[47] J. Trapp, The Biblical Illustrator, Electronic Database. Copyright @ 2002, 2003, 2006, 2011 by Biblesoft, Inc. Biblesoft.com

Peter ends this section of his letter with the eighth responsibility for us to follow. He says, on the contrary, we are to give a blessing. Blessing means to speak well of. We are to speak well of those who speak ill of us, and we are to pray for God's blessing upon them. One of the greatest blessings that Christ ever gave His enemies was from the cross, where He prayed to His Father on their behalf, in Luke 23:34, "Father, forgive them, for they do not know what they do." His enemies were mocking Him and yet He blessed them with a prayer. Can you and I pray that for those who are doing evil to us? Peter says there is a reason we are to give a blessing and it is because we are *called to this*. My friend, this is not an option for us! Peter says it is our calling to give blessings to those who do evil to us and slander us. Think of the context here, the suffering and persecution of these believers under the hand of Nero, and yet they were called to this! These readers would need to remember the Lord's abundant mercy, which, instead of paying back evil with evil, blessed others even to the point of granting them salvation. Because of the mercy that has been shown to us, we can show mercy to our enemies.

Not only are we called to this, but there is a benefit that comes from being obedient to this calling: we will *inherit a blessing*. Again, *blessing* here means to speak well of. What does it mean to *inherit* a blessing? A believer never earns a blessing. Rather, it is inherited. It is a gift. This could be the blessing of the Lord, "Well done, good and faithful servant." It could be some sort of earthly blessing. But, more than likely, it is the blessing of our salvation, as it proves the genuineness of our faith. As one put it so well: "Why should one who expects soon to be in heaven harbor malice in his bosom? Why should he wish to injure a fellow-worm? How can he?"[48]

---

[48]Albert Barnes, Barnes' *Notes: Hebrews to Jude* (Grand Rapids: Baker Book House, 1998), 165-166.

Summary

What are the responsibilities of the husband toward his wife? He is to dwell with her according to knowledge and he is to give her honor. He has three motivating factors to treat his wife this way. He is to treat her with honor because she is the weaker vessel, because she is an heir together with him in the grace of life, and so that his prayers won't be hindered.

What are the responsibilities we all have toward one another? We are to be of one mind; we are to have compassion for one another; we are to love one another; we are to be tenderhearted toward one another; we are to be courteous; we are to not render evil for evil; we are to not return reviling for reviling; but instead, lastly, we are to give a blessing to those who would revile us.

I realize you might want me to leave you with a zinger with which you can confront your husband, but I am not going to do that. I know for a fact that some of you live in difficult marriages and that your husbands do not honor you or live with you in an understanding way. But it is not up to me nor up to you to change your husbands. That is the Lord's business. Instead, I would challenge you with some questions that arise from these verses in 1 Peter, because these commands are for all of us to obey, even those of us who are wives. Consider the following questions:

Does your husband live with a wife who is adorned with a meek and quiet spirit? Are you graciously submissive, or do you challenge your husband on every decision he makes? Do you strive to be unified with your husband in your marriage? Are you of one flesh, one thought, and what are you doing to make sure that this is happening in your marriage? Do you show compassion toward your husband, trying to feel his hurts and pains? Do you show affection toward your husband, or do you give him the cold shoulder? Do you think of him more than you think of yourself? Are you courteous and respectful toward him? Are you tenderhearted, or do you use sharp words when you speak to him? If he is ugly to you in word or deed, do you repay him with evil or, on the contrary, do you give him a blessing and look for ways you can show kindness to him?

As I said earlier, I don't know of any godly woman that would not love to submit to a man who is leading in love and understanding. But I also cannot imagine any godly man who would not respond favorably to a woman who treated him in the manner that Peter is commanding in these verses. I would challenge you with the thought that you are not your husband's mother, nor are you his Holy Spirit, but you are your husband's helper. My prayer for all of you, whether you have a good marriage or a bad marriage, is that you would be like the Proverbs 31 woman, who did good to her husband, and not evil, all the days of her life.

Questions to Consider
The Rest of the Story!
1 Peter 3:7-9

1. (a) What are the responsibilities of the husband toward the wife, according to Ephesians 5:25-33; Colossians 3:19; and 1 Peter 3:7? (b) What do these passages tell us are the reasons these attitudes must be present?

2. Memorize 1 Peter 3:7. (*Not* to be quoted to your husband this week!☺)

3. (a) What does it mean to be of "one mind" (to live in harmony), according to the following verses? Acts 4:32; Romans 12:16-21; 15:5-7; 1 Corinthians 1:10-11; Philippians 1:27; 2:1-8; 3:16. (b) Which one of these passages is very similar to 1 Peter 3:8-12?

4. (a) Peter says in 1 Peter 3:9 that we are not to repay evil with evil. What do you see Peter doing in John 18:2-11? (b) What was the Lord's response to this here in John as well as in Luke 22:47-53? (c) Now read Acts 5:40-42 and note what Peter does when he is wronged. (d) Why do you think there is a change in Peter's attitude from the accounts in the Gospels to the account in Acts?

5. Peter mentions in 1 Peter 3:8 that we are to be compassionate toward one another. (a) Read Matthew 18:21-35. What question does Peter ask the Lord that prompts the Lord to give such a masterful illustration of being compassionate? (b) What things stand out to you as being sinful regarding the servant who owed 10,000 talents? (c) What can you learn about compassion from Christ's story, and how does what you learn from His story have application to your own life?

6. (a) How can we bless those who do evil against us, according to Matthew 5:43-48 and Romans 12:19-21? (b) What are some

other practical things that you have found helpful when others do evil or say evil things against you?

7. (a) How could you use 1 Peter 3:9 to instruct a child who hits back when he is hit, or speaks evil when he is spoken to in an evil manner? (b) Do you model this type of behavior before others, especially before your children and grandchildren?

8. (a) When you consider the five qualities of being like-minded from 1 Peter 3:8, which of them do you see as lacking in your life, and why? (b) What can you do to remedy that?

9. After considering question eight, please put your thoughts in the form of a prayer request asking for God's help in this area. (Then, put your prayer into *action* this week!)

Chapter 14

Five Keys to Loving Life
1 Peter 3:10-12

Someone once said that suicide is a permanent solution to temporary problems.[49] In fact, around 800,000 to 1,000,000 people commit suicide every year. In addition to that, there are also 10 to 20 million non-fatal attempted suicides every year. In the United States alone, suicide is the 10th leading cause of death. The questions I have are: "What is going on in the minds and hearts of those 800,000 to 1,000,000 people that would cause them to want to take the very life that has been given to them as a precious gift from God? Why do some not embrace and love life? Why do some see life as a burden and not a joy? Why does suicide seem to be the solution to those who take their own lives? Why do the trials of life prompt some to want to take their lives?"

For the believer in the Lord Jesus, our outlook on life should be very different from the world. We should not hate life. We should not want to take our own lives. We should not see life as drudgery, but as a blessing. What should be our outlook on life as believers? Peter writes that we should love life, not hate it. And if we don't love life, there is likely to be a clear reason why we don't. In fact, in 1 Peter 3:10-12, Peter will give us five keys to loving life. Let's read those verses together and discover these five keys to loving life.

1 Peter 3:10-12

> For "He who would love life and see good days, let him refrain his tongue from evil, and his lips from speaking deceit. 11Let him turn away from evil and do good; let him seek peace and pursue it. 12For the eyes of the Lord are on the righteous, and His ears are open to their prayers; but the face of the Lord is against those who do evil."

---

[49] http://kindnesshandbook.webs.com/suicide.htm

(It has been said that these verses were sung in the early church as a hymn. They have also been called "an ancient recipe for a happy life." They are also a quote from Psalm 34:12-16.)

> For He who would love life and see good days, let him refrain his tongue from evil, and his lips from speaking deceit. (1 Peter 3:10-12)

Peter begins with the word *for* or because. "For or because of what?" we might ask. Because of what Peter has just said in verse 9: for those of us who are saved, for those of us who will inherit the blessing of salvation, for those elected ones, there will be certain characteristics that are true about us, and those characteristics are the keys to loving life. This person, Peter says, *would love life*. The word *would* is a present participle that speaks of an action going on in present time. This loving of life is an act of our will that should be ongoing in the life of a believer. *Life* is a reference to life here on earth, not to eternal life. We don't have to be concerned about loving eternity in heaven—we will love that for sure! Peter is saying life here on Earth is a gift from God, and we should enjoy each and every day to its fullest. Some days are just harder than others, so we must choose to love life, whether God gives us good days or hard days.

Now, this loving of life is not loving the length of one's life, but the quality of it. We are to live life passionately by participating in everything that God puts before us each day with a full commitment to do His will with purpose and zeal. This would be manifested in a person who sees the best in every situation. "We can decide to endure life and make it a burden, escape life as though we were running from a battle, or enjoy life because we know God is in control."[50] We should make the most of every situation every day, even the ones that are most difficult. And remember who Peter is writing to. These readers had a particularly difficult challenge to loving life; many were losing their own lives or watching those they loved die at the hand of Nero. What Peter is saying here should encourage anyone going through trials, or anyone who is prone to being depressed or

---

[50] Warren Weirsbe, *Be Hopeful* (Colorado Springs: David C. Cook Publishing, 1982), pg 81.

discouraged. Just because things are rough for us as Christians does not mean that we give up on life. What can seem like a bad day can also be seen as a good day when viewed through the rule and reign of our Sovereign God. This certainly is the opposite of what the writer of Ecclesiastes said in Ecclesiastes 2:17: "Therefore I hated life because the work that was done under the sun was distressing to me, for all is vanity and grasping for the wind." Even though the readers of this letter were undergoing tremendous suffering, Peter admonishes them that life is a gift from God, and they should love it.

Not only does Peter remind them that they should love life, but that they should also *see good days*. Now what does this mean? The word *see* means to know; it is a verb that means to enjoy and experience. This means that you see your day as good. Even those days when it is hard to crawl out of bed, even those days when the kids are sick all day, even those days when everything goes wrong, even those days when we don't know how we are going to pay the bills, even those days when we get bad news—in all our days, we are to know that they are good! We should look at our days as beneficial, not as empty and meaningless. If we believe in a Sovereign God who works everything out for our good, even difficult days, then we truly can see our days as good. I was reminded of this even as I wrote this lesson, that even though my life is full of many pressures from many directions, I must continually remind myself of the goodness of God and that life is a good gift from Him.

You might be asking yourself, "Well, how do I do this? How do I look at my life as good, when it is so hard?" For one thing, we can believe what God says in Romans 8:28: "And we know that all things work together for good to those who love God, to those who are the called according to His purpose." This means that even in the unforeseen things that happen to us, we can know that our loving Father is working them all out for our good. We also can learn much from the apostle Paul about how to see our difficult days as good. Consider 2 Corinthians 6:4-10, along with 2 Corinthians 11 and 12. Even though his outer man was perishing, his inner man was being renewed day by day. He knew his light affliction was just for a moment, in light of eternity. Even though Paul went through hard days, he saw his life as given over to being a minister for the gospel, he saw God's grace as sufficient for each day—even the hard ones—and he knew that God's power was made perfect in his weakness.

Now, some of you may be saying to yourself, "I do all of that, but I still fail to love life and see my days as good." If that's the case with you, then it's possible that something is a bit out of kilter in your life, and so Peter continues on by giving five keys to loving life. *The first key to loving life that is needed is to refrain ones' tongue from evil.* The word *refrain* means to stop or quit. We are to stop using our tongue for anything wicked. This would include anything that is base and degrading in nature. This really goes right along with what he just said in verse 9 abound rendering evil for evil and slander for slander. This would also include any form of slander, gossip, swearing, flattery, coarse jesting, or any other kind of speech that is not fitting for a believer. It is hard to enjoy life and see it as good when we are using our mouths for anything other than praising God and edifying others. When we use our mouths wrongly, we not only feel shame and guilt for our sin, but that sinful speech also takes the enjoyment out of life! Peter wants these persecuted Christians to not to use their mouths for evil, to not revile back or slander back when being reviled or slandered by their persecutors.

The second key to loving life is to not use our lips for speaking deceit or guile. Interestingly, the word for *lip* means a gulf, a pouring place. That certainly describes our mouth from time to time, doesn't it? *Deceit*, or guile, means a misrepresentation of the truth. This would include anything that would lead others astray. Peter made mention of this in 1 Peter 2:1, and then he reminded us in 1 Peter 2:22 that deceit was never a part of our Lord's life. In fact, we know from Proverbs 6:16-19 that deceit is one of the things He hates the most: "These six things the LORD hates, yes, seven are an abomination to Him: a proud look, a lying tongue, hands that shed innocent blood, a heart that devises wicked plans, feet that are swift in running to evil, a false witness who speaks lies, and one who sows discord among brethren." Now, ladies, Peter knew the awful consequences of deceitful speech, because he denied that he knew the Lord three times, and it says in Matthew 26:75 that he went out and wept bitterly because of it. These readers needed to be reminded that in the midst of suffering for Christ they must not succumb to deceit to avoid being persecuted.

Since the first two keys to loving life have to do with our speech, it would perhaps do us all good to memorize the following poem:

> If your lips would keep from slips, five things observe with care: to whom you speak; of whom you speak, and how and when and where.[51]

In addition to this helpful little poem, some practical questions we would do well to ask ourselves before we speak are: Is what I am about to say true? Is it kind? Is it necessary? I would also encourage you to talk less, as Proverbs 10:19 tells us, "In the multitude of words sin is not lacking, but he who restrains his lips is wise." There were times when my husband would comment that I was quiet, to which I would reply, "I get in less trouble that way." We don't always have to give our opinion, and we don't always have to speak! I know that's a hard one for us as women, but it was John Calvin who said that talkativeness is a disease of women and that it gets worse with age! Perhaps we would all do well to pray with the Psalmist in Psalm 141:3, "Set a guard, O LORD, over my mouth; keep watch over the door of my lips." It is hard to enjoy life and see your days as good when you are practicing deceit.

Peter moves from these two admonitions regarding what we should avoid, speaking evil and speaking deceit, to three admonitions regarding what we should practice.

> Let him turn away from evil and do good; let him seek peace and pursue it. (1 Peter 3:11)

The third key to loving life is to turn away from evil. My friend, we

---
[51] Poem by William Norris; 1847-1925.

are to *turn away*, to shun, to avoid evil. The Greek word for *evil* is the same word used in verse 10. And the idea pictured in this verse is of one bending aside from his course at the approach of evil. He or she leans over or swerves aside to avoid an encounter with evil, just like you would get out of the way of an oncoming car headed right in your lane. That's how we should feel about evil; we should get out of its way!

I had this loudly illustrated to me once when I was in a room with several women who professed to be believers but whose talk and actions and the overall atmosphere were evil. I said my peace and quickly removed myself from the situation. It is said of Job in Job 1:1, "There was a man in the land of Uz, whose name was Job; and that man was blameless and upright, and one who feared God and shunned evil." Job avoided evil and got out of its way! Joseph is another man who got out of evil's way. When his master's wife pressed him to have sex with her, he responded in Genesis 39:9 with these words: "There is no one greater in this house than I, nor has he kept back anything from me but you, because you are his wife. How then can I do this great wickedness, and sin against God?" And in verse 12, after her continually pressing him day after day, it says Joseph fled and ran outside. Of course, his shunning of evil cost him, as he ended up in prison—but, my friend, it is better to suffer for doing what is right than to suffer for doing what is wrong (1 Peter 3:17)! In fact, this concept of shunning evil is so vital that Christ specifically prayed in John 17:15, in the High Priestly Prayer, that you and I would be kept from evil! When He was teaching about how to pray, He made it very clear that we are to ask the Lord to keep us from evil (Matthew 6:13 and Luke 11:4). Do you and I pray that God will keep us from evil and from the evil one? Do we ask God to help us shun evil? Perhaps we need to be praying that God will deliver us from evil and help us to hate it. When one is practicing evil, life cannot be good or enjoyable, that's for sure! These believers were not to allow their suffering to be a temptation to do evil.

The fourth key to loving life is to do good. This would, of course, be the opposite of doing evil. Doing *good* would include being involved in things that are good and beneficial, and it would be for the purpose of benefiting someone other than oneself. Doing good is one of the things an older woman is to teach a younger woman to do, according to Titus 2:3-5: "The older women likewise, that they be reverent in behavior, not slanderers, not given to much wine, teachers of good things—that they admonish the young women to love their husbands, to love their children, to be discreet, chaste, homemakers, good, obedient to their own husbands, that the word of God may not be blasphemed." Doing good reminds me of the Proverbs 31 woman, where it says in verse 20, "She extends her hand to the poor, yes, she reaches out her hands to the needy." We need to reach out and extend a helping hand to those who are in need, perhaps in our family, our neighborhood, or our church. Often, doing good involves sacrificing our time, energy, and even our resources. It might be visiting a shut in, spending the night at a hospital with someone who is in need, babysitting for a weary mom, mowing someone's yard who is unable to, taking a meal to someone who is in need. Again, it was imperative that these readers not take vengeance on their persecutors, but instead repay that evil with good. Those that enjoy life will just naturally do good.

Lovers of life will also have a fifth quality about them. *The fifth quality of a lover of life is that they will seek peace and pursue it.* The term *pursue* expresses a vigorous effort to chase or hunt down in order to obtain something. This command is not new to the New Testament. Paul states in Romans 14:19, "Therefore let us pursue the things which make for peace and the things by which one may edify another." Also, Paul states in 2 Corinthians 13:11, "Finally, brethren, farewell. Become complete. Be of good comfort, be of one mind, live in peace; and the God of love and peace will be with you." First Thessalonians 5:13 says, "Be at peace among yourselves." Second Timothy 2:22 tells us to "Flee also youthful lusts; but pursue righteousness, faith, love, peace with those who call on the Lord out of a pure heart." Last, but not least, Hebrews 12:14 tells us to

"Pursue peace with all people, and holiness, without which no one will see the Lord." It is interesting to me that peace and holiness are connected in this verse. The idea is that there can be no true peace without holiness. We should not go around pretending we are holy when we are really at war with one another. That is an impossibility! Jesus even declares them blessed who make peace, in Matthew 5:9: "Blessed are the peacemakers, for they shall be called sons of God."

There are times in our lives when peace seems impossible with others, and yet we are not to give up pursuing it until we have exhausted all efforts. We take comfort in Romans 12:18, which says, "If it is possible, as much as depends on you, live peaceably with all men." Unfortunately, there are times when it is impossible to be at peace with some people. This verse tells us that while it is sometimes impossible to be at peace with some people, we should nonetheless desire peace and endeavor to pursue it with all men.

Now, before we go on, I do want to say that pursuing peace cannot mean that we will seek peace at any price. Jesus is very clear in Matthew 10:34-36: "Do not think that I came to bring peace on earth. I did not come to bring peace but a sword. For I have come to 'set a man against his father, a daughter against her mother, and a daughter-in-law against her mother-in-law' and 'a man's enemies will be those of his own household.'" Our loyalty to our Lord may result in strife and separation from our family members; in such instances, we should still try to maintain peace but realize that it may not happen. Sometimes, we can work hard at being peaceful with others, especially our enemies, and it just doesn't happen. Many of Peter's readers may have been endeavoring to be at peace with their enemies, with no results. That may be why he encourages them in verse 12 that God knows and hears their cries for help.

> For the eyes of the Lord are on the righteous, and His ears are open to their prayers; but the face of the Lord is against those who do evil. (1 Peter 3:12)

Peter encourages his readers with the fact that *the eyes of the Lord are on the righteous*. The use of the word *eyes* here refers to a side glance with a jealous look. The word *on* means over or upon. In other words, the eyes of the Lord are directed in a favorable sense toward the good of those who are righteous, those who are innocent or holy. He watches us with a jealous eye and, my friend, that is an encouraging truth as we go through suffering. Second Chronicles 16:9 says, "For the eyes of the LORD run to and fro throughout the whole earth, to show Himself strong on behalf of those whose heart is loyal to Him." Proverbs 15:3 says, "The eyes of the LORD are in every place, keeping watch on the evil and the good." Peter's statement here would be a comfort to his first readers, and it should be to us as well, because while we already learned from 1 Peter 1:8 that we cannot see God, He still sees us. It's like those windows you can see out of, but the people on the other side are unable to see into. God is always watching us, and nothing escapes His attention. This would have been a real comfort to Peter's initial audience: that God knew what was happening to them and to their loved ones—He was watching!

But not only are His eyes watching; His ears are also listening. Peter says *His ears are open to their prayers*. This literally reads that God's ears are into the prayers or petitions of the righteous. What a picture of God bending down into the very prayers of His children, earnestly listening to their petitions, eager to answer them and come to aid those who pray! He hears even our whispers that we pray, as well as those prayers we utter only in our minds. In fact, did you know that God is more desirous to answer your prayers than you are desirous of Him answering them? Proverbs 15:8 states that "the prayer of the upright is His delight." And this principle is made perfectly clear in Matthew 7:7-11, where Jesus says, "Ask, and it will be given to you; seek, and you will find; knock, and it will be opened to you. For everyone who asks receives, and he who seeks finds, and to him who knocks it will be opened. Or what man is there among you who, if his son asks for bread, will give him a stone? Or if he asks for a fish, will he give him a serpent? If you then, being evil, know how to give good gifts to your children, how much more will your Father who is in heaven give good things to those who ask Him!" It is hard to say no to our children (and grandchildren) when they ask for things, isn't it? "Mom, can I have $5.00 for a school project?" or "Mom can I have a snack before dinner? I'm starving!" One of the most enjoyable things about our children's birthdays is buying gifts for them, and yet, God desires to give us gifts more than we desire to shower our children with gifts.

There are times that we can hinder the process of answered prayers. Many times, people will say to me that God does not answer their prayers, and it is worth considering that it may, perhaps, be because of one or more of those hindrances that Scripture mentions. But it is a marvelous thing to think that our Father hears our prayers.

There are, however, some individuals whose prayers God never hears. Peter closes with these words: *but the face of the Lord is against those who do evil*. The word *but* is a contrast. So, in contrast to the righteous we have the evil. God's face is against *those who do evil*, which means the front of His face is against those who do evil. The word for *evil* is the same word we have had in the last two verses. These are sobering words, as Peter is saying God's face—in other words, His providence and blessing—are turned away from the wicked, and He only looks upon them to abhor them, and to turn the arm of His justice against them. Proverbs 15:29 tells us, "The LORD is far from the wicked, but He hears the prayer of the righteous." This would be of great encouragement to Peter's readers. Many were being treated unjustly and persecuted, and Peter says the Lord is watching and His prayers are open to you, but He will be against those who are doing evil to you. It is interesting that Peter left off Psalm 34:16b, which is the rest of that quote, "to cut off the remembrance of them from the earth." Perhaps Peter was hoping that these evil men who were persecuting these believers would repent, and he wanted to encourage his readers that he took no delight in the fate of wicked men.

Summary

As we close this lesson, I would ask you: Do you love life and see your days as good? Or do you get out of bed in the morning, and say to yourself, "I just can't face another day here"?

If you have never had a love for life, there may be a more serious issue, and that is your heart. Perhaps your nature has not been changed. One who knows God will love the life God has graciously given them here, even when their days are filled with trials.

You might be thinking, "Well, I used to love life, but lately, it kind of stinks." Well, then I ask you, "Is something out of kilter in your life?" Honestly, ask yourself these questions:

- *Am I right now involved in any kind of gossip or slander?* Is there someone I need to go and ask forgiveness of for this terrible sin?

- *Have I been practicing deceit?* Do I color my stories a little to make myself or others look better than we are? That is deceitful! Am I practicing hypocrisy of any form? Saying one thing and doing another is hypocrisy, which is really deceit.

- *Do I avoid evil?* Am I taking the necessary measures to get out of its way? Do I perhaps have friends who are influencing me to do evil things?

- *Do I love good?* Do I look for ways to show kindness to others? Do I go out of my way to minister to those in need, or do I only minister when its convenient for my schedule?

- *Do I seek peace?* Is there anyone in my life right now with whom I am not on speaking terms? If so, have I made every possible effort to be at peace with them?

If God the Holy Spirit is speaking to you in regard to any of these questions, then I beg you to do whatever you need to do to get things right in your life. It would be an awful thing to have the Lord's face against you, to sense His hand of pleasure removed from you, to no longer have your prayers answered.

For those of you who do love life, what a joy it is to know that when we cry out to the Lord in time of trouble, He hears us and delivers us! My prayer is for each of us that we would love the life that God has given us, that we would see our days as good, and that we would richly enjoy all that God has given us as we go with our Master through the fiery furnace!

Questions to Consider
Five Keys to Loving Life
1 Peter 3:10-12

1. 1 Peter 3:10-12 is a quote from Psalm 34:12-16. Psalm 34 is written by David during the events in 1 Samuel 21. Read Psalm 34 and 1 Samuel 21 and answer the following questions. (a) What events happened in 1 Samuel 21 that caused David to fear? (b) What did his fear lead him to do, according to Psalm 34? (c) How do the events in 1 Samuel 21 help you to understand what David writes in Psalm 34? (d) How does Psalm 34 show that David was encouraged by the Lord during his trial? (e) How could these words encourage Peter's readers? (f) How do they encourage you?

2. Memorize 1 Peter 3:12.

3. (a) How does Romans 3:13-14 describe our speech? (b) How is our speech described in James 3:5-10? (c) What does James say in James 1:26 about those of us who cannot control our tongues? (d) Why do you think Peter writes in 1 Peter 3:10 that controlling our tongues is a key to loving life?

4. (a) To whom are we supposed to "do good" to, according to Galatians 6:10? (b) Why is "doing good" not always easy, according to Romans 7:18-25? (c) What do James 4:17 and 3 John 11 say about those of us who do not practice good? (d) Why do you think "doing good" is another key to loving life?

5. (a) What things can hinder our prayers, according to Psalm 66:18; Matthew 6:5-8; Mark 11:24-26; Luke 18:10-14; 1 Timothy 2:8; James 4:1-4; and 1 Peter 3:7, 12? (b) Are any of these things hindering your prayers? (c) What can you do to remedy that?

6. From what Paul writes in 2 Corinthians 6:4-10 and 2 Corinthians 11 and 12, how did Paul see his "bad days" as "good days"?

7. In what ways does 1 Peter 3:12 give you encouragement for when others are doing evil against you?

8. How could you use 1 Peter 3:10-12 to help someone who is not enjoying life and possibly even considering taking their own life?

9. (a) What are some practical ways that you have learned to control your tongue that you can pass on to others? (b) How are you (or how did you) train your children to control their tongue?

10. (a) Do you love life? (b) If not, what is hindering that? (c) Are any of Peter's admonitions hindering your love for life? Please come with a prayer request so that others might pray for your need to start loving life the way God intended!

Chapter 15

Six Keys to Being an Effective Witness
1 Peter 3:13-17

Many years ago, a gifted evangelist by the name of Tom Skinner wrote a book entitled *If Christ Is the Answer, What Are the Questions?*[52] As believers in Jesus Christ, we believe *He is* the answer. But, if Jesus is the answer, then what *are* the questions, and why don't more lost people ask us these questions about the hope within us? How many people have asked *you* about your faith in Christ in this past year? If no one has asked us, then perhaps you and I should ask ourselves, "Why don't very many people ask me about the hope within me? Does my life manifest anything that is noticeably different from the lost world, so that they stand in awe and wonder, 'Why is she so different?'"

In 1 Peter 3:13-17, Peter gives us some possible answers for why we may not be making a bigger impact on our world. There are six keys to being an effective witness, according to this passage. Perhaps as we look into this text, it will become apparent why more people don't ask about the hope within us, and we will be enabled to make the necessary changes so that our lives do live out the gospel of Jesus Christ. Let's read the verses together and discover the six keys.

1 Peter 3:13-17

> And who is he who will harm you if you become followers of what is good? [14]But even if you should suffer for righteousness' sake, you are blessed. "And do not be afraid of their threats, nor be troubled." [15]But sanctify the Lord God in your hearts, and always be ready to give a defense to everyone who asks you a reason for the hope that is in you, with meekness and fear; [16]having a good conscience, that when

---
[52] Zondervan (1974)

defame you as evildoers, those who revile your good conduct in Christ may be ashamed. ¹⁷For it is better, if it is the will of God, to suffer for doing good than for doing evil.

But, my friend, we must not fool ourselves into thinking that the day is far away for us that we too might be called upon to suffer for the sake of Christ. When you consider that same sex marriage is now the law of the land, when you consider that over 61 million abortions have taken place since *Roe v. Wade* (which means that over 61 million babies have been murdered), it can't be long before God's judgment will fall upon the earth. All you have to do is study history to know that once a nation turns its back on God, that nation is history! In the response to Covid-19, we have seen the unthinkable taking place, not to mention the riots and destruction of property and removal of monuments. The recent events in our nation are just a smidge of what is to come. For those of us who stand for moral absolutes in a wicked and perverse nation, we can be certain that we will be persecuted when we bring the gospel to bear upon the conscience of the unbeliever.

Peter encouraged us that the Lord is watching over us jealously and listening to our prayers. We are not to worry because God's face is against those who are doing evil. Peter has just given us encouragement about how to live in a hostile world, and now he's going to tell us how to be an effective witness in a hostile world. In verse 13, he continues talking about these evildoers; he says:

> And who is he who will harm you if you become followers of what is good? (1 Peter 3:13)

The word *and* is a connecting word, connecting what Peter was saying in verse 12 to what he is saying verse 13. Because God takes care of the righteous (verse 12), then *who is he* that will harm you (verse 13)? The word *harm* means to injure. In Romans 8:31, Paul captures the essence of Peter's words when he asks, "What then shall we say to these things? If God is for us, who can be against us?" I've heard it said that John Knox used to say, "With God on his side man is always in the majority." We know from our introductory lesson that some of Peter's first readers *were* being harmed, and many among them *were* murdered. So, what does Peter mean here? Peter is not guaranteeing that absolutely no harm will come to them (see also verse 17), but he is saying that if harm did come to them, God would vindicate them, as he's already mentioned in verse 12. He's saying that the likelihood of them suffering would be lessened, if they would simply follow that which is good.

What does it mean to *become followers of what is good?* The term *follower* refers to a zealot who was fanatical and pledged to liberate his native land by every possible means. Zealots burned with zeal to the point that they would risk their own lives, the comfort of their homes, and even their loved ones for their country. They were zealous not because they had to be but because they wanted to be. Peter is saying, "Love goodness with that passionate intensity with which the most fanatical patriot loves his country."[53] And, if indeed they loved goodness like that, then the chances of their being persecuted would be limited. It is true that Jesus went about doing good and was persecuted by wicked men. It is true that the apostles did much good and eventually were killed for their faith. But it is also true that those who live a life of integrity and goodness are less prone to persecution, even in a wicked world. This is the idea set forth in Proverbs 16:7: "When a man's ways please the LORD, he makes even his enemies to be at peace with him." Peter goes on in verse 14 to encourage those who are pursuing good and yet might still suffer, because that remains a possibility.

> But even if you should suffer for righteousness' sake, you are blessed.
> "And do not be afraid of their threats, nor be troubled." (1 Peter 3:14)

Peter says *but even if you should suffer for righteousness' sake.* In other words: there is a possibility you might still suffer for being righteous. The word *suffer* means to experience a sensation or

---

[53] William Barclay, *The Letters of James and Peter* (Louisville: Westminster John Knox Press, 1976), 229.

impression that is usually painful. This word is used more often in 1 Peter than in any other New Testament book. If we do suffer for righteousness, Peter says we *are blessed*, which means we are happy or fortunate. Those who suffer because of their stand for righteousness are spiritually prosperous. This does not mean that we find enjoyment or happiness in the persecution itself, but we do find it to be a blessed condition because we understand that it is a privilege to suffer for our Lord. As Peter will say later on, in 1 Peter 4:12-13, "Beloved, do not think it strange concerning the fiery trial which is to try you, as though some strange thing happened to you; but rejoice to the extent that you partake of Christ's sufferings, that when His glory is revealed, you may also be glad with exceeding joy."

It may be that Peter had in mind something he heard his Lord say in the Sermon on the Mount, in Matthew 5:10, "Blessed are those who are persecuted for righteousness' sake, for theirs is the kingdom of heaven." I remember the Lord illustrating this in my life with someone who stopped having a relationship with me because of my righteous stand on an issue. I was sad at the spiritual condition of that person whom I had known for a long time, but content in that I knew I had been salt and light for my Savior—and in that I could rejoice! As we saw when we were studying 1 Peter 1:5-6, we may not be able to rejoice in the trial, but we can rejoice in the certainty of our salvation. Remember the account in Acts 5 in which Peter and the apostles were beaten for sharing the gospel? It says in verse 41 that they went away rejoicing that they were counted worthy to suffer shame for His name.

It is probable that we will suffer for the sake of righteous living as the world around us declines morally—the ungodly world hates righteousness! But Peter says *do not be afraid of their threats, nor be troubled*. Sometimes people try to scare us with their threats, and in the case of Peter's initial readers, that was certainly happening. Peter says don't let them scare you. But not only are they not to be afraid of these threats; they are also not to *be troubled*, which means to stir or agitate. It describes the feeling of being tossed to and fro with feelings and distractions. It is easy to be troubled when people are trying to harm you, but we cannot allow our fears to run rampant. Jesus makes this clear in Matthew 10:28, where he says, "And do not fear those who kill the body but cannot kill the soul. But rather fear Him who is able to destroy both soul and body in hell." Instead of being troubled or fearful about this, Peter says in verse 15,

> But sanctify the Lord God in your hearts, and always be ready to give a defense to everyone who asks you a reason for the hope that is in you, with meekness and fear; (1 Peter 3:15)

Peter is alluding to Isaiah 8:12-14. And the allusion here from Isaiah is significant. Ahaz, who was the King of Judah, was facing a crisis because of an impending invasion by the Assyrian army. The kings of Israel and Syria wanted Ahaz to join them in an alliance, but Ahaz refused. So, Israel and Syria took vengeance on Ahaz and decided to invade Judah. Behind the scenes, though, we find Ahaz joining with Assyria. The Prophet Isaiah warns him against ungodly alliances and urges him to trust God for deliverance. That's where the allusion comes in: "The LORD of hosts, Him you shall hallow; let Him be your fear, and let Him be your dread." In other words: don't fear Assyria, but fear the Lord and put Him first. Peter takes this admonition from Isaiah to Ahaz and admonishes his own readers to not give into Nero's threats nor be tempted to abandon their faith and join up with ungodly men. These Christians Peter is writing to would naturally be tempted to give into fears because of their persecutors. But Peter says,"No! Instead, sanctify the Lord in your hearts and do not fear men or your circumstances. If the Lord is indeed the strength of our life, then of whom shall we be afraid? We should be fearful of Him, not of them!"

What does it mean to *sanctify the Lord God in your hearts*? *Sanctify* means to make holy, to set apart. We are to set apart Christ *as Lord in our hearts*. In other words, He is to have first place. He is to have first place in that inner sanctuary which is our heart. If Christ is first place in our hearts, then we will not fear what man can do to us. *So, number one on our list of things we must do to be effective in our*

...s: *We must have Christ first in our hearts.* This truth sets ...rs apart from the world because unbelievers do not have ...rst in their hearts. And this is the most important point if we are ...ing to be an effective witness for Christ! Why is this truth so important? If we do not have Christ in our hearts, if we do not have genuine saving faith, if we ourselves have not been changed by the amazing gospel, then how can we possibly be an effective witness? If we do not have the Holy Spirit within us, then we have no power to share the blessed gospel! This would be of utmost importance to Peter's readers because by having Christ first in their hearts and life they might have opportunity to be a vessel for sharing the gospel, which would make all their suffering worthwhile.

These readers were not only to set apart the Lord as first in their lives, though. They were also to be ready to give an answer to the persecutors who were attacking them. They were not to be afraid to speak of the hope within them. Peter says they should *always be ready to give a defense to everyone who asks you a reason for the hope that is in you.* This would be the second key to being an effective witness: *We must be ready to give an answer.* We must be prepared, we must be willing, we must be bold to share with those who might ask us about the hope we have! This might come at any time, and most often it happens when we least expect it.

I remember once being on my way home and stopping to get gas. The clerk said, "Wow, you sure are happy! What's the key?" I did not open my mouth for the gospel, much to my shame! And those opportunities don't usually come up again! We are to buy up those opportunities, as Paul says to the church at Colossae, when writing to them about how they are to behave toward the lost world (Colossians 4:5). In fact, he says in the very next verse, "Let your speech always be with grace, seasoned with salt, that you may know how you ought to answer each one" (Colossians 4:6).

The Greek word for *defense*, or answer, here in 1 Peter means an apology, but this does not mean we are to apologize for our faith. It is legal term which means a plea, an apology, a defense. It was used of an attorney who presented a verbal defense for his client that enabled him to be cleared of the charge against him. In fact, the theological term "apologetics" refers to that part of theological study that deals with the defense of the faith. As believers, we should be able to give a defense of our faith in Christ. We should know what we believe and why we believe it and be able then to tell someone else so that they can understand it. We should be able to defend any charges that the unbeliever may have against Christianity and present a clear verbal defense of the faith. Paul says in Acts 22:1, "Brethren and fathers, hear my defense before you now," and then he defends his faith in the next 20 verses. In the letter to the Philippians, we find Paul in prison for the defense of the faith (Philippians 1:7 and 17). Peter says this defending of our faith would be to *everyone who asks you* or inquires about it. Now, this does not mean that I do not have to share the gospel unless someone asks me how to be saved—I'm sure some of you were hoping that was what that meant! This cannot mean that we are only to share our faith with those who ask us about the hope we have, because Jesus clearly commands in Mark 16:15, "Go into all the world and preach the gospel to every creature." But I will say this: we also need to marry this command in Mark 16:15 with what Jesus says in Matthew 7:6, "Do not give what is holy to the dogs; nor cast your pearls before swine, lest they trample them under their feet, and turn and tear you in pieces." There is a time when we don't share the gospel and that is when people are violent and abusive. We must be wise as serpents and harmless as doves, as Jesus said in Matthew 10:16. But we must be ready when the opportunity does come to open our mouths and share the gospel.

Peter says that when the time comes, we should be ready and willing to share *the hope that is in you*. The hope within us is the gospel. Peter has already mentioned this in the introduction of this epistle, in 1 Peter 1:3: "Blessed be the God and Father of our Lord Jesus Christ, who according to His abundant mercy has begotten us again to a living hope through the resurrection of Jesus Christ from the dead." Peter says you have been blessed to be born again by the precious blood of Christ unto a living hope—now be ready to share that hope! This is a glorious hope which grants salvation

...ope of future glory! I imagine that those who were persecuting the Christians Peter was writing to would have been in awe at their courage and positive outlook, their hope in the midst of such awful suffering, and that would make them naturally curious as to how to attain such hope. Peter is admonishing his readers to have an intelligent grasp of this hope and skill in presenting it.

Peter goes on to show us three attitudes that ought to accompany our defense of the truth, and they are not arrogance, aggressiveness, and abrasiveness. As one man put it: "We are not prosecuting attorneys! We are defending the faith." We are not winning an argument. We are winning souls. *The first attitude we must have is meekness. This is also the third key to being an effective witness: We must have a spirit of meekness.* This means we must be gentle and humble. Paul states in 2 Timothy 2:24-25, "And a servant of the Lord must not quarrel but be gentle to all, able to teach, patient, in humility correcting those who are in opposition, if God perhaps will grant them repentance, so that they may know the truth." And then he gives a reason why in verse 26: "And that they may come to their senses and escape the snare of the devil, having been taken captive by him to do his will." *Meekness* entails gentleness and humility, but also strength under control. We must be strong in our sharing, but it must be under control. As we share the gospel, we should consider our own frailties as humans and our own unworthiness to be saved, and that should cultivate within us a spirit of meekness as we share our faith. We should realize that except for the grace of God, we too would still be steeped in wickedness and in darkness. This is the same attitude that a believing wife is to have toward her unsaved husband. She is not to preach at him but win him with her meek and quiet spirit, as Peter has already mentioned in 1 Peter 3.

The second attitude we should have as we share the gospel and the fourth key to being an effective witness is: We must have a spirit of fear. This is not a fear of man; otherwise, it would be a contradiction of verse 14. This refers to a fear of God; it means we must have a spirit of reverence, or respect toward God, as we share the gospel. In our gospel presentation, we should have a fearful and reverent spirit toward God because He sees and hears all. We should be reverent, because of the seriousness of the gospel, and cautious, lest we say anything that would not be accurate. God is listening to our gospel presentation, and we must keep that truth ever before our mind's eye. Martin Luther said, "Then must ye not answer with proud words and bring out the matter with a defiance and with violence as if ye would tear up trees, but with fear and lowliness as if ye stood before God's tribunal…so must thou stand in fear, and not rest on thine own strength, but on the word and promise of Christ."[54] It is possible that Peter is recalling his own failure of representing his faith in Matthew 26, when he denied the Lord out of fear and used words that were not gentle or respectful. It even says in Matthew 26:74 that Peter cursed and swore, saying, "I do not know the Man!" Peter failed in this point of being reverent and in being meek.

The third attitude that should accompany our defense of the faith, and the fifth key to being an effective witness is found in verse 16. Peter says,

> having a good conscience, that when they defame you as evildoers, those who revile your good conduct in Christ may be ashamed. (1 Peter 3:16)

This is the fifth key to being an effective witness and the third attitude that should accompany our defense of the faith: Must have a good conscience before God and others. Peter has already mentioned the importance of this in 1 Peter 2:19, and he will remind us again in 1 Peter 3:21. Our *conscience* is that internal judge that witnesses to us and lets us know whether we are doing good or evil. A good conscience will know right from wrong, and it will obey by acting on the good. Paul put it well in Acts 24:16, where he says he was always striving to have a conscience void of offense toward God and man. If one has a good conscience when undergoing persecution, that person will have courage because they know they are right with God and men. A good conscience also gives us peace. When we

---

[54]D. Edmond Hiebert, *First Peter: An Expositional Commentary* (Chicago: Moody Press, 1984), 214.

guilty or defiled conscience, it drains our energies and we cannot be bold for Christ, because we know we ought not preach what we do not practice! Profession without practice has no weight.

Why should we have a good conscience and a meek and reverent spirit when defending our faith? Peter says so *that when they defame you as evildoers, those who revile your good conduct in Christ may be ashamed*. (This is similar to what he said in 1 Peter 2:12.) The word for *ashamed* means to blush or to be disgraced. Peter says even though they *defame* you, which means continually slandering you and calling you evildoers, they will *see your good conduct* and be ashamed. *The sixth key to being an effective witness is: We must have good conduct toward others.* Paul says something very similar to the young men in Titus 2:7-8 where he commands them "in all things showing yourself to be a pattern of good works; in doctrine showing integrity, reverence, incorruptibility, sound speech that cannot be condemned, that one who is an opponent may be ashamed, having nothing evil to say of you." When a Christian's *conduct* or behavior is meek and reverent, when their conscience is clear and good, then the unbeliever is put to shame by their own slander. They will come to see that they were wrong regarding your character and they will be ashamed of themselves, and, perhaps, they may see that Christ is indeed who He says He is and repent and be saved!

Peter then ends this section with a principle he has stated numerous times throughout this epistle (see 1 Peter 2:19, 20; 3:14; 4:16, 19). Verse 17 is really a summary statement of where we have come from, as well as an introductory statement for the next set of verses. He says,

> For it is better, if it is the will of God, to suffer for doing good than for doing evil. (1 Peter 3:17)

Peter says *it is better, if it is the will of God*. *If it is the will of God* communicates not a probability in the Greek but a possibility. The word *better* means nobler; it is nobler or better *to suffer for doing good than for doing evil*. This is proof that it is God's will for some to suffer. Many times, I've had people tell me it is never God's will for one of his children to suffer. I'm not sure how they would interpret this verse, though, because it is clear not only here but in other places as well that God sometimes intends for us to suffer. In 1 Peter 4:19, Peter will say it is the will of God for some to suffer: "Therefore let those who suffer according to the will of God commit their souls to Him in doing good, as to a faithful Creator." Paul tells us in Philippians 1:29 that suffering is a gift. As we share the gospel of Jesus Christ with a lost and hostile world, we can count on the fact that most will not accept the gospel but reject it, and that will cause suffering for many of us. But we can take courage in the fact that many have gone before us, including the apostle Peter, who have suffered and even lost their lives for the sake of the gospel.

It is better to suffer persecution from men *for doing good* by living right and by sharing your faith boldly and clearly, than to encounter the judgment of God *for doing evil* by living unrighteously and by being ashamed of the gospel in this hostile world. This suffering for doing good could include the loss of family and friends, the loss of a job, or ridicule and persecution, but the judgment of God for doing evil would result in shame on judgment day. As one of my mentors has said to me many times, so now I say to you: "You will always regret doing what is wrong, but you will never regret doing what is right!"

Summary

My friend, are you making an impact on your world? Do people ask you, "What makes you different? Why are you so happy? Why are you so positive?" Peter's readers likely had a much bigger challenge than you and I do; they were undergoing tremendous suffering, the kind which would make these six areas significantly more challenging. Nevertheless, if you and I would make an impact on our society for the gospel of Jesus Christ, we must have these six keys in place to be an effective witness.

Christ must have first place in our hearts. Is Christ number one in your heart? If not, who or what is? Have you yourself embraced

Him as Lord and Savior? Has the gospel made a radical impact in your life? Does Christ have first place in your home, your marriage, your friendships, your time, and your activities? If He does, then it will make an impact on the unbelieving world around you!

We must always be ready to give a defense of our faith. Do you know how to share the gospel in a convincing and clear manner? If not, what is keeping you from being prepared? Why not get involved in some type of evangelism training: Discipleship Evangelism, Evangelism Explosion, or Way of the Master? *Tell the Truth,* by Will Metzger, is a great book which gives help on how to turn everyday conversations into spiritual conversations. It would even be a good idea to find someone who does know how to share their faith effectively and go out with them to a park, mall, or some other place to share the gospel. When is the last time you shared the gospel?

We must have a spirit of meekness as we share. As you share the gospel, do you come across as arrogant and aggressive, or are you gentle and humble as you share? If we asked the last person you shared your faith with, what would they say?

We must also have a spirit of reverence. When you share your faith, are you aware of God's awesome presence with you, and do you share in a reverent manner realizing His eye is watching and His ear is hearing all you say and do, even your motives in sharing the gospel?

We must have a good conscience before God and others. Is your conscience clear as you share the blessed hope? Is there anyone with whom you need to clear up a matter? Do you have unconfessed sin in your life that you need to get right with God? This reason here alone may perhaps be why the Lord doesn't use us more in sharing the gospel; we live in an era where sin is minimized and many have grieved or quenched the Spirit and desensitized their consciences. Holy living is archaic!

We must have good behavior, especially towards the lost world. Do unbelievers look at your life and see a difference in how you behave? Is your life any different than theirs? How does the lost world see you living, in the workplace, at the grocery store, the doctor's office, your child's school, in traffic? If you and I want to make an impact on our lost world, and if we want to expand the kingdom of God by fulfilling the great commission, then we must maintain the highest standard of Christian living and seize every opportunity to witness! And we must do it God's way and not ours!

We must have genuine faith ourselves. We must be ready to defend our faith. We must share with meekness, reverence, and with a good conscience. We must have holy conduct, and we must be ready to suffer for the gospel, if need be. We can take great comfort in the fact that we do this not on our own, but with our Master as we go with Him through the fiery furnace!

Questions to Consider
Six Keys to Being an Effective Witness
1 Peter 3:13-17

(You may need to use the KJV version of the Bible to answer some of these questions.)

1. (a) In 1 Peter 3:13-17, what qualities (of a Christian) do you see that Peter has already mentioned in this same chapter? (b) What connections do you see between what Peter says in verses 13-17 and what he says in verses 1-12?

2. Memorize 1 Peter 3:17.

3. (a) According to Isaiah 41:10-14; 51:12-13; Jeremiah 1:8; John 14:27; and 2 Timothy 1:7, what are some reasons we should not be fearful of our enemies? (b) Who should we fear, according to Luke 12:4-5?

4. Isaiah 7 and 8 are the setting for Peter's words in 1 Peter 3:15, "Sanctify the Lord in your hearts" (KJV, see Isaiah 8:13). (a) What is happening in these chapters? (b) What is the reason Isaiah says, "Sanctify the Lord of hosts himself"? (c) Why do you think Peter alludes to Isaiah in 1 Peter?

5. (a) Who is asking Peter of the "hope within him" in Acts 4:1-12? (b) How does Peter defend his faith? (c) Read over Acts 22 and 23 and write down how Paul defends his faith. (d) What can you learn from Peter and Paul about sharing your faith?

6. (a) What does our conscience do, according to John 8:9 (KJV)? (b) As believers, what kinds of consciences should we have, according to Acts 23:1; 24:16; Romans 9:1; and 1 Timothy 3:9? (c) What kind of consciences do unbelievers have, according to 1 Timothy 4:2 and Titus 1:15? (d) How does a good conscience

help believers in time of trial? (e) How does it help in opportunities for witnessing?

7. (a) Do you know how to defend your faith? In other words, can you share the gospel in a winsome and clear way, defending your faith in Christ? (b) What are some ways to defend your faith that you have learned that you could also pass on to others?

8. Does Christ have first place in your heart? If not, why not? If Christ does not have first place in your heart, who or what does have first place?

9. Please write a prayer request based on your answer from question 7 or 8.

Chapter 16

The Suffering and Longsuffering of Christ and God

1 Peter 3:18-22

Several years ago, a movie came out that was entitled *Noah's Ark*. Television and movies are not my favorite pastimes, but on the rare occasion that a show comes out that I think might actually have some substance to it, I might go watch it. So, when this *Noah's Ark* movie came out, I actually thought to myself, "Good! A movie that we can finally watch!" I was hoping, of course, that it was going to be biblical. Well, for those of you who watched that movie, you know it was bizarre! We actually gave up on it at some point and quit watching—it was that bad! The movie portrayed the destruction of Sodom and Gomorra occurring before the flood incident and Lot and Noah together during the flood. To make matters worse, not only were Noah and his family saved from the flood, but Lot was also. It was all very confusing! In fact, I felt about as bewildered about that movie as I once felt about these verses we are going to look at in the text for this lesson.

Before we study this text, I do want to let you know that the verses we're going to cover have caused more controversy than any other passage in this epistle. Even Luther did not know what Peter meant! He said of them, "A wonderful text is this, and a more obscure passage perhaps than any other in the New Testament, so that I do not know for a certainty just what Peter means."[55] Let's read these mysterious verses and see if we can make some sense of their meaning—the Lord willing!

---

[55] Martin Luther, *Commentary on Peter and Jude* (Grand Rapids: Kregel Publishing, 1982), 168.

1 Peter 3:18-22

> For Christ also suffered once for sins, the just for the unjust, that He might bring us to God, being put to death in the flesh but made alive by the Spirit, ¹⁹by whom also He went and preached to the spirits in prison, ²⁰who formerly were disobedient, when once the Divine longsuffering waited in the days of Noah, while the ark was being prepared, in which a few, that is, eight souls, were saved through water. ²¹There is also an antitype which now saves us—baptism (not the removal of the filth of the flesh, but the answer of a good conscience toward God), through the resurrection of Jesus Christ, ²²who has gone into heaven and is at the right hand of God, angels and authorities and powers having been made subject to Him.

Our outline for this lesson will include:

> *The Reason for Christ's Suffering* (vv 18-19)
> *The Reason for God's Longsuffering* (vv 20-21)
> *The Reason for Christ's Ascension* (v 22)

Let's look at the reason for Christ's suffering, from verses 18 and 19. Peter says:

The Reason for Christ's Suffering

1 Peter 3:18-19

> For Christ also suffered once for sins, the just for the unjust, that He might bring us to God, being put to death in the flesh but made alive by the Spirit, (1 Peter 3:18)

To begin, let's remind ourselves that Peter says *for Christ also suffered once for sins*. There is a continuation of the theme of suffering; Peter has referred to this already in 1 Peter 2:21. Notice the word *also*. Peter is reminding them that Christ also suffered, just as they are suffering. Peter is encouraging his readers that Christ Himself went through unjust persecution just as they were! Peter would have heard these words from the lips of his Lord in the upper room in John 15:20: "Remember the word that I said to you, 'A servant is not greater than his master.' If they persecuted Me, they will also persecute you. If they kept My word, they will keep yours also." Obviously, Christ's suffering was different from their suffering and from ours, in that His suffering provided our redemption. But Christ suffered for well-doing (just as Peter's readers did) when He died on the cross, and it provided the means to our salvation.

Now, Christ did not have to continually die for us. Peter states he suffered *once for* our *sins*. As Hebrews 9:12 states, "Not with the blood of goats and calves, but with His own blood He entered the Most Holy Place *once* for all, having obtained eternal redemption." And Hebrews 9:28, "So Christ was offered *once* to bear the sins of many. To those who eagerly wait for Him, He will appear a second time, apart from sin, for salvation." (Both emphases mine.) In the Old Testament, the High Priest would enter the Most Holy Place once a year to sprinkle blood to atone for the sins of the people. Likewise, Jesus suffered once for all for the sins of His people. This suffering was endured by the only One who is Just. The Holy One died for the wicked. The Innocent One died for the guilty. He is just in His character, and we are not.

Why did Jesus do this? *What is the reason for Christ's suffering? Peter says it was so that He might bring us to God!* The word *bring* means to lead one to and to gain an audience at court. At the court of kings, there was an official called the Introducer who would decide who would be admitted to the king's presence and then grant those individuals access to the king. Christ is the Introducer, so to speak, and He has brought us to God. Because of Christ's work on the cross, you and I now have access to God. This access to God describes a relationship with God that now makes us acceptable to Him and gives assurance that His favor is toward us. We may now come boldly to the throne of grace to find mercy in our time of need, as Hebrews 4:16 tells us. Peter has already mentioned several times that this redemption was for us (see 1:3, 10, 20, 21, and 25).

Peter goes on to describe this suffering as *being put to death in the flesh*. This phrase suggests a violent, painful death that was a deliberate termination of His life. But that wasn't the end of the story, praise be to God! Peter says also of Him: *but made alive by the Spirit*! The word *but* is word of contrast. Yes, Christ was put to death in His physical body, but He was also made alive by the Spirit. Now, there are two thoughts on what Peter means by this phrase. It could be that he is referring to the Holy Spirit or it could be that he is referring to Christ's human spirit. Remember, Jesus was fully man and so He had a spirit, and when He died on the cross He spoke these words to His Father, "Father, into Your hands I commit my spirit" (Luke 23:46). And then it says that "He breathed His last" or "He gave up His spirit." His spirit was made alive when He yielded it to God. His body was dead, but His spirit was alive.

Some translations, however, render this word as Spirit, referring to the Holy Spirit, which would then give it the same meaning as is conveyed in what Paul says in Romans 8:11: "But if the Spirit of Him who raised Jesus from the dead dwells in you, He who raised Christ from the dead will also give life to your mortal bodies through His Spirit who dwells in you." The idea would be that the Holy Spirit was involved in Jesus' resurrection.

I tend to hold to the first of these interpretations because the Greek word for spirit is the same Greek word that is used in verse 19; this would mean that Peter is referring to Jesus' human spirit and not the Holy Spirit. One man said of this verse that it is "one of the shortest and simplest, and yet one of the richest summaries given in the New Testament of the meaning of the cross of Christ."[56] Some scholars have even said that verses 18 and 19 may be fragments of a hymn the early Christians used to sing.

So, we turn from one of the simplest verses in the Bible to one of the most difficult verses in the Bible to understand. In that state of being made alive by the spirit, Christ went and preached to those spirits in prison.

---

[56] J. M. E. Ross, *The First Epistle of Peter in a Devotional Commentary* (London: Religious Tract Society, 1918), 151-152.

> by whom also He went and preached to the spirits in prison, (1Peter 3:19)

Before we try to unpack this verse, it might be helpful for you to know that there are more than 30 interpretations. Some of them are downright weird, about as weird as the movie *Noah's Ark*! Also, each of these words in the original language has been differently understood. The amount of literature that is out there on this verse alone is overwhelming.

There are some questions that might be coming to your mind as you reflect on this verse. Where is this prison? What was the message preached? Who are these spirits? When did this happen and who exactly preached to them? One man said, "It is a good rule that congregations should not be presented with a variety of interpretations, which can cause confusion,"[57] and I wholeheartedly agree with him! But there are three main interpretations of this passage, and I will do my best to explain those to you.

Some believe that between Jesus' death and resurrection He went to the prison where fallen angels are bound and He preached to them. These fallen angels, they say, were the ones mentioned in Genesis 6 who married the daughters of men. There, Christ did not preach the gospel but declared His victory. The word for *preach* is a Greek word for declaring or heralding something, not the Greek word for evangelizing. Some do say that He preached the gospel to them, giving them a second chance, but I don't find any support for that in Scripture. Nowhere in the Bible does it say that anyone is given a second chance after death. Luke 16:19-31 is pretty clear about that! That is the passage where the rich man in hell wants his tongue cooled with water by Lazarus, the beggar. He also wants someone to go and tell his family about how awful hell is. But Abraham says that if they won't believe Moses and the prophets, they won't believe it even if Lazarus comes back and tells them. You would have a pretty hard time proving that these angels (if they were really

---

[57] I. Howard Marshall, *1 Peter: The IVP New Testament Commentary Series* (Downers Grove:InterVarsity Press, 1991), 122.

angels) got married, because Jesus says very clearly in Matthew 22:30 that angels neither marry nor are given in marriage. This is a pretty weak view, in my opinion, in that it assumes that there were sexual relationships between angels and women; that would be a little difficult, since angels are spirits.

Some hold to the view that between Christ's death and resurrection He went to the place of the dead and preached to the spirits of Noah's wicked contemporaries. I will say there seems to be some weight to this idea, that is, that this is referring to Hades or Hell, a prison of sorts. Acts 2:27 says, "For You will not leave my soul in Hades, nor will You allow Your Holy One to see corruption." Hell or Hades or prison, as some call it, is the place of the punishment for the wicked. At death, Christians go immediately to be with the Lord; Paul states plainly in 2 Corinthians 5:8 that to be absent from our body is to be present with the Lord. But unbelievers go to Hades or hell or prison, which is a place of waiting until the judgment when death and Hades are cast into the lake of fire, which is the second death (see Revelation 20:11-15). This preaching would be a proclamation of Christ's triumph over these spirits.

A third possibility is this: Since one of the main themes of 1 Peter is suffering, Peter is reminding his readers of the conditions in Noah's day, that is, that God's people in Noah's day were suffering. They were being ridiculed. They were being mocked for building the ark. When Peter says *He went and preached,* he is referring to Noah being empowered by the Holy Spirit (vs. 18) to preach in his day to the wicked men of his day. These spirits are now in prison in the sense that they are held in a spiritual prison, Hell. This view has quite a bit of scriptural weight, especially when you consider that the verses which follow pertain to Noah, as well as the fact that Peter calls Noah a preacher of righteousness in 2 Peter 2:5. One man who holds to this view gives quite a bit of help here, so I want to share some of his thoughts with you. He states that this interpretation is appropriate because of the larger context.

- Noah and his family were a minority surrounded by hostile unbelievers; so are Peter's readers (vv. 13-14; 4:4, 12-13).

- Noah was righteous in the midst of a wicked world. Peter exhorts his readers to be righteous in the midst of wicked unbelievers (vv.13-14, 16-17; 4:3-4).

- Noah witnessed boldly to those around him. Peter encourages his readers to be good witnesses to unbelievers around them (vv.14, 16-17), being willing to suffer, if need be, to bring others to God (just as Christ was willing to suffer and die 'that he might bring us to God', v. 18).

- Noah realized that judgment was soon to come upon the world. Peter reminds his readers that God's judgment is certainly coming, perhaps soon (4:5, 7; 2 Peter 3:10).

- In the unseen "spiritual" realm Christ preached through Noah to unbelievers around him. By saying this Peter can remind his readers of the reality of Christ work in the unseen spiritual realm and the fact that Christ is also in them, empowering their witness and making it spiritually effective (*cf.*1:8, 11, 12, 25; 2:4). Therefore, they should not fear (v. 14) but in their hearts should "reverence Christ as Lord" and should "always be prepared" to tell of the hope that is in them (v. 15).

- At the time of Noah, God was patiently awaiting repentance from unbelievers, before he brought judgment. So it is in the situation of Peter's readers: God is patiently awaiting repentance from unbelievers (*cf.* 2 Peter 3:9) before bringing judgment on the world (*cf.* 2 Peter 3:10).

- Noah was finally saved, with "a few" others. Peter thus encourages his readers that, though perhaps few, they too will finally be saved, for Christ has triumphed and has all things subject to him (3:22; 4:13, 19; 5:10; 2 Peter 2:9).[58]

This is one of those verses that I hope we will understand more fully when we get to heaven! For now, let's move on from the reason for Christ's suffering to the reason for God's longsuffering, in verses 20-21.

The Reason for God's Longsuffering

1 Peter 3:20-21

> who formerly were disobedient, when once the Divine longsuffering waited in the days of Noah, while the ark was being prepared, in which a few, that is, eight souls, were saved through water. (1 Peter 3:20)

This verse seems to refer to those who were disobeying in Noah's day. Peter says they *formerly were disobedient*, he means that they were disbelieving. The people living during Noah's time rebelled against the message of God for 120 years as the ark was being built. God was very patient with these people; *the Divine longsuffering waited* for 120 years. *What was the reason for God's longsuffering? He hoped that man would repent.*

As sad as this is, people haven't changed one bit. Matthew 24:37-39 even tells us, "But as the days of Noah were, so also will the coming of the Son of Man be. For as in the days before the flood, they were eating and drinking, marrying and giving in marriage, until the day that Noah entered the ark, and did not know until the flood came and took them all away, so also will the coming of the Son of Man be." Mankind, obviously, has not changed since the day of Noah, and in many ways it seems as if it has become worse. Our world truly has gone mad! The word *saved* here is <u>diasozein</u>, which means to bring safely through. Peter says that only *eight souls* were saved. Those

---
[58] Wayne Grudem, *Tyndale New Testament Commentaries: 1 Peter* (Grand Rapids: Inter-Varsity Press, 1997), 160-161.

eight souls were Noah and his wife, their three sons, and their sons' wives. That was another erroneous thing about that movie: one of Noah's sons was trying to coax his wife to get into the ark and she wouldn't—so he hit her and knocked her out and dragged her in! Weird, to say the least! Peter goes on to use the picture of water to describe something that hopefully each of us has done, and that is to be baptized.

> There is also an antitype which now saves us—baptism (not the removal of the filth of the flesh, but the answer of a good conscience toward God), through the resurrection of Jesus Christ, (1 Peter 3:21)

When we think about baptism we have to ask the question, "What is baptism, and what does it represent?" Baptism is an act in which we depict that we have died to our old life and we are risen to new life in Christ. Baptism represents a breaking away from one's past life. As the flood wiped away the sinful world, so baptism pictures one's breaking away from his sinful life. Baptism to Christians in the New Testament meant a complete surrender of one's life to the Lordship of Christ, regardless of the cost. This often would include separation from friends, family, and even jobs. Unfortunately, much of what passes for 21st century Christianity has broken away from preaching the true gospel and has lost the meaning of not only the gospel but also the significance of baptism. I know people who claim to know the Lord and have never been baptized. That is unfortunate, as baptism should be one of our first acts of obedience after salvation!

Now, what does Peter mean when he says that baptism *saves us*? Let's look back first at what he says at the beginning of the verse. He mentions that baptism is *an antitype*, a like figure of something in the past, or figure of the reality, which is our salvation. Peter cannot mean literally that water baptism saves us, because Peter calls it an antitype or a like figure, a pattern or a model of something that has already taken place. Also, in Greek grammar, the gender goes back to the word *water*. This is an earthly expression of a spiritual reality, just like when Jesus said that we are to eat and drink His blood and body; He was not being literal, even though there are some religions that erroneously teach that. It was an antitype or a pattern. This cannot mean water saves us, because we know that we are saved by grace alone through faith alone in the precious blood of Christ alone; Peter has already been very clear on that in 1 Peter 1:18-19: "Knowing that you were not redeemed with corruptible things, like silver or gold, from your aimless conduct received by tradition from your fathers, but with the precious blood of Christ, as of a lamb without blemish and without spot." The water did not save Noah; the ark did. Water did not save Noah, and baptism does not now save us. They were saved by faith, just as you and I are saved by faith. In fact, Peter makes that clear that it is *not the removal of the filth of the flesh* that baptism accomplishes; rather, it is *the answer of a good conscience toward God*. No ceremony like baptism can save us, and no ceremony can affect our conscience. Hebrews 10:11-12 is pretty clear. "And every priest stands ministering daily and offering repeatedly the same sacrifices, which can never take away sins. But this Man, after He had offered one sacrifice for sins forever, sat down at the right hand of God." Water cannot wash away our filthy conscience, but the blood of Christ can. Baptism does not save us from sin; baptism is, rather, the expression of a good conscience toward God. Getting dunked in some water is not magical in itself—that would be the easy way to salvation! The harder thing to do is to have a good conscience before God! Peter has assumed that his readers have purified their souls by obeying the truth, as he mentioned in 1:22. That obedience to the truth is referring to their believing the gospel and turning to Christ for salvation. The result of that obedience is a good conscience before God. It is amazing how some people depend on their works to save them while their consciences remain stained with sin and guilt!

I had a friend when I was growing up who attended a Church of Christ, who held to the view that water baptism saved her. We would often sit and discuss our doctrinal differences. I remember asking her one time what would happen to her if she sinned on a particular day and then went out that same day and was killed in a car accident—would she go to hell? She told me that she would indeed go to hell and that every time she sinned, she had to be rebaptized. I remember thinking, "What bondage!" Peter is very clear in this verse that baptism cannot save us and forgive our sins. He says no, it is not water baptism which saves you, but it is the answer of a good conscience toward God. The word *answer* is a legal term meaning a pledge or a demand. When a person was signing a contract, he would be asked, "Do you pledge to obey and fulfill the terms of the contract?" He had to answer, "Yes, I do," or he would not be allowed to sign it. When converts were preparing for baptism in biblical times, they would be asked if they intended to obey God and serve Him and break from their sinful past. Questions would be asked of them, like: "Do you believe?" "Will you renounce?" "Will you obey?" If they had reservations in their hearts, they did not have a good conscience toward God. I wonder if maybe we should have these types of questions at baptisms in our day; perhaps, then, we would not take baptism so lightly. I am thankful that the church I belong to requires each one baptized to give a clear testimony of their conversion and faith in Christ.

Peter is reminding his readers of the importance of their baptismal testimony, which should encourage them to be true to the Lord. Water baptism does not save you, but the Holy Spirit baptism that comes at the moment of salvation does save you. Baptism is not only an outward expression; it is also an inward expression of God's grace, a cleansing not of the body but of the soul.

Another reason we know we are not saved by water baptism is because Peter says it's *through the resurrection of Jesus Christ*. That dynamite power that raised Christ from the dead is the same dynamite power that saved your soul. Baptism is a figure of what does save us: the resurrection of Jesus Christ. Without the resurrection there would be no salvation. If Christ is not risen, our faith is in vain! And

Peter says in verse 22 that after the resurrection, Christ ascended into heaven, and here we see the reason for His ascension.

The Reason for Christ's Ascension

1 Peter 3:22

> who has gone into heaven and is at the right hand of God, angels and authorities and powers having been made subject to Him. (1Peter 3:22)

After Jesus rose from the dead, He went *into heaven*. Mark 16:19 states, "So then, after the Lord had spoken to them, He was received up into heaven, and sat down at the right hand of God." Peter, who is writing this epistle, would have physically seen Christ ascend into heaven; he was an eyewitness, according to Acts 1. These words, no doubt, would have been of great comfort to these suffering believers, as they would realize that even though they might lose their lives, they too, just as their Lord, would soon be in heaven with the Father. That would be their greatest joy, to remember the example set before them in the Lord Jesus Christ, who, though He suffered terribly, is now in heaven seated at the right hand of the Father. *The right hand of God* would indicate the highest place of honor. And Peter makes it clear that *angels, authorities,* and *powers* have all been *made subject to Him* (see also Colossians 1:16 and Ephesians 1:20-21).

Peter has just given his readers the entire story of Christ's journey from his death to his accension. He died, He was made alive, and now He is gone into heaven.

Summary

What was the reason for Christ's suffering (vv 18-19)? To bring us to God! What was the reason for God's longsuffering (vv 20-21)? The hope that man would repent! What was the reason for Christ's ascension (v 22)? To be seated at the right hand of God, everyone and everything being subject to Him!

What are the main lessons from this passage? Well, I can tell you what they are not: Going and preaching to spirits in prison is not an application! Neither is coming up with yet another interpretation of this passage! Seriously, though, there are some important applications that we can take from this text:

1. *Christians can expect opposition* (verse 18). Jesus lived a perfect life. He was just. And yet, He was crucified like a common criminal. Jesus said to His disciples, "If they persecuted Me, they will also persecute you" (John 15:20).

2. *God is very long-suffering* (verse 20). One hundred and twenty years, actually, in Noah's day. Only eight were saved in Noah's day; how many in our day will be saved? Jesus said that hard is the way and few there be that find it (Matthew 7:13-14). We must not tread upon His goodness. If you are putting off committing your life to His Lordship, don't put it off any longer! Today, if you will hear His voice, harden not your heart! "Why choose to taste the sorrows of hell before you embrace the offers of mercy?"[59]

3. *Baptism is important* (verse 21). It identifies us with the Lord and testifies to the fact that we have broken from our old life. If you have never been baptized since your conversion, then I would urge you to do that soon! To take baptism lightly is a sin against God. If you want a clear and good conscience before God and man, then you must be obedient in this area.

4. *The exalted Christ is worthy of our worship* (verse 22)! The same Christ that you have submitted to as Lord of your life is also seated at the right hand of His Father interceding for you, and He is Lord over any opposition you might be facing today. Peter ends with an encouraging note as we finish out chapter three. Not only do we have the wonderful promise that our Master will be with us in the fiery furnace, but we also have the promise that He is now seated at the right hand of God interceding on our behalf!

---

[59]https://biblehub.com/commentaries/barnes/1_peter/3.htm

Questions to Consider

The Suffering and Longsuffering of Christ and God.
1 Peter 3:18-22

1. (a) Read the first three chapters of 1 Peter and list all the verses you can find that refer to the death and the resurrection of Jesus Christ. (b) From those verses, make note of any observations you see concerning Christ's death and resurrection. (For example: Christ's death was "once" in 1 Peter 3:18.) (c) Why do you think Peter so often emphasizes the death and resurrection of Christ?

2. Memorize 1 Peter 3:18.

3. (a) Why did God want to destroy mankind in the days of Noah, according to Genesis 6:5-13? (b) How long did He wait for mankind to repent while Noah built the ark, according to Genesis 6:3? (c) What does this teach you about God's patience with mankind? (d) Has mankind changed, according to Matthew 24:36-39?

4. (a) From the following scriptures, what do you notice about those being baptized? Matthew 3:6; Acts 2:38, 41; 8:36-38; 10:47; and 18:8. (b) According to Matthew 3:13-17, who was one of the first individuals to be baptized? (c) What did God say about Him in verse 17? (d) Why do you think God was pleased? (e) Have you been baptized since your conversion? If not, why not?

5. (a) What is Jesus doing at the right hand of God, according to Romans 8:34 and 1 Peter 3:22? (b) How long will He be there, according to Psalm 110:1? (c) When will this happen, according to what John records for us in Revelation 20:7-15?

6. What do *you* think 1 Peter 3:19 means?

7. (a) What do *you* think Peter means in 1 Peter 3:21, when he states, "even baptism does also now save us" (KJV)? (b) How do you personally deal with portions of God's Word that are difficult for you to understand?

8. (a) Would you say that you have a clear conscience before God and others? (b) Is there anything that you need to make right with God or another individual? If so, do so today!

9. In considering question three, how has God shown patience towards you? Put your words into a prayer of thanksgiving to God.

Chapter 17

The Past, the Present, and the Future Life of a Believer

1 Peter 4:1-6

C.S. Lewis once said, "God whispers to us in our pleasures, speaks in our conscience, but shouts in our pains: it is His megaphone to rouse a deaf world."[60] As we continue our journey through 1 Peter, I am sure Peter's initial readers could have identified with C.S. Lewis's comment. Some were suffering intense physical pain; some were going through emotional pain, being separated from family and friends; some, perhaps, were even going through spiritual pain, struggling with thoughts like, "Is this Christianity stuff really worth it? My life before Christ didn't seem that bad. Is this suffering *really* worth it?" As we begin chapter four of Peter's letter, we find him encouraging those reading his letter to not give up. Why? Because their present suffering doesn't even compare to what is yet to come in glory, and because their present suffering is joy compared to their sinful past. Let's read the first six verses together.

1 Peter 4:1-6

> Therefore, since Christ suffered for us in the flesh, arm yourselves also with the same mind, for he who has suffered in the flesh has ceased from sin, ²that he no longer should live the rest of his time in the flesh for the lusts of men, but for the will of God. ³For we have spent enough of our past lifetime in doing the will of the Gentiles—when we walked in lewdness, lusts, drunkenness, revelries, drinking parties, and abominable idolatries. ⁴In regard to these, they think it strange that you do not run with them in the same flood of dissipation, speaking evil of you. ⁵They will give an account to Him who is

---

[60]https://www.goodreads.com/quotes/623193-we-can-ignore-even-pleasure-but-pain-insists-upon-being#:~:text=God%20whispers%20to%20us%20in,man%20can%20have%20for%20amendment.

ready to judge the living and the dead. ⁶For this reason the gospel was preached also to those who are dead, that they might be judged according to men in the flesh, but live according to God in the spirit.

Our outline for this lesson will include:

> *The Believer's Present Life* (vv 1-2)
> *The Believer's Former Life* (vv 3-4)
> *The Believer's Future Life* (vv 5-6)

And now in chapter four, verse one, he continues to write regarding this theme of suffering.

The Believer's Present Life

1 Peter 4:1-2

> Therefore, since Christ suffered for us in the flesh, arm yourselves also with the same mind, for he who has suffered in the flesh has ceased from sin, (1 Peter 4:1)

Peter has just reminded his readers of Christ's suffering, and here he reminds them again that Christ suffered for them. The words *in the flesh* describe His suffering as a man here on earth. He had a fleshly body, just as we do. Peter says because *Christ* has *suffered for us*, then therefore, we are to arm ourselves also with the same mind. The words *arm yourselves* mean to equip yourselves, and they come from a term which describes a heavy-armed foot soldier putting on his heavy armor, including his weapons, which consisted of a large spear and a large shield. The idea here is that the Christian needs the heaviest armor he can get to withstand the attacks of the enemy of his soul. Peter will tell us in 1 Peter 5:8 that our enemy is always seeking whom he may devour! Because of this, we are to arm ourselves *also with the same mind*. What is Peter saying here? The *mind* refers to moral understanding, and the thought is that they are to arm themselves with the same moral understanding that Christ had during his suffering. What was His mindset during suffering? His attitude was one of humility. Peter himself would have had opportunity to practice this same attitude as he was crucified soon after the writing of this letter. We also know, according to church history, that Peter asked to be crucified upside down because he did not feel worthy to be crucified as his Lord had been. His humility was certainly exhibited by that request.

Peter goes on to say, *for he who has suffered in the flesh has ceased from sin*. *Suffered in the flesh* is the same idea as when Peter said,"being put to death in the flesh," in 1 Peter 3:18. When Peter indicates that this person has *ceased from sin*, the perfect tense of the verb indicates that this is a permanent eternal condition. Now, who is it that has ceased from sin here, and what is Peter talking about here? Some understand Peter to mean that suffering purifies the believer from sin. Others think that suffering disciplines the flesh so that it eventually becomes unable to exert sinful desires. Still others think suffering, for the believer, unites the believer with Christ, a union which is symbolized in Christian baptism, as we saw in our last lesson when we considered verses 20 and 21 from chapter three. In other words, when we were baptized, we were raised to newness of life, and part of that newness of life is suffering.

I personally think the correct interpretation is that those who belong to Christ endure suffering and, as a result, are drawn closer to Christ and not closer to sin! Suffering can have tremendously sanctifying results, if we allow it to. It's similar to what the Psalmist says in Psalm 119:67 and 71, "Before I was afflicted I went astray, but now I keep Your word, …. It is good for me that I have been afflicted, that I may learn Your statutes." A genuine believer has been freed from the power of sin, and so suffering pushes him or her closer to the Lord! We have looked many times at the importance of holiness already in our study of 1 Peter, and so we understand that when a believer completely identifies with Christ, he knows that he is done with sin and that he should act like a saint and not a sinner when it comes to suffering. We must refuse to give into sinful behavior! What a difficult task for these Christians—they were undergoing things you and I cannot imagine! How tempting it must have been to fight back and to give into sinful behavior. Would that all of God's children would be as Moses, who chose "rather to suffer affliction with the people of God than to enjoy the passing pleasures of sin" (Hebrews 11:25). So, what is the reason that during suffering we should arm ourselves with the same mind as Christ? Peter gives us the reason in verse 2.

> that he no longer should live the rest of his time in the flesh for the lusts of men, but for the will of God. (1 Peter 4:2)

The words *no longer* mean no further. The word *live* means to spend one's existence. And the word *rest* means what is left over. In other words, what Peter is saying is that we are to no longer live the rest of our earthly existence in sinful lusts. Remember, Peter has already reminded his readers of how brief their life is, in 1 Peter 1:24-25, when he said,"All flesh is as grass, and all the glory of man as the flower of the grass. The grass withers, and its flower falls away," and certainly, for many of them, life might end quicker than they think. Why waste the rest of our *time in the flesh*, our physical life, whatever is left of it, sinning?

What does Peter mean when he says they are not to live *for the lusts of men*? The word *lust* means a longing for what is forbidden. Peter will remind his readers of some of those lusts in the next verse but suffice it to say for now that Peter wants them to understand they should no longer live for those lusts *but*, rather, *for the will of God*. He has already mentioned this in 1 Peter 2:11, "Beloved, I beg you as sojourners and pilgrims, abstain from fleshly lusts which war against the soul." The word *but* here is <u>alla</u>, which is the stronger of the two Greek words for but. Our life before Christ was certainly consumed with our sinful passions and was pretty much a waste of time, as most of us can testify. In fact, often you hear of men and women embracing Christ as Lord late in life, and a commonality among most of them is the regret of a wasted life. The idea here is that God has broken the power of sin at the time of our conversion, and so we should no longer live for things that are forbidden, but for that which is the will of God. We should delight to do the will of the

Father and that will, whatever it may be, should not be a burden, as John explains in 1 John 5:3.

As we think about what a believer's present life should look like, it should resemble two things, according to these two verses: suffering for Christ, from verse 1; and living for Christ, from verse 2. Are you suffering for Christ, my friend, and are you living for Him? How have these both been manifested in your life recently?

Next, Peter reminds his readers just how ugly their former life was, just in case some were thinking they might want to return there. What did their former life look like? Peter reminds them in verses 3 and 4.

The Believer's Former Life

1 Peter 4:3-4

> For we have spent enough of our past lifetime in doing the will of the Gentiles—when we walked in lewdness, lusts, drunkenness, revelries, drinking parties, and abominable idolatries. (1 Peter 4:3)

Peter says *we have spent enough* time in the past *doing the will of the Gentiles*. *Past lifetime* would indicate an activity that has terminated. The Greek tense used here implies that the course is closed and done, as if they are looking back upon it as a standing and accomplished fact. The Christian should look at his life before Christ as a closed matter. The Christian died with Christ and has been raised to newness of life. The old is gone, the new has come. This would include old habits, old friends, places we used to go, and everything having to do with our old life. It is done away with, it is gone.

Sometimes, we look back at our life before Christ, and all we can remember is the pleasure of sin and not the bondage of sin. There are things I look back from my life before Christ and I wish I could forget them, but I can't. I certainly don't want to go back to that way of life. Peter says in our former life there was *enough* time, sufficient time, to go the limits of sin, but we don't need to go back there. Peter says you have already given enough time to wickedness. It's as though he's saying, "That's enough!" We might say we've "been there, done that, and don't need to do it again!" We don't need to go back and do what we did when we were heathens, which is what the word *Gentiles* means here. Peter says you've wasted enough years in worldliness, but now you should spend the rest of your time doing the will of God.

Peter then goes on to describe how his readers used to live. He reminds them of their ugly past. First, he says *we walked in lewdness*, or lasciviousness, your translation might say. This means we walked in filthiness. This would include actions that excite, disgust, and shock public decency. These would be acts done by people who want to flaunt their freedom and go beyond whatever is recognized as allowable. It reminds me of times past when "streaking" was popular—and even more recently as some Americans think they have the right to go nude in public! Lewdness would also include open acts of sex or homosexuality. I remember my daughter telling me several years ago that she was walking through a park and came upon two people having sex where all could witness it! That is lewdness!

Secondly, Peter says you walked in *lusts*. Lusts are longings for what if forbidden. This is not just sexual sins, but anything for which you might have a passionate desire. It might be drugs, alcohol, food, even someone else's things or even a person.

Thirdly, Peter says they were involved in *drunkenness*, which means an excess or overflow of wine. I don't need to remind you what God says about this sin, but let me remind you that as older women one of the character qualities we should possess, according to Titus 2, is to not be given to much wine.

The fourth area of sinfulness that Peter mentions is *revelries*, which is a word we don't use often, but it means rioting, letting loose, luxurious feastings, and village merry-making. One man helps us here: "In the cities such entertainments grew into carouses, in which the party of revelers paraded the streets with torches, singing, dancing, and all kinds of frolics. These revels also entered into worship of religious gods. Their excitement would include dancing and clamorous prayers of the god. They were said to tear animals from limb to limb, to devour the raw flesh, and to cut themselves without feeling the wound. The men yielded to a similar impulse by noisy revels in the streets, sounding the cymbals and tambourine, and carrying the image of the god in procession"[61] These were wild and furious parties, which kind of remind me of Mardi Gras in New Orleans! We also have witnessed this in recent years in the riots and the plundering of our cities and businesses and the tearing down of statues and monuments. These would certainly be revelries!

The fifth area of pagan living is similar to the fourth, and Peter calls it *drinking parties*. This would involve carousing, gluttony, or excessive eating.

The last of the deadly sins Peter mentions (and believe me, this list is not extensive!) is *abominable idolatries*. This word refers to illegal image worship. These were idolatries that were forbidden even by Roman law, and yet people would still practice them in secret. "Going beyond the inner sense of what was proper, their idolatries led to evils that tended to make men shudder."[62] Peter then, in verse four, tells his readers what their former friends, who still do such things, think of them.

> In regard to these, they think it strange that you do not run with them in the same flood of dissipation, speaking evil of you. (1 Peter 4:4)

Peter is saying, "Your old companions think that it is weird that you don't do the things you used to do. They think it strange that you don't hang out with them, and they're surprised that you have given

---

[61] PC Study Software—1993-1997—Vincent's Word Studies of the New Testament—not word for word.

[62] D. Edmond Hiebert, *First Peter: An Expositional Commentary* (Chicago: Moody Press, 1984), 246.

up the gratification of the flesh for something spiritual." I know unbelievers who will not come to Christ because they don't want to give up their wicked lifestyle. They think Christianity is made up of a bunch of fuddy-duddies. They have no idea how much joy comes from knowing Christ! The words *think it strange* mean to be surprised or astonished; the Greek verb tense also indicates that they are continually surprised. It was a normal part of their life back then to be involved in heathen worship, so their peers naturally would think them to be strange now for no longer doing so. It is the same way today. The world doesn't think it is strange when people wreak havoc on their bodies. They think that this is normal and that doing these sinful things is just human nature. What they don't realize is that Christians have been given a new nature, a divine one, which is now the motivating factor in their lives. Christians now hate the things they once loved and love the things they once hated. I am sure that these unbelievers were especially astonished at these Christians who not only were giving up their past, but who also were willing to suffer and even die for their newfound religion!

What does it mean to not *run with them* anymore? Well, it doesn't mean that you don't jog at the park with them anymore; it means that you don't rush together or hastily assemble with them. You don't keep company with them anymore. They are not your best friends anymore. Christians realize what Paul means in 1 Corinthians 15:33, where he says, "Do not be deceived: 'Evil company corrupts good habits.'" And Peter says you don't run with them *in the same flood of* dissipation, which means an overflowing or pouring out of a substance that springs up and flows down as lava from the crater of a volcano. *Dissipation* is a squandering of money, energy, or resources. This flood of dissipation perfectly describes their unrestrained wickedness!

Because these Christians did not run with the crowd, so to speak, then they were *evil spoken of*, Peter says. (See also 2:12, 3:16.) "The Christians were compelled to stand aloof from all the social pleasures of the world, and the Gentiles bitterly resented their Puritanism, regarding them as the enemies of all joy, and therefore of the human race"[63] This happened to Christ in Mark 3:21, when his friends said, "He is out of His mind." It happened to Paul in Acts 26:24 before Governor Festus; who said with a loud voice,"Paul you are beside yourself! Much learning is driving you mad!" In other words, "You're nuts, Paul!" And I imagine the unbelieving world says the same thing about you and me as well. I am sure they think we are crazy. In fact, I had a woman tell me that even her "Christian" family thought she was weird and too narrow because of her stand for holiness!

What did the believer's former life look like, according to verses 3 and 4? It looked like walking in all sorts of putrefying wickedness! My dear friend, I pray this does not describe you! If it does, some serious spiritual self-examination is in order!

The Believer's Future Life

1 Peter 4:5-6

> They will give an account to Him who is ready to judge the living and the dead. (1 Peter 4:5)

The first question that might come to mind here is: Who is Peter speaking about when he says *they will give an account*? It could mean the saved, or it could mean the unsaved, and both would be true statements. Both the saved and the unsaved will stand before the judgment seat of Christ. Hebrews 9:27 says, "And as it is appointed for men to die once, but after this the judgment." Also, Paul says in 2 Corinthians 5:10, "For we must all appear before the judgment seat of Christ, that each one may receive the things done in the body, according to what he has done, whether good or bad." However, it is more likely that Peter is referring to the unsaved here, that the persecutors of these Christians will give account to God. Those who speak evil of these Christians will give account to God! The word *account* comes from the world of book-keeping, and it means to pay back. These unbelievers will spend all eternity paying back for the wickedness that they have done. Paul tells the persecuted

---

[63]PC Study Software—1993-1997—Robertson's Word Pictures in the New Testament

church at Thessalonica something similar in 2 Thessalonians 1:6, "Since it is a righteous thing with God to repay with tribulation those who trouble you." This would have been of some comfort to these persecuted Christians, to know that their persecutors would be called to account by God, and He will *judge the living and the dead*. Peter also mentions that He is *ready* to do so; this is a continued readiness as One fully qualified to exercise decisive judgment. *The living and the dead* would be those that are now living and those who have died. Knowing that the unsaved will give account on that day should cause us to pray for them and to have compassion on them. Knowing that we also will one day be judged should also cause us to live in holy fear here and not get caught up in past sins and be willing to suffer as a saint—and not as a sinner!

Peter then goes on to talk about some of these Christians who have already died.

> For this reason the gospel was preached also to those who are dead, that they might be judged according to men in the flesh, but live according to God in the spirit. (1 Peter 4:6)

Now verse six is a very difficult verse to interpret, almost as difficult as the spirits in prison from 1 Peter 3:19! I will give you the three main interpretations, and then tell you which one I think is right. Some think that Christ went into hell and preached to those there and gave them a second chance. I don't find any support biblically for this view. It cannot mean that dead people get a second change with the gospel, as that is not taught anywhere in Scripture, as we brought out in our last lesson. Others think that the dead are the believers in the Old Testament who did not live during the New Testament and had to wait for Christ to preach the gospel to them. There is no biblical support for this view, either. Still others think that this refers to the preaching of the gospel to those who had since then died. Those who are dead, then, would refer to those Christian believers who had already died. The Gospel was preached to them while they were living, they believed, and they have since then died. Remember, many of those reading this letter had already lost believing family members and friends to death by suffering and persecution. I believe this third view is correct because it makes more sense with the rest of the verse.

Notice that Peter goes on to say that they might be judged according to men in the flesh, but live according to God in the spirit. The result of their believing the Gospel was that while they were here on earth they were judged by men. This judgment was in the form of persecution because of their claim to Christ. When God brings judgment on a nation, He usually begins with His own people, as Peter will mention later on in verse 17. Just as Christ has suffered in the flesh, as we saw in verse 1, these Christians too were being judged in the flesh by suffering in their flesh. But, praise God, they live now according to God in the spirit. Many of them were martyred for their faith and are now living in heaven. These Christians may suffer persecution here, but who cares?! One day soon, they will live with God! Paul says in 2 Corinthians 4:17, "For our light affliction, which is but for a moment, is working for us a far more exceeding and eternal weight of glory." In fact, consider some of the martyr's prayers, and you will see that they knew this was true: "I know what must be done. Only now am I beginning to be a disciple. May nothing of powers visible or invisible prevent me that I may attain unto Jesus Christ. Come fire and cross and grapplings with wild beasts, the rending of my bones and body. Come all the torments of the wicked one upon me. Only let it be mine to attain unto Jesus Christ!"[64] Another: "There is but one king that I know, It is He that I love and worship. If I were to be killed a thousand times for my loyalty to him, I would still be His servant. Christ is on my lips, Christ is on my heart; no amount of suffering will take Him from me."[65] Yet another: "I ask nothing more than to suffer for the cause of my Lord Jesus Christ and by this to be saved. If I can do this, then I can stand in confidence and quiet before the judgment seat of my God and Savior, when, in accordance with His will, this world passes away."[66] And another: "Let the estates I own be ravaged, or

---

[64] Duane W. H. Arnold, *Prayers of the Martyrs* (Grand Rapids: Zondervan Publishing House, 1991), 26.
[65] Ibid; 29.
[66] Ibid; 33.

given to others: Let me loose my life, and let my body be destroyed, rather than I should speak one word against you, O Lord, who made me. If they take from me a small portion of this earth and its wealth, I shall exchange it for heaven."[67] Do you sense their attitude as they were being killed for their faith in Christ? Who cares if we suffer in the flesh, as long as we can live with God in the spirit for all eternity? The tables will be turned in the end, right? Those who now live in the flesh and slander believers will one day be judged and suffer eternally. Those who now suffer in the flesh and endure such persecution will enjoy life eternally.

What does the believer's future life entail, according to verses 5 and 6? Judgment to come, yes, but life with God eternally! What a blessing for us to meditate upon—we will be with God in heaven forever!

Summary

I don't know what suffering you are going through this day. Maybe some of you are being persecuted by your unsaved husband or by other family members that think you have lost your marbles. Perhaps your old friends think you're a fuddy duddy, and they do not understand why you don't participate in their ungodly activities. Maybe you have been tempted to turn back to your old way of life. Regardless of what you are facing, I want to encourage you this day to turn your face towards the Savior and look to the One who knows your pain! I want to encourage you to remember four things as we close out this lesson:

1. *Remember to arm yourself with the same mind Christ had during suffering.* Are you doing that? How have you done that? Do you saturate your mind with God's Word so you know how He would respond to suffering?

2. *Remember that your former way of life is not worth it because it has no lasting value.* What was your life like before Christ? Are you still participating in those evil deeds? If so, why?

---
[67]Ibid; 36.

3. *Remember that you will give an account to the One who is ready to judge.* God's Word says that we will all stand before Him and give account on the Day of Judgment. Are you ready for that? Do you pray for those who are persecuting you that they will repent before the Day of Judgment comes?

4. *Remember that you have a place prepared in heaven for you.* The suffering you are experiencing today pales in comparison to the joy you will have in heaven. "The pain now is part of the happiness then. That's the deal."[68]

These should be motivating factors for us to suffer righteously as we go through the fiery furnace with our Master!

The story is told of a man named George Matheson who was to be married to his college sweetheart. Before the wedding, he found out that he had some physical problem that would eventually lead to him becoming blind. His bride-to-be informed him that she did not wish to be the wife of a blind preacher and so she broke off the engagement. You can only imagine the rejection, the pain, and the suffering this man went through. But instead of becoming bitter and resentful, he turned his eyes upon Jesus and wrote a beautiful song, *Oh Love that Wilt Not Let Me Go.*

> Oh love that will not let me go
> I rest my weary soul in thee
> I give thee back the life I owe
> That in thine ocean depths its flow
> May richer fuller be.
>
> Oh joy that seekest me through pain
> I cannot close my heart to thee.
> I trace the rainbow through the rain
> And feel the promise is not vain
> That morn shall tearless be.[69]

---

[68] Words by C.S. Lewis from "Shadowlands."
[69] Words by George Matheson.

Questions to Consider
The Past, the Present, and the Future Life of a Believer
1 Peter 4:1-6

1. (a) As you read 1 Peter 4:1-6, try to put yourself in the shoes of these persecuted Christians. How would these verses be an encouragement to you? (b) How would they be a warning to you?

2. Memorize 1 Peter 4:2.

3. (a) Peter says in 1 Peter 4:2 that we are to suffer with the same mind (attitude) as our Lord did. What was the attitude that Christ displayed during suffering, according to Matthew 26:38-46; Luke 23:33-46; Philippians 2:5-8; 1 Peter 2:21-25? (b) Which of these attitudes is especially difficult for you when encountering suffering?

4. (a) What are some *biblical reasons* that we should not live as we used to live before we became Christians, according to 1 Corinthians 6:9-20; Galatians 5:19-22; Ephesians 4:17-32; 5:1-8; and 1 John 5:4? (b) What are some *practical reasons* that you can think of that we should not walk as we "once walked"?

5. (a) Who in Luke 15:11-32 was involved in "riotous living"? (b) Was it satisfying to his soul? Prove your answer with scripture. (c) Did he repent of his sinful life? Again, prove your answer with scripture. (d) What principles can you glean from this parable regarding "riotous living"?

6. (a) What are the reasons we should not get drunk, according to Proverbs 23:29-35 and Ephesians 5:18? (b) What are we do to instead, according to Ephesians 5:18? (c) What are some practical reasons that you can think of that we should not get drunk?

7. (a) What sins listed in 1 Peter 4:3 do you see mentioned also in Exodus 32? (b) What did God want to do to His people, according to Exodus 32:9-10? (c) What happened to them for their disobedience, according to Exodus 32:25-35? (d) What makes the Israelite's behavior especially grieving?

8. What are some principles for suffering from 2 Corinthians 4:8-18 that you could use to encourage yourself and others when encountering suffering?

9. How do you personally handle ridicule from others for your attachment to Christ?

10. Are you currently suffering because you are a Christian? Please write your need in the form of a prayer request.

Chapter 18

How to Occupy Until He Comes
1 Peter 4:7-8

I have some very vivid memories of growing up in a Baptist minister's home, especially a minister whose love was the return of our Lord. I remember specifically one Sunday evening coming out of the church and noticing that the sky looked quite unusual. I was standing next to an older lady who was looking up at the sky, and I clearly remember her saying, "Maybe it will be tonight! Wouldn't that be great?!" I remember sudden fear gripping my heart. "No way!" I thought, "I'm not ready! Why, I haven't graduated from high school, I'm not married, I haven't had children yet!" And a myriad of other excuses went through my mind. Years went by, and after graduating from high school, I went to Bible College, where I met my soon-to-be husband. I also have a vivid memory of sitting with him in the school cafeteria one day when the subject of the rapture came up. I immediately began to cry and said, "Don't bring that up, please!" He looked at me strangely, and I excused my fear by saying that Bible prophecy was all I heard growing up and I did not want to hear about it. Little did I know that I was fearful because I did not know the One who was coming one day from heaven to take His children home. I was self-deceived, thinking I was one of His children when I was not. We got married, had children, and life went on, and so did my fears regarding the Lord's return. It wasn't until around the age of 30 that the Lord plucked me from the pit, showed me my wretched self, and I repented of my sin and committed my life to the Lordship of Jesus Christ.

It was such an encouragement to me after my salvation, when I was studying 1 John 4:18, to read that John says, "There is no fear in love; but perfect love casts out fear, because fear involves torment. But he who fears has not been made perfect in love." John is talking about that time in heaven when we stand before God and we will have no terror of judgment. What a joy it was to my heart to finally realize why all those years I had been so terrified of the Lord's coming. I was scared for all those years because I hadn't really known Him, the One who is coming. I have no fear now of the time when He will come and take me home. In fact, you can talk to me about the rapture all you want and I won't cry, but I'll probably say, "Even so, come Lord Jesus!" The Lord's Coming—a theme that runs throughout much of the New Testament, and now here in 1 Peter. Let's hear what Peter has to say about this event!

1 Peter 4:7-8

> But the end of all things is at hand; therefore be serious and watchful in your prayers. ⁸And above all things have fervent love for one another, for "love will cover a multitude of sins."

Peter writes about what we are to do while we wait for the Lord's return. Because the end is near, then Peter says we are to be about certain things; we are to occupy in four different ways. And those four ways are not to eat, drink, do drugs, and party on! These are the kinds of things we did before salvation, as we saw in our last lesson. We will consider three of these four things in this lesson, and then in the following lesson we will cover the fourth thing we are to be about as we wait for our Lord's return.

> But the end of all things is at hand; therefore be serious and watchful in your prayers. (1 Peter 4:7)

The word *but* introduces a new train of thought, which is suggested by the mention of judgment that Peter has been talking about in the previous verses. Judgment would remind us of the Lord's coming! Peter reminds his readers that judgment is not that far off by the words *the end of all things is at hand*. The word *end* refers to a consummation, a goal achieved. What is this goal achieved that Peter is talking about? When we consider what Peter has been writing about—a living hope (1:3); the last time (1:5); the appearing of Jesus Christ (1:7); the revelation of Jesus Christ (1:13); and the judgment of the living and the dead (4:5-6)—then we can see that the end of all things is the Christian's hope, which is Christ's return.

The Greek word that is translated as *of all things* is in the emphatic position, meaning that it has the emphasis in the sentence. So, it would read, "of all things the end is at hand." *At hand* means that it is near, it is approaching. It's similar to what we saw in 1 Peter 4:5, where we learned that God is ready to judge the living and the dead. It is similar to what Paul says in Romans 13:11-12, "And do this, knowing the time, that now it is high time to awake out of sleep; for now our salvation is nearer than when we first believed. The night is far spent, the day is at hand. Therefore let us cast off the works of darkness, and let us put on the armor of light." And, as Paul states in Philippians 4:5, "Let your gentleness be known to all men. The Lord is at hand." Even James reminds his readers of this fact, in James 5:8, when he writes, "You also be patient. Establish your hearts, for the coming of the Lord is at hand." The idea here is that He is at the door ready to open it. (Also, other passages to consider are 1 John 2:18 and Revelation 22:20.) The Christians in the early church expected Jesus to return in their lifetime. Acts 1:11 states, "This same Jesus, who was taken up from you into heaven, will so come in like manner as you saw Him go into heaven." During the Reformation, believers thought that the end was near. And today, because of international happenings and the moral decline of our own nation, we often hear believers saying, "Surely, it can't be much longer!"

The fact that Christ has not yet returned does not mean He won't. Peter says in 2 Peter 3:3-10,

> knowing this first: that scoffers will come in the last days, walking according to their own lusts, and saying, "Where is the promise of His coming? For since the fathers fell asleep, all things continue as they were from the beginning of creation." For this they willfully forget: that by the word of God the heavens were of old, and the earth standing out of water and in the water, by which the world that then existed perished, being flooded with water. But the heavens and the earth which are now preserved by the same word, are reserved for fire until the day of judgment and perdition of ungodly men. But, beloved, do not forget this one thing, that with the Lord one day is

as a thousand years, and a thousand years as one day. The Lord is not slack concerning His promise, as some count slackness, but is longsuffering toward us, not willing that any should perish but that all should come to repentance. But the day of the Lord will come as a thief in the night, in which the heavens will pass away with a great noise, and the elements will melt with fervent heat; both the earth and the works that are in it will be burned up.

There will be some who think He's not going to come again. But Peter reminds his readers that one day is with the Lord as a thousand years and a thousand years as one day. Time is nothing to God; He is eternal. The hours pass by neither fast nor slowly to Him. He is not slack or tardy concerning His promise to return. He will come when it is the appointed time. We also know from Matthew 24 that there are certain things which must happen first before the coming of Christ.

Notice that here in 1 Peter, Peter does not set a date for the end, as some in our day are doing. Matthew 24:36 says that no man, not even the angels in heaven, know the day or the hour of Christ's return, except the Father. He is the only one who knows. And when He tells the Son to come and get His children, then the Son will come. Regardless of when it will be, you and I must be ready at all times, because you and I do not know when it will be. But we do know this, that with each passing day the coming of our Lord is nearer than the day before.

So, what should be the attitude of these readers, and us, in light of the Lord's return? Should we eat and party as much as we can? No! *Because the end is near, Peter says we should first of all be serious or soberminded. This is the first thing we must be doing while we are waiting for the Lord's return.* If we really thought that the Lord's coming was today, we would be serious. We would sober up, wouldn't we? And yet, we are to live as though it could be today. The word *serious*, or sober, is a word we learned of when we were studying 1 Peter 1:13, and it means to be of sound mind or to be clear-headed. The temptation for many of these readers would be to have all kinds of fears and worries, which would lead them to make hasty and wrong decisions. They must have sobriety of mind. Peter says, be alert! Don't dull your mind with drink—and I would add with drugs. My friend, we are living in an age that has a drug addiction, whether it be prescription drugs or illegal drugs. We are far from being soberminded!

Again, Peter is not the only writer of Scripture who addresses our need for sobriety in light of the Lord's return. Consider 1 Thessalonians 5:1-8:

> But concerning the times and the seasons, brethren, you have no need that I should write to you. For you yourselves know perfectly that the day of the Lord so comes as a thief in the night. For when they say, "Peace and safety!" then sudden destruction comes upon them, as labor pains upon a pregnant woman. And they shall not escape. But you, brethren, are not in darkness, so that this Day should overtake you as a thief. You are all sons of light and sons of the day. We are not of the night nor of darkness. Therefore let us not sleep, as others do, but let us watch and be sober. For those who sleep, sleep at night, and those who get drunk are drunk at night. But let us who are of the day be sober, putting on the breastplate of faith and love, and as a helmet the hope of salvation.

Also Titus 2:12-13, "teaching us that, denying ungodliness and worldly lusts, we should live soberly, righteously, and godly in the present age, looking for the blessed hope and glorious appearing of our great God and Savior Jesus Christ." These passages all agree with the idea that being soberminded is necessary for the Christian, especially in light of the Lord's coming. Peter is saying: We must have our wits about us, so to speak. It always amazes me when I see more and more people turning to drugs and alcohol to alleviate their fears and worries. People cannot face the reality of life and death, so they turn to numbing drugs. But, for the Christian, we have a different place to turn, and that is the second thing we should be about in light of the Lord's return.

Peter goes on to write that we are to be watchful in our prayers. This is the second thing we must do in light of Jesus' return. This is not the first time Peter has talked about prayer in this epistle. He drew our attention to this necessary practice in 1 Peter 1:17; 2:4; 3:7; and 3:12. What does it mean to be *watchful in your prayers*? The word *watchful* means to be sober, to abstain from wine, to be calm and collected in spirit. So the idea is that we are to be sober so that we can pray. If we are drugged or drunk, we likely are not apt to pray. The need for sobriety is so that we can pray. The temptation would be to drown one's sorrows in wine, but instead, Peter says one must turn to prayer. We see this same propensity in our own culture even now as people are turning to drugs and alcohol for consolation. Instead of repenting before a Holy God, they are rebelling by becoming more engrossed in evil. People's lives are increasingly difficult because of moral decay and so they are more and more willing to turn to drugs. But that should not be the case for the child of God! Drugs and alcohol dull one's mind and keep them from facing reality. "Temperance promotes wakefulness; both promote prayer. Drink makes drowsy; drowsiness prevents prayer."[70] Peter's readers must be discreet and sober so that they can pray. "The Christian who is always on a tear, whose mind is crowded with fears and worries, who is never at rest in his heart, does not do much praying"[71] These believers during their time of persecution would need their wits about them so that they could be prayerful. Think about it: if our minds are confused with drink or drugs, then we will be confused when we pray. I have counseled many women who are on some type of psychotropic drug, and it is difficult at times because their minds are so cloudy they can't think or reason. Paul communicates a similar truth in Philippians 4:6-7 "Be anxious for nothing, but in everything by prayer and supplication, with thanksgiving, let your requests be made known to God; and the peace of God, which surpasses all understanding, will guard your hearts and minds through Christ Jesus." Peter, of course would know the heartache of this admonition, because he himself was not watchful unto prayer with His Lord, in Mark 14:32-38:

---

[70] PC Study Software—1993-1997; (from Jamieson, Fausset, and Brown Commentary)

[71] Kenneth Wuest, *Word Studies in the Greek New Testament, Volume II* (Grand Rapids: Eerdman's Publishing Company; 1973), 115.

> Then they came to a place which was named Gethsemane; and He said to His disciples, "Sit here while I pray." And He took Peter, James, and John with Him, and He began to be troubled and deeply distressed. Then He said to them, "My soul is exceedingly sorrowful, even to death. Stay here and watch." He went a little farther, and fell on the ground, and prayed that if it were possible, the hour might pass from Him. And He said, "Abba, Father, all things are possible for You. Take this cup away from Me; nevertheless, not what I will, but what You will." Then He came and found them sleeping, and said to Peter, "Simon, are you sleeping? Could you not watch one hour? Watch and pray, lest you enter into temptation. The spirit truly is willing, but the flesh is weak."

Also, in Ephesians 6:18, Paul says, "Praying always with all prayer and supplication in the Spirit, being watchful to this end with all perseverance and supplication for all the saints." And then again, in Colossians 4:2, "Continue earnestly in prayer, being vigilant in it with thanksgiving."

It is interesting that the word for *prayer* here in 1 Peter is plural, which would indicate that it refers to prayers. Peter does not explicitly state what they should be praying for, but certain things do come to my mind as I think about the end of all things drawing near. Prayers of thanksgiving would be in order, for sure—for the fact we have been chosen and are going to escape the awful torment of hell. We should also be expressing gratitude that we have a place in heaven prepared for us. We should be much in prayer about living holy lives in preparation to meet the Lord. We should be asking Him how we should live until He comes. We should be confessing any known sin to Him and to others. We should be praying for those who do not know the Lord, for the salvation of their souls. We should be praying for those who would be left behind. And the list goes on and on of prayers we should be offering up to God. If we really thought the end was near, that Christ might return *today*, don't you think we would be more prayerful? I think we would! My dear sister, we must be praying at all times and for all things.

The third thing we must be about as we wait for our Lord's return is found in verse 8.

> And above all things have fervent love for one another, for "love will cover a multitude of sins." (1 Peter 4:8)

Peter says *above all things*, which means prior to or in front of all things, we are to have *love* for each other. This does not mean that love is preeminent over prayer. It means that love is the heading to all we do. It's like in Colossians 3, where Paul has a list of put-offs and put-ons and then he says in verse 14, "But above all these things put on love, which is the bond of perfection." In other words, love bathes everything else we do. Or, like Paul writes in Galatians 5:22-23 regarding the fruit of the Spirit. The first thing he mentions is Love! "But the fruit of the Spirit is love, joy, peace, longsuffering, kindness, goodness, faithfulness, gentleness, self-control. Against such there is no law." Love is the preeminent fruit from which all of the others flow. It is also as Paul mentions in 1 Corinthians 13, where he lists all these things we can do, like speak in tongues, prophesy, give our bodies to be burned, give everything to feed the poor, and yet he says if we don't do these things in love we are a big zero!

Notice that Peter doesn't just say love, he says *fervent love*. This is the same way he put it in 1 Peter 1:22, where he told his readers to love one another fervently. We saw then that the word *fervent* means to be intent, to be stretched out. It was used of an athlete who would strain to win a race—you've probably seen that very thing in the Olympics. The idea is that of a love that stretches out to reach the one loved. It gives of himself or herself for others. It is willing to spend and be spent for others, as Paul says in 2 Corinthians 12:15. Notice also that this love is among themselves, *for one another*. Peter has already mentioned the importance of this to them previously in several places: 1 Peter 1:22; 2:17; and 3:8.

Peter then gives a reason why his readers are to have fervent love among themselves. He says *love will cover a multitude of sins*. Now, what does this mean? There are some erroneous ideas about this, so let's look at it carefully. The word *cover* means to conceal or hide. The word *multitude* means a large number or a bundle. Peter knew the idea of a bundle; when he asked the Lord in Matthew 18:22

how many times he had to forgive someone—like seven, maybe?—Jesus responded with, "How about 70 x 7, Peter?" Now, that's a bundle in deed! I'm not sure if I have ever forgiven someone that many times for the same offense! Again, Peter is not the only writer to mention this idea. Similar ideas are found in Proverbs 10:12, "Hatred stirs up strife, but love covers all sins." And Proverbs 17:9, "He who covers a transgression seeks love, but he who repeats a matter separates friends." Even James mentions in James 5:20, "Let him know that he who turns a sinner from the error of his way will save a soul from death and cover a multitude of sins." Most of us have heard the phrase "love is blind," and how true that notion is! Love certainly blinds us to the faults of others. I remember when I first met my husband, I could not see one fault of his. My love for him overlooked any faults he might have had. When trying to help young women who are considering marriage, you realize that any counsel you give might go right over their heads because they are blind to any faults others might see in their soon-to-be spouse. One man describes it like this:

> There in your local church there is Ann, who doesn't know much about hygiene and is frankly smelly. Billy wears you out with incessant talking. Cathy is unspiritual. Don doesn't get along with Evelyn. Fred treats his wife badly. Gene is a gauche teenager who never knows how to act with courtesy and discretion. Hilary often grumbles. Irene has a different set of interests and values (she can't come to the Tuesday evening prayer meeting because it clashes with the local Amnesty International group.) Then there is Kevin, to be sure, who is really quite saintly but rather drab as a person. And so it goes on. None of them is very easy to love at full stretch. [72]

And yet we are commanded to do so. By the way, this writer also adds that he is probably on someone's list too as well as a difficult person! My husband and I have often talked about various family members who we think are a little odd, but then we chuckle, saying that they are probably talking about us as well and how weird we are!

---

[72] I. Howard Marshall, *IVP New Testament Commentary Series: 1 Peter* (Downers Grove: IVP Academic, 1991), 143.

What Peter is saying here is that we should be forgiving and patient and we should accept others, even with all their faults. Peter sure knew about this from personal experience, when he was questioned by the Lord three times about his love, in John 21. Jesus could have said, "Come on, Peter, give me a break! You don't love me! Why, you denied me three times! Do you expect me to believe that you love Me?" But Jesus' love for Peter covered Peter's sins and overlooked his weaknesses. I am sure Peter remembered that conversation as he wrote these words in his epistle. When we truly love each other, we will not publish each other's sins, but will instead cover them. "Where love is lacking, every word is viewed with suspicion, every action is liable to misunderstanding, and conflicts abound—to Satan's perverse delight."[73] "How much gossip is eliminated when we love each other."[74] The person that doesn't love others the way Christ would have them to is often critical and judgmental.

Now, let me clarify here that love does not deceptively cover up sin, nor does it conceal sin when the sinner goes on sinning. Those ideas are really reading into the text things that Peter does not intend. Jesus' point in Matthew 18, that whenever sin occurs, love deals with it according to the principles that Jesus set up for us to follow. But when repentance occurs, then we are to do what Jesus told Peter, to forgive 70 x 7, and we don't hold others' sins against them. We don't keep records of wrongs done to us.

I also would like to say another word about Matthew 18, because as a pastor's wife for many years, I came to see that people often will share with their pastor and his wife the sins of others without first going to the sinning person and following the steps laid out in Matthew 18. Please follow the steps in Matthew 18. What do you do when you hear of someone's sin? What is your first reaction? Do you call a friend? Do you think the worst of the person? Do you call them to see if what you heard is really true? Or, do you expect the best and want to protect them from further exposure? Are you

---

[73] Wayne Grudem, *Tyndale New Testament Commentaries: 1 Peter* (Grand Rapids: Eerdman's Publishing Co.), 173-174.

[74] Kenneth Wuest, *Word Studies in the Greek New Testament, Volume II* (Grand Rapids: Eerdman's Publishing Company; 1973), 115.

willing to confront sins when necessary and help the sinning person? How you react to such things really shows the quality of your love.

When we think about the return of our Lord, we certainly should be focusing on loving the brethren. In fact, the writer to the Hebrew says in 10:24-25, "And let us consider one another in order to stir up love and good works, not forsaking the assembling of ourselves together, as is the manner of some, but exhorting one another, and so much the more as you see the Day approaching." As the end of the age winds down, we must be about loving one another more and more!

So Peter says, while we wait for His return, love each other, stay clear-headed, and be alert in prayer. The end is at hand, and when it comes, what will you have done for the glory of God?

Summary

What should we be doing while we are waiting for the Lord to return? What are *you* doing while you wait for His return? Are you sitting up late to watch the latest tragedy in our nation and becoming hysterical about it all, or are you working on having a level head and being soberminded? Are you worrying about what will happen to those you love who will be left behind, or are you spending that time in prayer for them? Are you stirring up trouble and holding grudges, or are you loving others to the maximum?

I don't know what you believe concerning the end times. You may be a postmillennialist, an amillenialist, or a premillennialist. You might believe in a posttribulational, midtribulational, or a pretribulational return of Christ. Or you may be none of the above and hold to a "pan-millenialist" view—that is, that it will all pan out in the end! Believe me, I am not trying to prove an eschatological system—but I am encouraging you to be prepared till He comes. As one man has said, here's what you don't do: "You don't whip up a white robe and buy a helium-filled balloon with angels painted all over it. And, if you're a Californian, don't quit work and move to Oregon for fear you'll miss Him because of the smog. And for goodness' sake, don't try to set the date because of the 'signs of the times!'"[75] The fact that He is coming should motivate us to live holy lives. We should be living soberly and righteously. We should be watching with an attitude of prayer, and loving one another fervently and using our spiritual gifts, as we will see in our next lesson. We should love each new day as if it were our last and live each day as if it were our last—and, my friend, it just might be!

Perhaps, as I said in the beginning of this lesson, you are terrified of the Lord's return. Maybe you don't want to talk about it with others, and you find it hard to share in their excitement. And so, perhaps the issue for you is that you are like I was, you're not ready to meet the Lord. If your life is not consistent with your profession of faith, then the coming of the Lord will naturally be a dreaded event for you. May I plead with you? If you're not ready to go, then get ready! But don't wait. Today, if you will hear His voice, do not harden your heart. Don't put off committing your life to His Lordship—or you may find yourself looking back and not up. And then, my friend, it will be too late.

---

[75]Charles Swindoll, *Come Before Winter* (Portland: Multnomah Press, 1985), 341.

Questions to Consider
How to Occupy Until He Comes
1 Peter 4:7-8

(You may want to glance at question 8 first)

1. (a) Read 1 Peter 4 and list all the commands you find. (b) How many did you find? (c) List the reasons why Peter perhaps gives these commands.

2. Memorize 1 Peter 4:7.

3. (a) In light of the Lord's return, what should we be doing, according to Matthew 25; Mark 13:32-37; Romans 13:11-14; 1 Corinthians 15:58; 1 Thessalonians 5:1-11; Hebrews 10:19-25; James 5:8-12; 1 Peter 4:7-11; 2 Peter 3:1-14, and 1 John 2:28? (b) What are some ways you are "occupying your time" until the Lord's return?

4. (a) Why should we avoid predicting dates for the Lord's Second Coming, according to Matthew 24:36-44? (b) According to Matthew 24:4-31 what things have to happen first?

5. (a) Who covered another's sin in Genesis 9:20-23? (b) What was the sin that was committed? (c) Who covered another's sin in 1 Samuel 25? (d) What was the sin that was committed? (e) What happened to the sinner, according to verses 36-38? (f) What principles can you glean from these two stories about covering the sins of others?

6. (a) What should we do when someone is in sin, according to Leviticus 19:17 and Matthew 18:15-20? (b) What should we do if they don't repent, according to the Matthew passage, and 1 Corinthians 5:9-13 and 2 Thessalonians 3:6, 14-15? (c) How

does this reconcile with what Peter says in 1 Peter 4:8, that "love will cover a multitude of sins"?

7. (a) Why is church discipline (Matthew 18:15-20) a loving thing to do? (b) Why do you think most churches do not practice this command from God?

8. Examine your prayer life this week and answer the following questions: (a) Do you pray from a sense of duty or are you compelled to pray? (b) Do you pray infrequently or briefly? (c) Do your prayers center on your needs or the needs of others? (d) Do your prayers center mainly on spiritual matters or earthly concerns?

9. Look over your answers from question three, and then write a prayer request on how you might better "occupy your time till He comes."

Chapter 19

Knowing and Using Your Spiritual Gifts for the Glory of God

1 Peter 4:9-11

The human body is often referred to as a machine—in fact, the most wonderful machine ever built! Of course, we know that our bodies *are not* machines but have been created by our wonderful Creator and have been created in His image. However, we can compare our bodies to machines in the sense that our bodies are made up of many parts, and each part, like a machine, has a special job. All the parts of our bodies work together so that our bodies run smoothly, just as all the parts of a machine must work together so that the machine will run smoothly. As an example, let's take a car, which is a machine: if you don't have gas in your tank, you're not going anywhere because the car won't work. If your brakes malfunction, you can almost guarantee a wreck. The windshield wipers need to work, the transmission, the tires, and so on. All the parts need to be working for the car to run properly. So it is with our physical bodies. As Paul says in 1 Corinthians 13, the eye cannot say to the hand, "Hey, get lost!" (my paraphrase), nor can the head say to the foot, "I don't need you!" All the parts of a body have a job to do, and they all work together. What happens when one of our bodily parts malfunctions, like in a brain injury, or a broken leg, or some type of cancer? Well, the whole body suffers, and the whole body doesn't work properly. You might be wondering, "Susan, what is your point?" My point is this: Everyone who knows the Lord is a part of His body, and each of us has at least one function, one spiritual gift, that is to be used to make the body of Christ run as it ought to.

What happens when one person in the body doesn't use the gift or gifts God has given them to benefit and to help the body of Christ run smoothly? Well, the spiritual body malfunctions, and there is an unnecessary strain on the rest of the body of Christ. It is my earnest prayer for all of us, and for the body of Christ worldwide, that we would discover our spiritual gifts and use them to God's glory. To do so is to lead a fulfilled life to the glory of God. To not do so, is to lead an unfulfilled life, put strain on the rest of the body, and bring shame to the name of Christ.

What are the Spiritual Gifts?
Selected Scriptures

First of all, what are the spiritual gifts? To see what the gifts are, let's read together the passages of Scripture that specifically address them:

> For as we have many members in one body, but all the members do not have the same function, so we, being many, are one body in Christ, and individually members of one another. Having then gifts differing according to the grace that is given to us, let us use them: if prophecy, let us prophesy in proportion to our faith; or ministry, let us use it in our ministering; he who teaches, in teaching; he who exhorts, in exhortation; he who gives, with liberality; he who leads, with diligence; he who shows mercy, with cheerfulness. (Romans 12:4-8)

> There are diversities of gifts, but the same Spirit. There are differences of ministries, but the same Lord. And there are diversities of activities, but it is the same God who works all in all. But the manifestation of the Spirit is given to each one for the profit of all: for to one is given the word of wisdom through the Spirit, to another the word of knowledge through the same Spirit, to another faith by the same Spirit, to another gifts of healings by the same Spirit, to another the working of miracles, to another prophecy, to another discerning of spirits, to another different kinds of tongues, to another the interpretation of tongues. But one and the same Spirit works all these things, distributing to each one individually as He wills. ... And God has appointed these in the church: first apostles, second prophets, third teachers, after that miracles, then gifts of healings, helps, administrations, varieties of tongues. (1 Corinthians 12:4-11, 28)

> And He Himself gave some to be apostles, some prophets, some evangelists, and some pastors and teachers, for the equipping of the saints for the work of ministry, for the edifying of the body of Christ. (Ephesians 4:11-12)

> Be hospitable to one another without grumbling. As each one has received a gift, minister it to one another, as good stewards of the manifold grace of God. If anyone speaks, let him speak as the oracles of God. If anyone ministers, let him do it as with the ability which God supplies, that in all things God may be glorified through Jesus Christ, to whom belong the glory and the dominion forever and ever. Amen. (1 Peter 4:9-11)

All the gifts listed in the Word of God, in these passages in Romans 12, 1 Corinthians 12, Ephesians 4, and 1 Peter 4, fall under two categories, speaking gifts or serving gifts. Now, as they are listed in the New Testament, there are 19 spiritual gifts. It's possible that there have been other gifts given, but they are not mentioned in the New Testament. Let me say, before I explain these gifts, that there is a lot of differing opinion on some of these gifts, and I am not the expert on these things. In fact, my son took a class on spiritual gifts when he was in seminary and he told me that he was more confused after that class about what the gifts were, and that the class raised a lot of questions in his mind. What I would encourage you to do is to be a good Berean and study this subject on your own. What I am going to do here is to briefly list the gifts and define them for you.

These first five gifts were given to the apostles and the prophets in the early church for the purpose of confirming the gospel. They were temporary gifts.

1. **Healing.** This gift was given to Christ and the apostles; it included a word or touch that caused complete healing to all that were touched by it. It was not a partial healing, nor did those possessing this gift have to attempt several tries at it. The healing was instant, it was thorough, and it was permanent. It also included raising the dead. In Matthew 4:23, we read that Jesus went about healing the sick and, according to John 11, He

raised Lazarus from the dead. In Matthew 10:1, Jesus gave the twelve apostles the power to heal all kinds of sickness and all kinds of disease. No Christian today has the gift of healing, or else they would be clearing out the hospitals. However, let me say that I believe God is still in the business of miraculously healing whomever He wills, whenever and however He wills.

2. **Miracles.** This was a supernatural intrusion into the natural world and its natural laws, explainable only by divine intervention. Examples of such miraculous events include the turning of water into wine in John 2, and the feeding of the 5000 and 4000 in Matthew 14 and 15. These were miraculous abilities given to the apostles and other early Christians to authenticate God's message. No person today possesses the gift of miracles, but I believe that God can and does do miraculous things when it pleases Him to do so!

3. **Tongues.** The Greek word for tongues is <u>dialekto</u>, from which we get our English word dialect, and it means human languages. This is the supernatural gift of speaking in another language without its having been learned or previously known. We know this from Acts 2, where the people heard the disciples of Jesus speaking in their native languages—not a heavenly gibberish, as is claimed by many today. Paul also tells us in 1 Corinthians 14:22 that tongues were given as a sign for the unbeliever, to confirm the authenticity of the gospel message. The gift of tongues was given for the authentication of the gospel among those who had not yet believed it.

4. **Interpretation of Tongues.** This was a special gift of the Spirit given in conjunction with the gift of tongues. The person with the gift of interpretation of tongues possesses a supernatural ability to interpret the message given by the person speaking in a tongue; like the one speaking in a previously unknown tongue, the interpreter would also not have previously known the tongue spoken. Many who were endowed with the gift of tongues did not know the language they were speaking in when

they utilized their gift, and so it had to be interpreted by one who possessed the gift of interpreting such tongues.

5. **Apostleship.** This, too, was a gift given only to the early church. According to Acts 1:21-23 and 1 Corinthians 9:1-2, an apostle must have had personal contact with Jesus and been an eyewitness of His resurrection. If someone tries to tell you today that they are an apostle, take them to these passages to demonstrate to them the error of their thinking.

The remaining 14 gifts were permanent gifts given for the purpose of equipping and edifying the body of Christ in an ongoing way.

6. **Wisdom.** The gift of wisdom is the ability to apply wisdom to the body of believers in difficult situations, and knowing what is right and wrong. This person simply knows how to rightly apply the truths discovered in God's Word. These people usually make good counselors and pastors.

7. **Knowledge.** A person who has the gift of knowledge can perceive and understand the truths of God's Word. These people usually make good scholars and professors.

8. **Prophecy.** The word prophecy simply means to speak forth or to proclaim. A prophet is one who simply speaks forth God's Word and proclaims it. Now, I will say that there is some debate on this gift; some think it is the gift given to the prophets in the Old Testament who were able to foretell the future and preach against impending judgment. But that seems to be different than what Paul is speaking of in 1 Corinthians 12. A prophet is simply someone who heralds the truth. I know I have the gift of prophecy, of proclaiming the truth of God's Word, but not in the sense of foretelling the future.

9. **Distinguishing of Spirits or Discernment.** The person who possesses this gift has a special ability to discern whether

something is demonic or divine, whether something or someone is genuine and or spurious. First John 4:1-3 provides us a test for how we can discern the true from the false, but individuals with this gift seem to have a divinely-given enabling in this regard.

10. **Faith**. The gift of faith consists of a special ability to believe God concerning anything. This person is known for bringing everything to God in prayer in great trust.

11. **Evangelism.** A person who possesses the gift of evangelism has an unusual ability to persuade lost people to embrace Christ as Lord and Savior and put their faith in Him. These people usually have persuasive abilities, and while they do not have 100% success rates in their evangelism, they certainly have a far better average than those who do not have this gift. My dad had this gift, and he rarely let an opportunity go by without sharing the gospel, even up to his death at the age of 96!

12. **Teaching.** A person with the gift of teaching has the ability to grasp, arrange, and present truth effectively and in an organized manner so that their audience is able to clearly understand the Scripture.

13. **Pastor/Teacher.** This gift is related to the gift of teaching but also includes shepherding gifts. The person who possesses this gift is someone who expresses pastoral care for the sheep that God has given them. This gift not only includes the feeding of one's flock but also looking out for and tending to the needs of those who are sick, in sin, discouraged, or the like. You might have heard the phrase, "He has a pastor's heart," to describe a person with this gift. That would be a pretty good indication that such a person has the gift of pastor-teacher.

14. **Exhortation.** A person with the gift of exhortation has a special ability to call others to action and to convince others to get their lives back in harmony with God's will. They do this by

both admonishing and encouraging. People with the gift of exhortation often make good counselors.

15. **Helps or service.** This gift encompasses both desire and effectiveness in assisting and laboring behind the scenes. A person with this gift would be someone who excels at tasks such as running the sound booth, setting up and tearing down after events, managing the nursery, and things like that. This person does not necessarily like to be seen, but simply enjoys serving.

16. **Showing mercy.** This person would be one who effectively relieves the distress and suffering of others, aiding those who are in some kind of misery, pain, or anxiety.

17. **Giving.** The gift of giving is evident in a person who has a special ability to invest material substance in spiritual undertakings, such that they are able to reap maximum spiritual dividends. Those with this gift are also apt to give sacrificially in order to meet the needs of others.

18. **Administration or Ruling.** This person possesses the ability to organize and wisely direct people and projects. Those with this gift often head up committees, teams, functions, and events.

19. **Hospitality.** The gift of hospitality shows up in a person who loves strangers, loves to make people feel welcome and included, and is effective at both. They enjoy opening their home to people, even people they do not know, and making them feel welcome.

There are spiritual gift tests out there that a believer can take to help him or her get some idea of their giftedness; some of those tests are fairly good, and some I would not recommend. But I don't think the New Testament saints took any sort of spiritual gifts tests; rather, like us, they were simply given gifts by the Holy Spirit and they used them. We are endowed with these gifts, as Paul says in 1 Corinthians

12:11; the Holy Spirit distributes to each one individually as He wills. So, every believer in Jesus Christ has at least one gift; many have more than one gift.

Now, you may be wondering how one would come to know what gift they have been blessed with—especially if there isn't a test to determine one's gift! I believe one way we come to know what our gifts are is that God begins to impress upon us the need to serve Him, and as we yield to those promptings we excel in whatever He has gifted us to do for His glory. Another way we come to know our gifts is to ask those close to us—our husbands or good friends, who watch our lives and know us well.

For example, my main gifts are teaching, prophecy, and exhortation. Those are my strongest gifts. How did I know that? I have a love to study the Word and to understand it and to pass it on. I have a burning desire to help people when they are struggling with sin. I have a desire to admonish in love so that those who are erring might get back on track spiritually. Now, I have sharpened my gifts over the years, and so should you; first, because the Lord would have us do everything with excellence, and, second, because He has commanded us to do everything heartily, as unto Him. Once you know what God has gifted you to do, then it is your responsibility to sharpen those gifts to the glory of God and the maximum impact of His kingdom. Jesus told us in John 15:16 that we have been ordained to bring forth much fruit, and Paul states in Titus 2:14 that we are to be zealous for good works.

Those are the gifts given by the Spirit of God. But there are certain attitudes that must also accompany our gifts as we use them. The apostle Peter gives us five attitudes that must be present as you and I serve our Lord with the gifts He has given us.

Five Attitudes That Must Be Present as We Use Our Spiritual Gifts

1 Peter 4:9-11

> Be hospitable to one another without grumbling. ¹⁰As each one has received a gift, minister it to one another, as good stewards of the manifold grace of God. ¹¹If anyone speaks, let him speak as the oracles of God. If anyone ministers, let him do it as with the ability which God supplies, that in all things God may be glorified through Jesus Christ, to whom belong the glory and the dominion forever and ever. Amen.

Let's look at the first attitude that must be present as we serve.

> Be hospitable to one another without grumbling. (1 Peter 4:9)

Peter says we are to *be hospitable to each other without grumbling*. *Hospitable* means to be fond of guests or friendly to strangers. Hospitality in biblical times is not what we think of as hospitality in the 21st century. Our definition of hospitality is having friends and family over for dinner and a night of fellowship. We might also throw in some occasional overnight company with some relatives or friends from out of town. That was not how it was in biblical times. Hotels were a rare commodity, and even the inns that were available were filthy, notoriously immoral, and basically unsafe. So there was a great need for travelers to find a safe place to rest and eat. Christians, above all people, should be hospitable, and should be hospitable to other believers in need. (Acts has some great examples of this for you to study on your own sometime: Acts 16:15; 16:32-34; 21:7; and 28:14.) This hospitality that Peter is commanding would also be a willingness to hold church services in one's home, since there was no such thing as a church building in New Testament times. Official church buildings did not exist until almost 200 years after the church began. Instead, churches met in homes, or rented buildings, which were also used for other purposes, and so there was a need for homes which had big rooms to hold congregations. (Other passages that mention such hospitality, that I'd encourage you search out on your own sometime, include Romans 16:23;

1 Corinthians 16:19; and Colossians 4:15.) Now, in our day, we don't have much need to hold a formal church gathering in our homes, nor do we have much need for strangers to stay with us who are traveling through town and need a place to stay, because there are nice accommodations available in most cities. But, nonetheless, we should still be hospitable, especially to those in need. For example, missionaries might need a place to stay; people who live alone might need a place to live or a family to join for the holidays; or a family may be in dire need of accommodations. Interestingly, one of the qualifications of a church elder, according to Titus 1:8 and 1 Timothy 3:2, is that they be hospitable.

There is also an attitude that should accompany our hospitality, and Peter says it is no *grumbling* or murmuring. The Greek term denotes a muttering or low speaking as a sign of displeasure. It would be a natural temptation to be resentful of frequent strangers who need food and lodging night after night after night. But we should not complain about the inconvenience on our time and schedule; we should not murmur about the extra work load, the cooking and cleaning, and even the extra money it takes to be hospitable. We should not even grumble in our thoughts! Peter is challenging us to see these opportunities for hospitality as opportunities to serve the Lord. How would you feel if you knew that the person's house you were staying at considered you nothing more than trouble and inconvenience? Now, I confess to you, even though I love company and visitors, I usually prefer to know that they're coming somewhat ahead of time. So, this would definitely be a test for me and many women, I am sure.

The story of Sarah amazes me, when Abraham told her to go and prepare for those three unexpected guests, and she just did it with no complaining. That's what Peter is saying here. Complaint spoils hospitality. And, of course, it goes without saying that it is not only hospitality that should be performed without grumbling, but all of our gifts. *Attitude number one is serve the Lord without grumbling.* Paul says in Philippians 2:14, "Do all things without complaining and disputing." Consider this: What if I started complaining to the Lord and to my husband about all the time it takes to teach and write? What if I said, "I'm sick of doing women's Bible studies and traveling and doing conferences! I just want to stay home!" or "I'm tired of all the time and study teaching requires!"? Our attitude in serving must be one of gratitude to the Lord, not grumbling. In fact, James tells us in James 5:9 that we are not to grumble lest we be judged. Even inward attitudes of murmuring will be judged one day. It is a privilege to serve our Lord who saved us and we should do it with a joyful heart!

Peter also gives a second attitude that should be present in our service to God, in verse 10.

> As each one has received a gift, minister it to one another, as good stewards of the manifold grace of God. (1 Peter 4:10)

What Peter is saying here is in whatever quality or quantity of gift God has given you, use it to minister, and in so doing be a good steward of what God has given you. A *gift* is a spiritual endowment or enablement that is given by God. A gift is not something you can conjure up yourself, but rather God gives it. So, if you don't have a certain gift, you should not fret over it or be jealous of others' gifts. God will give you the gift or gifts that He knows will best suit you and will glorify Him. Also, let me say here that even though you may not have the gift of evangelism, you still should be sharing the gospel. If you don't have the gift of mercy, you still should be merciful to others. So, don't make excuses and say, "Well, I don't have the gift." We all should be pursuing Christlikeness and the command to be holy as He is holy which is given in the Word. The point is not what gifts you have been blessed with; the point is using them, as Peter says.

Peter says *minister it to one another*. Here we have *one another* again. Just like the hospitality is to be shown to one another, so the using of our gifts is to be for one another. The exercise of our gifts is not about us; it is for the edification of the body of Christ, as Paul states in Ephesians 4:12. Our use of our gifts is for the benefit of the whole body. It is always a shame to be involved in a body where only a minority are doing all the work and service for God. How much easier it is when all are using their gifts freely and generously for God's glory and the edification of the saints!

The word *minister* is the same word as for deacon, which means to be a table waiter. We use our gifts to serve, just as a waiter or waitress serves you at a restaurant. Gifts are not given to you to build you up, but for you to be of service to others. *So, the second attitude that must be present as we serve the Lord with our gifts is the attitude of a servant's heart.*

Paul finishes this verse by saying we minister *as good stewards of the manifold grace of God*. A *steward* was a manager, one who governs a household. This is not ownership, but it is stewardship of what God has graciously entrusted to you. A steward had no wealth of his own but would distribute his master's wealth according to his master's will and direction. The same is true for us. We have nothing of our own but only what God, and God alone, has given us, and we should distribute what He has given us according to His will and direction. We have a responsibility to properly use what has been entrusted to us. Paul speaks of this in 1 Corinthians 4:1-2, "Let a man so consider us, as servants of Christ and stewards of the mysteries of God. Moreover it is required in stewards that one be found faithful."

What does Peter mean when he says that we are to be good stewards *of the manifold grace of God*? The world *manifold* means various in character, or rich in variety. It is the *grace of God* that grants many varieties of gifts and also the variety of ways in which those gifts can be used. You may have the gift of teaching, for example, and He may grant you a variety of ways to use that gift, and the ways you use your gift of teaching might be very different from the ways someone else uses their gift of teaching. That is a gift from God, from his manifold, or varied, expressions of grace. Or, you might have the gift of mercy, and the manner in which you extend mercy might be very different from the manner in which someone else extends mercy. Praise the Lord, we are not robotic in the use of our gifts!

Now, as we end with verse 11, Peter gives us the last three attitudes that must accompany the use of our spiritual gifts. He says,

> If anyone speaks, let him speak as the oracles of God. If anyone ministers, let him do it as with the ability which God supplies, that in all things God may be glorified through Jesus Christ, to whom belong the glory and the dominion forever and ever. Amen. (1 Peter 4:11)

Peter says *if anyone speaks, let him speak as the oracles of God*. Peter is saying if you have speaking gifts, then let what you say be as if it were words spoken by God Himself. *The third attitude we should possess as we use our gifts is the attitude that all we do is as unto the Lord.* We would do well to ask ourselves, "Would the Lord say this?" or "Would the Lord do this?" We should do everything as unto the Lord, whether it is our words or our deeds, as Paul says in Colossians 3:17 and 23. If you have a speaking gift of teaching, preaching, evangelism, or exhortation, you should be conscious of what you say because you are to be speaking God's message, not your own. It should not be your opinion you put forth, but under the leadership of the Holy Spirit, it should be God's Word you deliver. That's why it is essential to be in a church where the Word is taught. Man's ideas only get people into trouble. It is the Word of God that teachers are to speak, not empty and vain philosophies. It was said of one great preacher: "First he listened to God, and then he spoke to men."[76] Also, if you have a speaking gift, you should remind yourself often of James 3:1, where James tells us that teachers will receive a stricter judgment for the things they teach. So, you want to study hard to accurately understand and teach the truth, and to live out what you teach.

Next, Peter gives us the fourth attitude that must be present as we use our spiritual gifts. He says, *if anyone ministers, let him do it as with the ability which God supplies*. The word *minister* here is the same word as in verse 10; it means to be a table waiter, a server. Whatever your gift is, you should use it with a conscious understanding that it is done not with your human ability or cleverness, but with the

---

[76] William Barclay, *The Letters of James and Peter* (Louisville: Westminster John Knox Press, 1976), Pg 256.

ability that God gives. The word *ability* means power or strength. When you try to use any spiritual gift in your own strength, you will fail, in one way or another. Without Him, you can do nothing. Paul says in 1 Corinthians 4:7, "For who makes you differ from another? And what do you have that you did not receive? Now if you did indeed receive it, why do you boast as if you had not received it?" Everything we're able to do is because God gives us the ability. *Attitude number four that must be present as we serve is the attitude that it is not our own abilities that enable us to serve, but the abilities that God gives.* If you had ever told me in time past that I would be a teacher of the Word of God today, I would have told you that you were crazy. I did not like to get up in front of people and I did not enjoy studying—at all. But after God saved me, He gave me certain gifts, and I must always remind myself that it is not Susan who has the ability, but it is God who gives me the ability or strength.

Peter goes on: *that in all things God may be glorified through Jesus Christ, to whom belong the glory and the dominion forever and ever. Amen.* This is the ultimate reason why we use our gifts and the fifth attitude that must be present as we do so. *What is that fifth attitude that must be present as we serve Christ? The goal of glorifying God.* Why do we use our gifts, anyway? Is it to receive some pat on the back or the praise of men or acknowledgment in the church bulletin? No! Peter says that *God* in all things *may be glorified through Jesus Christ*! Everything we have is from God and so it should be used for His glory. We have been made for His glory and for the pleasure of His will. And Peter even ends the verse with *amen*, which means so be it. This word was used to put a strong affirmation on what has just been said. It was used in the early Christian worship services as an expression of agreement with what was being said. Being raised in a Baptist minister's home, I heard this word a lot in our worship services! This is obviously an emotional response from Peter, and yet it is not the end of his epistle. What Peter is saying is use these gifts to the glory of God—Amen! So be it!

Before we end with some closing thoughts, allow me to offer a simple reminder that Peter is writing these words to persecuted Christians. Going through fiery trials didn't give them an excuse to stop serving God. And, my friend, the same is true for us! You might be going through some difficulties or an unusually stressful time in your life, but that does not give you license to stop serving the Lord. In fact, I have noticed that the more suffering and trials and pressure I encounter, the more the Lord shows Himself strong!

Summary

Ladies, are you using your gifts for the glory of God? If not, why not? Maybe you do not know what your gifts are. If you don't, then discover your gifts and start using them. But for those of you who do know your gifts, are these attitudes present in your serving?

1. No complaining.
2. A servant's heart.
3. Ministering as unto the Lord.
4. Serving with the ability the Lord gives you.
5. The desire to glorify God.

Maybe you know what your gifts are, but you don't like what God has called you to do, and you're jealous of the gifts and ministries that others have. Paul says in 2 Corinthians 10:12 that those who compare themselves among themselves are not wise. I look at people who have other gifts and marvel at their abilities, yet I don't have the same giftedness. For example, I look at people who work with children, and wonder how they do that? It is a gift from God and yet God has not called me to do that! God gives us each different gifts and different creativity in how to use those gifts best to His glory. I recognize my limitations and focus on what God has called me to do. Be thankful for those who have different gifts than you and pray for them as they use their gifts to minister to others.

Perhaps you are upset that you only have one gift, or maybe you're upset because you think you have too many gifts. It doesn't really matter how many gifts God chooses to give you, does it? What does matter is that each one is used for His glory! If you are not using the spiritual gifts that God has given to you, I would challenge you to do so.

Some of you may know what your gifts are, you don't struggle with jealously over another person's gifts, you are using them, but quite frankly you're weary and tired. I have a word for you too from 1 Corinthians 15:58 "Therefore, my beloved brethren, be steadfast, immovable, always abounding in the work of the Lord, knowing that your labor is not in vain in the Lord." When I'm feeling weary in serving, I try to remember this verse, along with Hebrews 6:10, "For God is not unjust to forget your work and labor of love which you have shown toward His name, in that you have ministered to the saints, and do minister." I want to encourage you as women to discover your gifts, accept your gifts, and use your gifts, and thus show others what a godly woman looks like.

Frances Havergal, who wrote my favorite hymn, *Take My Life and Let It Be*, lost her mother when she was only 11 years old. Her mother's final words to this young girl were, "Fanny dear, pray to God to prepare you for all He is preparing for you." Have you and I—and *are* you and I—prepared for what God has prepared for us in this life? Do we know what He has called us to be and to do and are we using what He has given us for His glory? *Take My Life and Let It Be* is a wonderful song of dedication, mentioning many of the spiritual gifts we've just studied. I would challenge you to think seriously as you read the words to this song. Will you dedicate yourself anew to be all God has for you to His glory?

> *Take my life, and let it be consecrated, Lord, to Thee.*
> *Take my moments and my days; let them flow in ceaseless praise.*
> *Take my hands, and let them move at the impulse of Thy love.*
> *Take my feet, and let them be swift and beautiful for Thee.*
> *Take my voice, and let me sing always, only, for my King.*
> *Take my lips, and let them be filled with messages from Thee.*
> *Take my silver and my gold; not a mite would I withhold.*
> *Take my intellect, and use every power as Thou shalt choose.*
> *Take my will, and make it Thine; it shall be no longer mine.*
> *Take my heart, it is Thine own; it shall be Thy royal throne.*
> *Take my love, my Lord, I pour at Thy feet its treasure store.*
> *Take myself, and I will be ever, only, all for Thee.*[77]

---

[77] Words by Frances R. Havergal.

Questions to Consider

Knowing and Using Your Spiritual Gifts for the Glory of God

1 Peter 4:9-11

1. (a) Read Romans 12:3-8; 1 Corinthians 12; Ephesians 4:11-13; and 1 Peter 4:9-11. List the spiritual gifts you find mentioned in these four passages. (b) Looking over the list, define as many of these as you can, either by what you know or by what you can research.

2. Memorize 1 Peter 4:9.

3. (a) According to Ephesians 4:12-13 and 1 Peter 4:11, why are spiritual gifts given? (b) According to 1 Corinthians 12:11, who gives these gifts to us? (c) How do Romans 12:4 and 1 Corinthians 12:4 answer whether we all have the same gift(s)? (d) What does 1 Corinthians 13:1-3 say regarding the attitude that should be present in us when using our gifts?

4. Read Matthew 25:14-30. (a) What can you learn from this parable regarding the seriousness of not using the gifts God has given to you? (b) What other observations do you see in this parable regarding talents? Write down as many as you can. Examples: 1) God gives one gift to some, many to others, verse 15. 2) Fear keeps us from using what God has given us, verse 25.

5. (a) Do you know what your spiritual gifts are? If so, what are they? (b) How are you using them for the Lord? (c) How are you refining them? For example, if you have the gift of teaching, are you learning and growing and sharpening that gift for God's glory? If you have the gift of mercy, are you looking for individuals to whom you can show mercy, as well as thinking of creative ways to be merciful? (d) How can you encourage others to use their gifts for the Lord?

6. (a) What attitude should accompany our hospitality, according to 1 Peter 4:9? (b) Who is commanded to be hospitable, according to Romans 12:13 (see especially verse 1); 1 Timothy 3:2; 5:9-10; and Titus 1:7-8? (c) According to Matthew 25:31-46 and Hebrews 13:1-2, what are some reasons you should want to be hospitable?

7. What are some practical tips you have learned that help you to simplify and to enjoy having people in your home?

8. After prayerfully considering this lesson, how might we pray for you regarding spiritual gifts or hospitality? Please write down your request.

** For a rich blessing this week, read over these beautiful doxologies (perhaps a few each day) and worship the Lord: Romans 9:4-5; 11:33-36; 16:27; Galatians 1:4-5; Ephesians 3:20-21; Philippians 4:20; 1 Timothy 1:17; 6:16; 2 Timothy 4:18; Hebrews 13:20-21; 1 Peter 4:11; 5:11; 2 Peter 3:18; Jude 24-25; Revelation 1:6; 5:13; 7:12.

Chapter 20

What to Do in the Furnace: Part 1
1 Peter 4:12-14

When I was three years old, my family moved to Tulsa, Oklahoma. For most of my life, Oklahoma has been "home" to me. When I travel to various places to speak, a question I'm often asked is, "Where are you from?" or, "Where did you grow up?" When I say, "Oklahoma," those who've inquired often immediately think of the musical "Oklahoma," or the Oklahoma City bombing, which destroyed the Federal Building on April 19, 1995, or some of the largest tornadoes in history, the F5 tornadoes that hit May 3, 1999 and May 20, 2013. In fact, Oklahoma is most often recognized for its tumultuous weather and has been referred to by many as the heart of Tornado Alley. Many of the storms and tornadoes that arise here in Oklahoma are unexpected; some even appear suddenly and seemingly out of nowhere.

The weather storms that come up in Oklahoma are often like the spiritual storms that come into our lives. They often arise suddenly and unexpectedly, and it sometimes feels as if they've come out of nowhere. Much of our life is filled with unexpected storms. Some of them come to us in the form of a mist, like a broken arm, a sick child, or a day in which everything goes wrong. Other storms come to us in the form of steady rain, like a child who is sick for days and days, the betrayal of one whom you thought was your best friend, or an unexpected move. Still other storms in life are a little more severe. They come in the form of thunderstorms, like an unfaithful husband, a rebellious child who leaves home, or a family member or friend who discovers they have a life-threatening illness. Probably the most frightening of all of life's storms are the tornadoes and the hurricanes of life. These storms might involve persecution or separation from a friend or family member because of your faith in Christ, the sudden death of a child or spouse, or a catastrophe of some sort which affects a whole city or region or even the entire world. Life is filled with storms. That is a fact.

When these storms come into our lives, what is one of the first questions that we Christians usually ask? "Why, Lord, is this happening?!" But sometimes we don't know why, and sometimes it is not for us to know why. Another question we might ask when we're going through these storms is, "How, Lord, am I to respond to this storm?" Where is a Christian to go for the answers to all the whys and hows of life's storms? For the believer in Christ Jesus, we go to the Word of God. And I can think of no better place in the Word of God to go than 1 Peter for the answers to these questions.

As we study 1 Peter 4:12-19, we are going to discover that there are 7 answers to the question, "Why, Lord, is this happening?" We'll also discover that there are 5 answers to the question, "How, Lord, do You want me to respond to this storm?" We will take two lessons to cover this material and for this lesson we will cover verses 12-14. Let's read what Peter has to say.

1 Peter 4:12-14

> Beloved, do not think it strange concerning the fiery trial which is to try you, as though some strange thing happened to you; [13]but rejoice to the extent that you partake of Christ's sufferings, that when His glory is revealed, you may also be glad with exceeding joy. [14]If you are reproached for the name of Christ, blessed are you, for the Spirit of glory and of God rests upon you. On their part He is blasphemed, but on your part He is glorified.

As we approach these next few verses, I want to remind you that the storms Peter's initial readers were encountering were very different from the storms most of us encounter. They were suffering because of their attachment to Christ, something most of us have never had to go through—at least, not yet. And yet, the message is still the same for all of us, no matter what storms we face. Peter begins by writing,

> Beloved, do not think it strange concerning the fiery trial which is to try you, as though some strange thing happened to you; (1 Peter 4:12)

It would have been of great comfort to Peter's readers that Peter begins this section of his letter about suffering by calling them *beloved*. The term means beloved ones, and it would remind these suffering Christians that the Lord loved them. Remembering this love would help them to endure the sufferings they were going through. It helps you and me, as well, as we go through trials, to know that our Father loves us, even when it seems as if all are against us. "What a sweet pillow upon which to rest our weary hearts, just to know that our Father loves us."[78] The word beloved is also the beginning of a new thought with the apostle Peter, as he moves from spiritual gifts to suffering.

After reminding his readers of the Father's love for them, Peter then reminds them not to think of their trials as strange: *do not think it not strange* or, literally, "stop thinking it is a thing alien to you." Now, we need to understand the context here. Gentile converts to Christianity would not have been used to persecution because of their religious beliefs. They would have been inclined to think it out of place and contrary to the blessings of being a Christian. In fact, I have met people who think the same thing today; they equate Christianity with a sort of "No worries, mate" kind of life. I'm not sure where that idea hatched, but it's certainly not from the Bible! When Peter wrote these words, Jesus had already made very clear while He was here on Earth that attachment to His name would mean troubles. He said, "If the world hates you, you know that it hated Me before it hated you. If you were of the world, the world would love its own. Yet because you are not of the world, but I chose you out of the world, therefore the world hates you. Remember the word that I said to you, 'A servant is not greater than his master.' If they persecuted Me, they will also persecute you. If they kept My word, they will keep yours also. But all these things they will do to

---

[78] Kenneth Wuest, *Word Studies in the Greek New Testament: Volume II* (Grand Rapids: Eerdman's Publishing Co., 1973), 118.

you for My name's sake, because they do not know Him who sent Me" (John 15:18-21).

When Peter tells his readers to not think it strange that they are going through fiery trials, the Greek tense is in the present imperative, which means that it forbids a continued reaction of being puzzled. We must all admit that usually when a trial comes, our first reaction is like, "Whoa, I can't believe this is happening to me!" But what Peter is saying is that we should not continue in that state of being shocked. When we continue to stay puzzled about our trial, we're not able to accept the trial and deal with the test. When we remain in a state of shock over our trial, we don't stop to ponder what God may be trying to accomplish in and through us. I have watched some people going through trials over longs periods of time and I often wonder why they are never able to accept it; they seem to continually fight with God, struggling to accept what He has allowed. And yet I have watched others who adjust and begin to humble themselves in their trial, and these are the ones that seem to come forth as gold and are used by God to glorify Himself and help others!

So, the first answer to the question, "Why is this happening, Lord?" is, "It is to be expected." It's a part of the course you enrolled in, you might say, when you signed up to be a Christian. Some of us, perhaps, don't consider this cost, but nonetheless it is a part of the cost of being a disciple of Jesus Christ. I heard about a father whose son was killed in a car wreck, and at the funeral he went up to the minister and asked, "Where was God when my son was killed?" The minister replied, "The same place He was when His son was killed." God is still on the throne in our trials and we must not forget that as we go through them. Trials are a part of life.

Notice that Peter calls these trials fiery. The word *fiery* means a burning or a furnace, and indicates something that is ignited. This particular Greek word is used only here, in 1 Peter, and in Revelation 18:9, 18, where it speaks of Babylon's destruction and calls it the "smoke of her burning." Many believe that Peter's use of the word fiery refers to a literally burning, which is very probable. We must remember that many of Peter's first readers were literally going through fire as some were covered with pitch and lit on fire to be used as living torches to light Nero's garden at night. Many were literally burned to death. But we know that not all of them were burned to death, so this could also refer to simply being tested as by fire, because Peter does say that the purpose of these fiery trials is *to try you* or test you. Peter has already mentioned these testings in 1 Peter 1:7 where he refers his readers' faith as being tested by fire: "That the genuineness of your faith, being much more precious than gold that perishes, though it is tested by fire, may be found to praise, honor, and glory at the revelation of Jesus Christ." Peter refers to this testing there as a refining process in which gold is melted until all the impurities are skimmed off and it becomes pure. In Psalm 66:10, the Psalmist refers to this very thing when he says, "For You, O God, have tested us; you have refined us as silver is refined." When Job was going through the storms of his life, he said in Job 23:10, "But He knows the way that I take; when He has tested me, I shall come forth as gold." We might say today, "Boy, he or she is going through the fire!" What we mean by that is, of course, that they are going through a rough time right now and that they are being tested in a great way.

So, the second answer to the question, "Why, Lord, is this happening?" is, "There is a purpose, and that purpose is to test (try) you." This word for *try* has the idea of probation or a putting of something to the proof. We understand the concept of probation in our culture; it is a time to see if someone is going to behave correctly. In the spiritual sense here, God tests us to see if our faith is real and to purify the sin from our lives. We have already seen in 1 Peter 1:7 that trials are sent to test us to see if our faith is genuine. Will we persevere? Will we deny our Lord? The storms of life show us what we are really made of. Are we really leaning on the everlasting arms? Are we really a child of the King? Or are we leaning on our own strength? Have we been faking it all these years? These things come out as we go through the difficulties of life. As one man says, "Suffering does not destroy us, but purifies us."[79]

---

[79] John R. W. Stott, *The Message of 1 Peter* (Downers Grove: Inter-Varsity Press, 1988), 190.

Peter goes on to say: don't think of these trials *as though some strange thing happened to you*. Again, why do we think trials are foreign to believers? Why do we think that God has promised a life of ease and comfort? In fact, the phrase *think it not strange* is a strong Greek word that means "God forbid that you would think it strange!" Nothing just happens in the life of a believer. Persecution and suffering are not accidents. Everything is a part of His divine plan, and His children are not exempt from trials of many kinds. Instead of spending our time sitting around thinking it strange that we are being tested with a trial, Peter says we are to rejoice.

> but rejoice to the extent that you partake of Christ's sufferings, that when His glory is revealed, you may also be glad with exceeding joy. (1 Peter 4:13)

The word but here indicates a contrast; in fact, in the Greek it is a very strong contrast. And in this verse we find the first answer to the how question, "How, Lord, do I go through a trial?" The answer is: "You go through it rejoicing!" The word rejoice means to be cheerful. Peter is going to mention four times in the next two verses the joy we should have in the midst of our trials, and he uses words like rejoice, be glad, exceeding joy, and happy or blessed. The Greek tense here also indicates that this is not a one time rejoicing, but a continuous attitude that we have in the trial. But why should I rejoice? Peter says because we partake of Christ's sufferings. "Faith realizes that the ground for rejoicing does not lie in the sufferings themselves but in the fellowship with Christ that they bring."[80] This is the third answer to the why question, "Why, Lord, am I suffering?" The answer is: "So that you can be a partaker of His sufferings." And notice that Peter says to the extent, which means inasmuch, or in so far as, or in the measure of. What Peter is saying is that not all his readers had been called to suffer to the same degree. Some suffer to a greater degree; some a lesser degree. We see the same in our day, don't we? Why God calls some of us to suffer to greater degrees is a mystery to me, but I do see Him giving much grace to those

---

[80] D. Edmond Hiebert, First Peter: An Expositional Commentary (Chicago: Moody Press, 1984), 207.

He places in that position. But whatever the degree of suffering He calls you to, it will allow you to partake in His sufferings, His pain, which means to share with Him in close fellowship. Paul explains in Philippians 1:29, "For to you it has been granted on behalf of Christ, not only to believe in Him, but also to suffer for His sake." Paul is saying there that suffering is a gift! Now, I know that suffering is not number one on your birthday list this year, but it is a gift. Remember what Paul says in Philippians 3:10? "That I may know Him and the power of His resurrection, and the fellowship of His sufferings, being conformed to His death." Paul's desire was to so identify with his Lord that he wanted to fellowship in Christ's sufferings, to be a partaker of His sufferings.

You might be thinking, "Why would anyone want to do that? Are they crazy?!" I remember one of the first times that being a partaker of Christ's sufferings truly impacted me. Many years ago, the Lord allowed my husband and me to go through tremendous suffering for the name of Christ. It involved some very close friends of ours who hurt us very deeply. I remember during that time trying to see the good in the painful ordeal, and I remember being grateful to finally get a small taste of what my Lord endured and suffered when His disciples forsook Him and fled, when Judas betrayed Him, when Peter denied Him. And I finally could say, "Thank you, Lord, thank you for letting me partake a little bit in Your sufferings and so identify with You in Your sufferings." My friend, suffering allows us to identify with our Lord, and that is a privilege, a gift. In fact, Paul says something even more profound in Colossians 1:24, "I now rejoice in my sufferings for you, and fill up in my flesh what is lacking in the afflictions of Christ, for the sake of His body, which is the church." Paul desired to be so much like his Lord that he pursued a course of life which allowed him to suffer in some of the same ways as his Lord. And isn't that really what Paul is saying in Philippians 3:10, when He says "That I may know Him and the power of His resurrection, and the fellowship of His sufferings, being conformed to His death"? Paul wanted to be closely identified with his Lord in every way. And, really, that should be the desire of all of us who know God. Getting to know Him intimately comes not just by reading the Word and praying and worshipping but also by suffering.

Notice that Peter is not saying to rejoice in the suffering itself, but to rejoice because you can share in Christ's sufferings. He doesn't say enjoy the trial, but find joy in it. Some people like trials because it brings sympathy from others, or because they get attention. But Peter says the motive behind the rejoicing is the blessing of identifying with Him. Part of the blessing of partaking in His sufferings includes partaking in the results of His sufferings. Peter puts it this way: *that when His glory is revealed, you may also be glad with exceeding joy.* When Christ is revealed in glory we will share in that glory, just as we have shared in His sufferings. What Peter is saying here is that present rejoicing now during our trials prepares us to fully experience joy in the future in glory. Paul states in 2 Timothy 2:12, "If we endure [or suffer, KJV says], we shall also reign with Him. If we deny Him, He also will deny us." And then in Romans 8:18 he writes, "For I consider that the sufferings of this present time are not worthy to be compared with the glory which shall be revealed in us." Peter says we will *be glad with exceeding joy*, which means to jump with joy. It is a great burst of joy that will sweep over us at Christ's return. *Exceeding joy* would include things like jubilation, skipping, and bubbling over with shouts of delight. That will certainly be a divine intervention for those of us who have more refined personalities! And the present tense here of this exceeding joy means that it is enduring, because it is forever and ever.

So, the second answer to the question of how we are to respond to trials is, "Rejoice, knowing that glory will follow." Life's trials will seem very small when we see Christ; Paul helps us see that in 2 Corinthians 4:17, "For our light affliction, which is but for a moment, is working for us a far more exceeding and eternal weight of glory."

Peter continues with his theme of being happy in trials by saying,

> If you are reproached for the name of Christ, blessed are you, for the Spirit of glory and of God rests upon you. On their part He is blasphemed, but on your part He is glorified. (1 Peter 4:14)

The word *if* does not indicate a hypothetical situation; rather, it means since, or in view of the fact that, you are reproached for the name of Christ. Being *reproached for the name of Christ* means to be insulted. This would include attacks that were verbal as well as physical. They were reproached because of their attachment to Christ, as Peter will mention here. He also mentions it again in verse 16, when he writes, "Yet if anyone suffers as a Christian, let him not be ashamed, but let him glorify God in this matter." Peter is saying that if you are attacked, either physically or verbally, *blessed are you*, or happy are you, which means to be spiritually well-off, we might say. In Matthew 5:11-12, Jesus said something similar, "Blessed are you when they revile and persecute you, and say all kinds of evil against you falsely for My sake. Rejoice and be exceedingly glad, for great is your reward in heaven, for so they persecuted the prophets who were before you."

Why should we be happy when we're persecuted? Why is it that we are we blessed when we're persecuted? Peter says: *for the Spirit of glory and of God rests upon you*. The word *rest* is an interesting Greek word that means to refresh. It speaks of a farmer resting his land by sowing light crops on it. He relieves the land of the necessity of producing heavy crops, and therefore gives it an opportunity to recuperate its strength, to rest. In fact, Leviticus 25 talks about 6 years of sowing and reaping and then one year of allowing the land to rest. The idea is that the indwelling Holy Spirit rests and refreshes the believer when the world is persecuting him or her. He strengthens us and refreshes us in ways beyond our understanding. "He rests upon the Christian as the Shechinah rested on the tabernacle, and brings a foretaste of that glory which is fully given at the Revelation."[81] This is probably the same idea mentioned in Matthew 4, where we

---

[81] Rev Charles Bigg, *The Epistles of St Peter and St Jude* (Scotland: Morrison and Gibb Limited, 1978), 172.

read of Christ being tested by the devil in the wilderness; it states in verse 11 that when the test was over the devil left Him and then angels came and ministered to Him. Also, in Acts 6:15, we see that when Stephen was being persecuted for his attachment to Christ, his face looked like that of an angel. And right before they stoned him to death, it says in Acts 7:54-55, "When they heard these things they were cut to the heart, and they gnashed at him with their teeth. But he, being full of the Holy Spirit, gazed into heaven and saw the glory of God, and Jesus standing at the right hand of God." And so it is for us; many of you could testify that just as Christ and Stephen were refreshed and strengthened by the Spirit in their hour of trial, so are we. I remember one lady who told me that when her son was on the brink of life and death after a tragic accident, she felt an awareness and sense of Christ's presence and a closeness that was not there at other times.

So, we have a third answer to the question of "How do I respond to life's storms?" The answer is, "With assurance, knowing that the Holy Spirit will strengthen and refresh you." As Paul says in 2 Corinthians 12:9 regarding his thorn in his flesh that the Lord would not remove,"Therefore most gladly I will rather boast in my infirmities, that the power of Christ may rest upon me."

Peter ends with these words: *on their part He is blasphemed, but on your part He is glorified.* Interestingly, this portion is not in the original manuscripts. But if it were in the original manuscripts, Peter is basically saying this: while these unbelievers blaspheme God by persecuting His people, His people, on the other hand, by their faithful and obedient lives, bring glory to Him.

Summary

In our next lesson we will continue with the whys and hows of life's storms. But let's review what we have learned thus far.

Why do we have storms in this life? First, it's a promise; it's to be expected. Do you expect trials? Do you see them as part of your being a child of God? Or are you under the myth that trials are not for believers? Second, there is a purpose, and that purpose is to test you. What trials have you encountered in the past year, the past week, or even today? How have they been used by God to bring you one step closer to His image? Third, we have trials in order to allow us to be partakers of, or to participate in, Christ's sufferings. Is this a comfort to you, to be able to fellowship with Christ in His sufferings?

How are we to respond to these difficulties? First, with an attitude of rejoicing. Is this your response to the trials that God allows in your life? I know it might not be your immediate response, but are you eventually able to be joyful, knowing that God is doing something in your life that is for your good? Second, we are to rejoice, knowing that glory is to follow. When life hits you with a trial, do you allow your mind to drift to heaven and what is to come, to glory? Do life's trials seem small to you compared to eternity and seeing Christ? Third, we respond with an attitude of assurance, knowing that the Holy Spirit will strengthen and refresh us. How did the Spirit strengthen and refresh you in your last trial?

I know there may be many of you who are facing storms in life this very day. For some of you, it may be only a mist; for some, it is steady rain; for some, it is thundering and lightening; and for some of you, it is a real tornado that has come into your life. Whatever type of trial God is allowing, whether small or great, will you allow it to bring you closer to the Master as He walks with you in the fiery furnace?

Questions to Consider

What to Do in the Furnace: Part 1
1 Peter 4:12-14

Please begin by glancing at Question 8.

1. (a) As you read 1 Peter 4, which themes do you discover that Peter has already written about in the previous three chapters? (b) Why do you think he repeats these themes?

2. Memorize 1 Peter 4:12.

3. (a) Who in the Bible comes to your mind as an example of someone who suffered for Christ? (b) What do you learn from his or her example about how to go through suffering?

4. (a) Peter writes of suffering for the name of Christ in 1 Peter 4:14. What types of suffering for Christ are mentioned in Matthew 19:29; Acts 5:40-41; Acts 21:13, and Revelation 20:4? (b) How do these compare to your present sufferings?

5. (a) What was Paul's desire in Philippians 3:10-11? (b) Why did he desire this? (c) Is this *your* desire? (d) What does Paul say about suffering in Philippians 1:29? (e) Do *you* view suffering as a gift?

6. (a) In their epistles, Peter and Paul both mention rejoicing in our sufferings (1 Peter 4:13 and Colossians 1:24). What are the reasons they give for rejoicing? (b) What do you think Paul meant when he wrote, "fill up in my flesh what is lacking in the afflictions of Christ, for the sake of His body, which is the church"?

7. According to Matthew 5:11-12; Acts 5:41; 16:25-34; Romans 5:3-5; 2 Corinthians 4:17; 12:9-10; and James 1:2-4, what are some other biblical reasons we should rejoice in our sufferings?

8. (a) Observe your responses this week to the trials that come your way. How did you respond? (b) Were you surprised by your trials or by your reaction to them? (c) Did you respond with an attitude of joy? (d) What did you learn about yourself and your attitude toward life's difficulties?

9. What is difficult for you during a trial? Is it your attitude? Your endurance? Is it something else? Put your need in the form of a prayer request.

Chapter 21

What to Do in the Furnace: Part 2
1 Peter 4:15-19

The following is a true story told by a pastor who was flying in an airplane. All was going well on the flight, until the plane was descending to its final destination and the pilot realized that the landing gear would not engage. The flight attendants instructed the passengers to place their heads between their knees and grab their ankles just before impact. It was definitely one of those I-can't-believe-this-is-happening-to-me experiences. Suddenly, the pilot announced over the intercom, "We are beginning our final descent. At this moment, in accordance with Aviation Codes established at Geneva, it is my obligation to inform you that if you believe in God you should commence prayer."[82]

Now, I do want you to know that all ended well and the plane landed safely. But, I find it very interesting that even the "Aviation Codes established at Geneva" would recognize that in a crisis it might be a good idea to pray to God. For the life of the unbeliever, a crisis is about the only time they call upon God, isn't it? But for the believer in Jesus Christ calling upon Him and committing our souls to Him in a crisis should be as normal as breathing. Let's read together the last part of chapter four, verses 15-19, where Peter addresses this very thing.

1 Peter 4:15-19

> But let none of you suffer as a murderer, a thief, an evildoer, or as a busybody in other people's matters. ¹⁶Yet if anyone suffers as a Christian, let him not be ashamed, but let him glorify God in this matter. ¹⁷For the time has come for judgment to begin at the house of God; and if it begins with us first, what will be the end of those

---
[82]Charles Swindoll, *Seasons of Life* (Portland: Multnomah Press, 1983), 273-274, paraphrase.

who do not obey the gospel of God? ¹⁸Now "If the righteous one is scarcely saved, where will the ungodly and the sinner appear?" ¹⁹Therefore let those who suffer according to the will of God commit their souls to Him in doing good, as to a faithful Creator.

As we continue to answer the why and how questions concerning the storms of life, we will discover four more answers to the why question and two more answers to the how question. But before we unpack the meaning of verse 15, I want us to consider James 1:13-15, which says, "Let no one say when he is tempted, 'I am tempted by God'; for God cannot be tempted by evil, nor does He Himself tempt anyone. But each one is tempted when he is drawn away by his own desires and enticed. Then, when desire has conceived, it gives birth to sin; and sin, when it is full-grown, brings forth death." In the first part of James 1, James writes about trials and the fact that we should consider it all joy as we go through them and that we should endure through the process (James 1:12). But then, James turns and writes verses 13-15, which we just read. We might wonder why he warns his readers of temptations while instructing them regarding trials. He does this because if we are not careful, a trial can be turned into a temptation to sin. We may go through a difficulty and grow weary or impatient and allow ourselves to become angry with God or with a particular person. Remember Job's wife? She allowed the trial she and her husband were going through to get the best of her, and she told her husband to curse God and die. She allowed their suffering to be an excuse for sin. This is where we find ourselves as we end chapter four of 1 Peter. Let's consider verse 15 together.

> But let none of you suffer as a murderer, a thief, an evildoer, or as a busybody in other people's matters. (1 Peter 4:15)

Peter writes in verse 15 that they should avoid suffering for wrongdoing, and he lists some of those wrongdoings. The first one he mentions is being *a murderer*, which means one who kills intentionally. The second one is *a thief*, which is someone who steals. The third offense is being *an evildoer*, which is someone who does anything bad, any type of crime. The last one Peter mentions is being *a busybody in other people's matters*, which refers to someone who thinks they need to oversee another's matters. The idea is that of one who spies out the affairs of other men. Peter lets his readers know that just because they were suffering under terrible persecution, they have no excuse for lawlessness. When you think about it, these particular sins could be a temptation under the given circumstances. Peter has already told them not to render evil for evil in 1 Peter 3:9. If some among them were being killed, and they were, others should not retaliate by killing back. If their property was taken away from them, and it was, they should not retaliate by stealing themselves. Certainly, in their condition, they may be in need of food or clothing, but they were still not to steal. They were also not to participate in any kind of criminal act, any type of evil doing at all, which, in their situation, could have included slander, sinful anger, lack of compassion, lying, and the like. And certainly they were not to meddle in other people's business. They were not to meddle in the matters regarding their persecutors so as to cause disruption and revolts—they were not to carry around signs and protest their persecution! (See 1 Peter 2:13-20 and 3:17.) Obviously, this would have been a difficulty for some of them, and many would have been tempted to fall back into their old way of life, as we have already seen in 1 Peter 2:11 and 4:3.

So, the fourth answer to why the Lord allows us to suffer is this: "Sometimes, it's because of our own sin." Now, of course, this is not always the case, but many times our suffering is because of our own evil-doing. As Peter says in 1 Peter 3:17, it is better to suffer for doing what is right than to suffer for doing what is wrong. One of my mentors once told me, "Susan, you will never regret doing what is right, but you will always regret doing what is wrong!" "There is very little comfort in sufferings when we bring them upon ourselves by our own sin and folly. It is not the suffering, but the cause, that makes the martyr."[83]

I think of David and his sin of adultery with Bathsheba. He certainly suffered for his sin; his child died, and a myriad of other problems

---
[83]Matthew Henry—PC Study Software—1993-1997.

came into his life. If you recall, one of David's sons, Amnon, raped his half-sister Tamar; another son, Absalom, secretly plotted a revolt against the throne of his father David and started a rebellion against him. And so it is in our lives. Sometimes, the trials in our lives are due to the fact that we bring them upon ourselves, and it would be a good thing when we're going through such suffering to ask ourselves if it may be due to some sin in our life. Peter tells us here in verse 15 that we are not to behave like that. Instead of behaving sinfully, he says,

> Yet if anyone suffers as a Christian, let him not be ashamed, but let him glorify God in this matter. (1 Peter 4:16)

Peter indicates in this verse that there is a contrast between suffering for committing sin and suffering for being a Christian. *Christian* is a word that is only used three times in the New Testament—here, and in Acts 11:26 (the disciples were first called Christians in Antioch) and Acts 26:28 (when Paul was appealing to Herod Agrippa regarding his soul, and Agrippa tells Paul that he has almost persuaded him to be a Christian). To be a Christian means to be a follower of Christ, and actually, the pagans gave this name to believers and often called them "little Christs," though they intended it to be derogatory. The simple fact of being known as a Christian would often be enough to incur persecution. We must remember that during this time in history it cost to be a Christian! Christians were looked down upon and persecuted for the name of Jesus, which is something most of us have never encountered—at least not yet. And Peter says, if one suffers for being a Christian *let him not be ashamed*, which means don't feel shame for yourself. Paul says in Philippians 1:20, "according to my earnest expectation and hope that in nothing I shall be ashamed, but with all boldness, as always, so now also Christ will be magnified in my body, whether by life or by death." Paul wasn't ashamed at all, but was bold in his witness—so much so that he didn't care if he lived or died! His only concern was glorifying God! In fact, Paul states in 2 Timothy 1:12, "For this reason I also suffer these things; nevertheless I am not ashamed, for I know whom I have believed and am persuaded that He is able to keep what I have committed to Him until that Day." Paul was not ashamed to suffer for Christ because he knew what he believed and who he believed in, and he committed it all to Him.

So, the fourth answer to the question of how we are to respond to a trial or suffering is this: "Unashamed." We should not be ashamed for suffering for Christ, my friend! But we should feel shame if we suffer for doing any of the things that Peter mentioned in verse 15. Peter knew the shame of denying his Lord repeatedly (see Mark 14:66-72) and yet, later on in his life, as he matured in the Lord, we find him in Acts 5:41 willing to be beaten because of his faith in Christ: "So they departed from the presence of the council, rejoicing that they were counted worthy to suffer shame for His name." Maybe some of you are going through a trial today that does involve suffering for the name of Christ and you are struggling with being ashamed of Him. Jesus gives us some very sobering words to consider. Mark 8:38 says, "For whoever is ashamed of Me and My words in this adulterous and sinful generation, of him the Son of Man also will be ashamed when He comes in the glory of His Father with the holy angels."

Instead of thinking about how ashamed we are for being a Christian when we're suffering, Peter says we are to glorify God. He puts it like this: *but let him glorify God in this matter.* Instead of feeling sorry for ourselves, we are to bow our heads in shame and we are to praise God that we bear His name! The Greek tense here indicates a habitual response of glorifying God. What Peter is saying is: The experience of suffering for Christ is to be looked at by the believer as the foundation for giving glory to God. *Number five, then, in answer to why we suffer is this: "To glorify God."* Paul says in Philippians 1:20 that he wants to glorify God in his body, whether it is by life or by death. Is that your desire this day as you go through difficulties? Is God being glorified through your trials? Some people go through the storms of life and bring shame upon the name of Christ, and yet there are others who use their difficulties as opportunities to give praise to the Lord and draw upon His strength. Peter goes on, with still more for us to consider:

> For the time has come for judgment to begin at the house of God; and if it begins with us first, what will be the end of those who do not obey the gospel of God? (1 Peter 4:17)

Now, it's possible you are reading this wondering what Peter is talking about and what this has to do with trials. The word for *judgment* here in the Greek is krima, which is an action or a process, rather than the more usual idea of judgment, which is a judicial verdict. It has more of the idea of affliction or distress. The term *house of God* is a reference to the true disciples of Jesus Christ. Peter has already referred to them as this building of God in 1 Peter 2:5-8, where he refers to them as a spiritual house and calls them living stones. This judgment Peter is referring to would have been the persecution these saints were undergoing, which would be a disciplinary kind of judgment, a fiery trial, sent for the purpose of purifying their lives. God is holy and cannot condone sin, even when His judgment might affect His own children. The readers here would need to understand this momentary affliction or persecution in light of coming judgment. God was testing them to see if they were genuine, to see if they were really a part of the house of God. "God acts first to remove all that is inconsistent with His holy nature in His people."[84] That is, the starting place of the judgment is the Church, and from there the judgment goes on its way to the unsaved.

So, the sixth answer to the question, "Why, Lord, do we suffer?" is: "Because God judges His people first." In biblical times, when God was about to pour out some general judgment, he began by afflicting his own people in order to correct them, that they might be prepared for the overflowing scourge. Ezekiel 9:6 is a good example of this; God orders the destroyer to slay both old and young in the city, and tells him to "begin at My sanctuary." Providence has always been this way; when God brings great calamities and judgments upon whole nations, He begins with his own people, testing them and trying their faith to purify them for Himself. Many people believe that God has begun to pour out His judgment on America, and I personally believe that is true. If so, we as believers will not

---
[84]D. Edmond Hiebert; *First Peter: An Expositional Commentary* (Chicago: Moody Press, 1984), 274.

be exempt from being chastened; the righteous many times suffer with the unrighteous. This judgment on the house of God purifies the church and removes the chaff from the wheat, separating the true believers from the false. Even now, as our nation is experiencing some degree of judgment, we hear of so-called "Christians" vacating the church due to fear. They are proving who they really are.

Peter goes on to say *and if it begins with us first, what will be the end of those who do not obey the gospel of God?* If God brings such fiery trials on *us* who know Him, then *what will be the end* of those who do not know Him? Our suffering here is mild compared to their coming eternal suffering, right? Augustine said, "If the sons are chastised, what have the most malicious slaves to expect?"[85] Another man says, "If God so strongly and painfully judges His church which He loves, what will be His fury on the ungodly?"[86] If it foremost begins with us, what will be the final fate of those *who do not obey the gospel of God?* To *not obey* means to disbelieve willfully and perversely. (We had this same idea in 1 Peter 2:8 and 3:1.) Peter is trying to convey to his readers that even though their present sufferings were severe, those sufferings still fell short of what awaited the real enemies of God. The punishment of the wicked is merely delayed. Many times, we wonder why God allows the wicked to go unpunished. It seems to us that the righteous suffer while the wicked seem to never suffer. Maybe you often think the same thing. Perhaps you think, "Lord, I am going through all these storms and trials and my ungodly neighbor or family member is just going on with life and everything is hunky dory for them." Did you know that David felt this way too? Take some time to contemplate Psalm 73, looking especially at verses 1-5, 16-17, and 19. David felt like this too, until verse 17, where he says, "Until I went into the sanctuary of God; then I understood their end." And then in verse 19, he writes something even more sobering, "Oh, how they are brought to desolation, as in a moment! They are utterly consumed with terrors." David is saying: I don't understand why I suffer and the ungodly don't. But, having gone to the house of God, I now understand, because I now realize what their end is—an eternity

---

[85] https://www.studylight.org/commentaries/lcc/1-peter-4.html
[86] https://www.preceptaustin.org/acts-5-commentary

of terror! The unbeliever will be punished in the life to come, with eternal judgment in hell. Christians, on the other hand, are tried here and prepared through their trials for eternal glory.

Peter goes on to repeat in verse 18 what he has just said, only he uses different words.

> Now "If the righteous one is scarcely saved, where will the ungodly and the sinner appear?" (1 Peter 4:18)

Some believe that this is a quote from Proverbs 11:31, and it could be. Proverbs 11:31 says, "if the righteous will be recompensed on the earth, how much more the ungodly and the sinner." What does Peter mean here about the *righteous* being *scarcely saved*? The word *scarcely* means with difficulty. It could be that Peter is using *saved* here in the sense of being saved spiritually, but he could also be using it in the sense of being delivered physically. If the righteous are with difficulty delivered, where will the ungodly and the sinner appear? We know from what David said in Psalm 73 that they will be cast down to destruction and utterly consumed with terrors! And so to conclude Peter's remarks about suffering from chapter four, he ends with verse 19.

> Therefore let those who suffer according to the will of God commit their souls to Him in doing good, as to a faithful Creator. (1 Peter 4:19)

Peter says *therefore*, because of what was previously said in verses 17-18, *let those who suffer according to the will of God commit their souls to Him in doing good, as to a faithful Creator*. Notice the suffering here is *according to the will of God*. And *so we find here number seven on our list of why God allows suffering: "Because it is His will."* Their suffering did not come as chance but as divine choice. Peter says, as you suffer according to His will, then commit the keeping of your soul to Him. The word *commit* means to give in charge, much as a deposit is given to the bank. It was used in biblical times to describe the giving of one's money to a friend to keep in a safe place. In the biblical world, there were no banks, so when people would travel on long journeys they would commit or entrust their monies to a trusted friend. They didn't want to travel with it or leave it in an empty house, for fear of theft. Exodus 22:7 refers to this idea: "If a man delivers to his neighbor money or articles to keep, and it is stolen out of the man's house, if the thief is found, he shall pay double." The word commit was also used by Christ in Luke 23:46, where He said, "Father, into Your hands I commit My spirit." One author said this: "When you deposit your life in God's bank, you always receive eternal dividends on your investment."[87] Also, the Greek tense indicates that this is not a one-time act of committing something to Him, but a constant attitude of committing it to Him. We may commit something to Him, only to get off our knees and take it right back and carry it around with us all day! That is not what Peter is suggesting we do! To repeat what Paul said in 2 Timothy 1:12, "For this reason I also suffer these things; nevertheless I am not ashamed, for I know whom I have believed and am persuaded that He is able to keep what I have committed to Him until that Day."

The fifth answer to how we should respond to our trials is: "By committing our souls to our Creator." Peter tells us how to commit ourselves to Him, and he says it is by *doing good*. As we go through a difficulty of life, it is easy to commit our souls to Him when we are doing what is right, isn't it? But if we are sinning as we go through our trial, then it becomes difficult to commit our ways to Him. Peter goes on to say that we do this *as unto a faithful Creator*, which means a trustworthy founder. Maybe you wonder why Peter doesn't call God a faithful Judge or faithful Savior. Consider Matthew 6:25-34 for the answer, especially looking at verses 26, 28, and 30.

> Therefore I say to you, do not worry about your life, what you will eat or what you will drink; nor about your body, what you will put on. Is not life more than food and the body more than clothing? *Look at the birds of the air, for they neither sow nor reap nor gather into barns; yet your heavenly Father feeds them. Are you not of more value than*

---

[87]Warren W. Wiersbe, *Be Hopeful: How to Make the Best of Times Out of Your Worst of Times* (Colorado Springs: David C. Cook, 1982), 136.

they? Which of you by worrying can add one cubit to his stature? *So why do you worry about clothing? Consider the lilies of the field, how they grow: they neither toil nor spin;* and yet I say to you that even Solomon in all his glory was not arrayed like one of these. *Now if God so clothes the grass of the field, which today is, and tomorrow is thrown into the oven, will He not much more clothe you, O you of little faith?* Therefore do not worry, saying, "What shall we eat?" or "What shall we drink?" or "What shall we wear?" For after all these things the Gentiles seek. For your heavenly Father knows that you need all these things. But seek first the kingdom of God and His righteousness, and all these things shall be added to you. Therefore do not worry about tomorrow, for tomorrow will worry about its own things. Sufficient for the day is its own trouble (emphasis mine).

As we go through the storms of life, we can entrust ourselves to our Creator, the One Who made us. He will protect us and care for us as He does the birds and the flowers. He made us, so He knows what is best for us and for all whom He has created. We can commit ourselves to our Faithful Creator. As Peter will tell us in 1 Peter 5:7, you and I are to throw our cares upon Him, to roll them over and don't take them back. Why?! Because He cares for you!

Summary

Let's review what we have learned in these two lessons. First, the seven reasons why we go through suffering:

1. *It is a promise; it's to be expected* (v 12). Do you expect trials and suffering? Or are you under the myth that suffering is not for you?

2. *There is a purpose, and that purpose is to test you* (v 12). What trials have you gone through recently and how did you do in those tests?

3. *In order to allow you to participate in Christ's sufferings* (v 13). Have you been able to see the benefit of identifying with Christ in your sufferings?

4. *Sometimes because of your own sin* (v 15). Do you stop to examine yourself when trials and sufferings come, to see if it might be something you have brought upon yourself?

5. *To glorify God* (v 16). How was God glorified in the last trial you went through?

6. *God judges His people first* (v 17). Are you under the myth that God will not scourge His own people when judgment comes?

7. *It is His will* (v 19). Have you bought into the heretical teaching that it is not God's will for His children to suffer?

Second, the five answers to how should we respond as we go through suffering:

1. *With an attitude of rejoicing* (v 13). In your trials do you find yourself rejoicing or complaining?

2. *Rejoicing in the knowledge that glory is to follow* (v 13). As you go through trials, do you meditate on the fact that this will be only a brief affliction compared to glory?

3. *With an attitude of assurance, knowing that the Holy Spirit will strengthen and refresh you* (v 14). How has the Holy Spirit refreshed you in your past sufferings?

4. *Unashamed* (v 16). When you suffer for Christ's sake, are you disappointed that you are a follower of His?

5. *Committing your soul to Him* (v 19). When you go through a trial, do you commit all of it to the One who made you, the One who allowed it to come up, the One who knows how it will end because He and He alone knows the beginning and the end?

What storm of life are you going through this day? Do these attitudes characterize you? Are you committing your trials to Him? There is no other place we can turn to in a crisis but to Him!

Annie Hawks, who knew well of life's storms, wrote a hymn that I know has touched many of our lives. Of it, she wrote: "One day as a young wife and mother of 37 years of age, I was busy with my regular household tasks. Suddenly I became filled with the sense of nearness to the Master and I began to wonder how anyone could ever live without him, either in joy or pain. Then the words were ushered into my mind and these thoughts took full possession of me." And she proceeded to write her beloved hymn, *I Need Thee Every Hour*. Sixteen years later, her husband died, and again she wrote of her experience: "I did not understand at first why this hymn had touched the great throbbing heart of humanity. It was not until long after, when the shadow fell over my way, the shadow of a great loss, that I understood something of the comforting power in the words which I had been permitted to give out to others in my hour of sweet serenity and peace."[88] As we close with this song, let us think about our trials, our sufferings, and the storms of our lives, and let us commit our souls to Him as unto a Faithful Creator.

> I need Thee every hour, most gracious Lord;
> No tender voice like Thine can peace afford.
> I need Thee, O I need Thee; every hour I need Thee;
> O bless me now, my Savior, I come to Thee.
>
> I need Thee every hour, stay Thou nearby;
> Temptations lose their power when Thou art nigh.
> I need Thee, O I need Thee; every hour I need Thee;
> O bless me now, my Savior, I come to Thee.
>
> I need Thee every hour, in joy or pain;
> Come quickly and abide, or life is in vain.
> I need Thee, O I need Thee; every hour I need Thee;
> O bless me now, my Savior, I come to Thee.

---

[88] Facts taken from: http://cyberhymnal.org/htm/i/n/ineedteh.htm

I need Thee every hour; teach me Thy will;
And Thy rich promises in me fulfill.
I need Thee, O I need Thee; every hour I need Thee;
O bless me now, my Savior, I come to Thee.

I need Thee every hour, most Holy One;
O make me Thine indeed, Thou blessed Son.
I need Thee, O I need Thee; every hour I need Thee;
O bless me now, my Savior, I come to Thee.[89]

---

[89] Words by Annie Hawks, 1872.

Questions to Consider

What to Do in the Furnace: Part 2
1 Peter 4:15-19

1. Read 1 Peter 4 and summarize it in three sentences or less.

2. Memorize 1 Peter 4:17.

3. What things do you see that are similar in 1 Peter 4:17-19 and Romans 2:1-10?

4. (a) Peter writes in 1 Peter 4:17 that "the time has come for judgment to begin at the house of God." According to what you read in the following verses, what would you say Peter is referring to? Isaiah 10:12; Jeremiah 25:29; Ezekiel 9; Amos 3. (b) Why does God's judgment first begin with God's own people, according to these verses?

5. (a) Read 1 Peter 4:18 and then read Genesis 18:16 – 19:29 to better understand the meaning of what Peter is saying in 1 Peter 4:18. Who were the righteous that were scarcely saved in this story? (b) What happened to the ungodly and the sinner in this story? (c) How does this story also help you to understand 1 Peter 4:17?

6. (a) Peter encourages his readers to commit the keeping of their souls to their faithful Creator. What else should we commit to Him, according to Job 5:8; Psalm 37:5; Proverbs 16:3; 2 Timothy 1:12; and 1 Peter 2:23? (b) Do you commit these things to Him? (c) Why is it difficult at times to commit our ways to God?

7. (a) Why do you think Peter refers to God as a "faithful Creator" in 4:19? (b) Does this have any special significance to his readers? (c) Does this have any special significance to you?

8. Recall a time when you suffered for doing something wrong. Recall a time when you suffered for being a Christian. What was the difference between the two, in regard to the lessons that you learned?

9. (a) Are you suffering because you are a Christian? (b) What is your attitude? Are you rejoicing? Are you unashamed? Are you committing your soul to Him? (c) How can we pray for you? Write down your request to share with your group.

Chapter 22

What Does a Good Pastor Look Like?

1 Peter 5:1-4

There was once a young man attending seminary who had all the credentials of pastoring a church. Hearing that there was a church back in his hometown that was without a pastor, he decided he would send them his resume. He soon followed it up with a phone call to see if the church might be interested in considering him as their pastor. Much to his surprise, one of the elders of the church, who took his call, replied, "We're sorry; we won't consider your application. You see, we're looking for a pastor who is tall, dark, and handsome, and you don't fit that description." The seminary student was baffled and shocked! He thought to himself, "Tall, dark, and handsome?! Are those the requirements of a pastor according to what Scripture teaches?"

Tall, dark, and handsome. If those are the requirements of a pastor, do you know that the apostle Paul wouldn't even have been qualified?! Second Corinthians 10:10 says this about him: "'For his letters,' they say, 'are weighty and powerful, but his bodily presence is weak, and his speech contemptible.'" Instead of tall, dark, and handsome, Peter lists for us some qualities of elders or pastors that are slightly different. Let's begin chapter five of 1 Peter and find out what they are! Let's read verses 1-4.

1 Peter 5:1-4

> The elders who are among you I exhort, I who am a fellow elder and a witness of the sufferings of Christ, and also a partaker of the glory that will be revealed: ²Shepherd the flock of God which is among you, serving as overseers, not by compulsion but willingly, not for dishonest gain but eagerly; ³nor as being lords over those entrusted to you, but being examples to the flock; ⁴and when the Chief Shepherd appears, you will receive the crown of glory that does not fade away.

As we begin chapter five of Peter's epistle, and we move from the theme of suffering to the role of the pastor, you might have asked yourself the question, "Why does Peter write these words to the shepherds?" There are several possibilities. The first possibility is this: Because of what he has already written in 1 Peter 4:17, that judgment begins at the house of God, it would be natural for his readers to look to their spiritual leaders during these times of intense persecution—and so Peter wants those shepherds to remember that they must be living out their calling. They also must be readily available to shepherd their sheep during such tumultuous times. A second reason, perhaps, is that in times of persecution those spiritual leaders would have a special challenge to be faithful and not run away. When things get intense, some shepherds (and sheep) flee or apostatize, which, of course, would prove that their faith was never genuine to begin with. As we consider what a good pastor should look like, we will consider the following outline:

The Meaning of the Word "Pastor" (v 1)
The Ministry of the Pastor (v 2a)
The Mindset of the Pastor (vv 2b-3)
The Motive of the Pastor (v 4)

Let's consider the meaning of the word pastor in verse 1.

The Meaning of the Word "Pastor"

1 Peter 5:1

> The elders who are among you I exhort, I who am a fellow elder and a witness of the sufferings of Christ, and also a partaker of the glory that will be revealed: (1 Peter 5:1)

First of all, we need to define what an elder is. The word *elder* comes from the Greek word, presbyteros, from which we get our English word Presbyterian. This word means one who is an overseer and whose duty it is to exercise spiritual oversight and authority over its members; it is also the meaning of the word pastor. Elders were men who are older in age, usually over 40. It would only be reasonable that the older men would be appointed to this office, because with age comes wisdom and maturity. It's the same idea in Titus 2 where older men teach younger men, and older women teach younger women.

The concept and role of elders can actually be traced back to Exodus 18, when Moses' father-in-law Jethro counseled him to appoint elders to help with the burden of exercising leadership over all the people of Israel. In fact, it was mentioned then that these men should be able men who fear God, men of truth who hate covetousness. We also find the mentioning of elders in Numbers 11. When we come to the New Testament, we also find numerous mentions of elders. It was customary for Paul to ordain elders in every town in which he would preach. Usually, each church also had a plurality of elders. The elders would counsel the people in their church and administer church matters. They would pray for the sick, anoint them with oil, lead their people, teach them the Word of God, and pray with them and for them. We are told in 1 Timothy 3:1, that if a man desires the office of an elder, he desires a good thing. This is an honorable ministry! But with that honored position comes some required qualities and responsibilities.

Peter says *the elders who are among you I exhort*. The word for *exhort* means to call near. This is not a stern command, but a calling near so as to call to action. Peter is persuading, not imposing his authority. He goes on to say that he is *a fellow elder*. He was a fellow elder with a fellow feeling and he did not put himself above these men. He could identify with the joys as well as the difficulties of the pastorate, because he was one, as well. But in this statement by Peter is a good life principle for all of us: we should all, like Peter, put ourselves on the same level with those we exhort. We are not above anyone. To put one's self on a level with those we exhort gives weight to our exhortations. If you and I are going to exhort one another, it always helps to say, "Hey, you know, I am just a sinner saved by grace, just like you. I may come to you this week, but you may be coming to me next week." That is part of the beauty of Christian relationships. Iron sharpens iron! In fact, just today, I was speaking with someone and needed to say some hard things, but I mentioned that I too had just been rebuked regarding something and it was good for me to be reminded of this; I had not previously considered the things that person had said to me and I realized, because of her exhortation, that I needed some help in that particular area.

Peter was not only a fellow elder, but he was also a witness of the sufferings of Christ. To witness refers to the act of seeing, as well as to the act of testifying to what one has seen. Peter is not just claiming to having seen the sufferings of Christ but to also give testimony to what he had seen. He speaks of this in Acts 2:32, "This Jesus God has raised up, of which we are all witnesses." And again, in Acts 3:15, where he's preaching and says to the men of Israel, "and killed the Prince of life, whom God raised from the dead, of which we are witnesses." Also, in Acts 5:32, he says, "And we are His witnesses to these things, and so also is the Holy Spirit whom God has given to those who obey Him." In Acts 10:39, he speaks similar words, "And we are witnesses of all things which He did both in the land of the Jews and in Jerusalem, whom they killed by hanging on a tree." Even in his second epistle, he makes mention in 2 Peter 1:16, "For we did not follow cunningly devised fables when we made known to you the power and coming of our Lord Jesus Christ, but were eyewitnesses of His majesty." Peter had been a witness of the very sufferings he has been writing about in 1 Peter. He was with Christ in the garden; he was with Christ when he was apprehended; and he was with Christ in the high priest's hall. Whether he followed him to the cross or not, we don't know for certain; but we can probably assume he did not, because in the hall of the high priest, Peter denied Christ and then went out and wept bitterly. More than likely, Peter withdrew to some private place, to humble himself before God and to beg for mercy. We cannot be dogmatic about that, though, as Peter may have been present as a spectator of Christ's suffering on the cross, perhaps watching from a distance. We also get our word martyr from this word witness, so Peter may have been indicating that he was to be a martyr for Christ, which we know he went on to be, and would be crucified not all that long after writing this epistle, as the Lord predicted in John 21:18.

Peter, however, knew that his life would not end with suffering; he knew that suffering was only the beginning to something far more glorious—glory! Numerous times in this epistle, he has mentioned this glory that is to follow (see 1:7, 11, 19-21; 4:11, 13-14; and he will mention it again in 5:10). And so he mentions that he is also, in addition to being a fellow elder and a witness of the sufferings of Christ, a partaker of the glory that will be revealed. Peter knew that he would one day be a partaker of Christ's glory; he knew he would soon be with His Lord in heaven, after his own crucifixion would take place. The word partaker means to share in something. Just as we share in His sufferings, we will share in His glory, and Peter says, one day that glory will be revealed. The word revealed means to take off the cover. John puts it so beautifully in 1 John 3:2, "Beloved, now we are children of God; and it has not yet been revealed what we shall be, but we know that when He is revealed, we shall be like Him, for we shall see Him as He is."

After Peter reminds the elders he's writing to that he is a fellow elder, a fellow pastor, he then reminds them of the ministry of the pastor in verse 2. Let's consider verse 2.

The Ministry of the Pastor

1 Peter 5:2

Shepherd the flock of God which is among you, (1 Peter 5:2a)

Shepherd the flock means to feed the flock. *The ministry of the pastor is to feed the flock.* And notice, it is to feed the flock, not fleece the flock. The *flock* of God would be those precious people who have been bought with Christ's precious blood that Peter wrote about in 1 Peter 1:19. Notice also, it is the flock of God; it is God's flock, not theirs. Some shepherds think they own their flock, but they need to remember that these are God's sheep that have merely been entrusted to them for a time. It's just like those of us who are parents; we might think our children are ours, but they are on loan to us and are gifts from God that have been entrusted to us for a time.

Peter goes on to remind his readers that this flock they feed is *among them,* which means these shepherds are near their sheep or with them. He also mentioned this in verse 1, as well. This indicates that the shepherd should have a close relationship with his sheep, and that they should be around him. A man who shepherds a flock should be near them and with them; he should not wander off and leave his sheep; he should be with them, watching them very closely and protecting them and caring for them. I know some pastors who are never with their sheep and are not relational at all. Their motto is: "Don't bother me. Don't call me. I'm unavailable." (I know some shepherds' wives like that too!) It is rare indeed to find pastors faithfully feeding their sheep, in the pulpit and in personal ministry; often, we find them off doing all kinds of other things. This should not be, as they are to be among their sheep; they are, after all, one of them. (I would also add this brief note, since I spent many years as a shepherd's wife: it is also nice when the sheep actually allow the shepherd to minister to them and endeavor to have a relationship with them.)

How do these shepherds feed the flock? Obviously, the main job of a shepherd would be to make sure his sheep get food and water. Without proper nourishment, they would die. But the feeding or tending of the flock in the spiritual sense would not only include spiritual food, but it would also include guiding, guarding, discipline, leading, prayer, exhortation, and example. Jeremiah 3:15 talks about the shepherd feeding his sheep with knowledge and understanding. A shepherd must know how to teach; Titus 1:9 says that an elder must be able to teach. Also included in this feeding would be a balanced diet. If the shepherd only teaches on one subject in the Bible or one book of the Bible and doesn't give his people the whole counsel of God, then they will become spiritually anemic. Also, a faithful shepherd will protect his flock from false teachers, as like a shepherd protects his sheep from snakes, pits, poisonous plants, and dangerous animals, like wolves. (And, by the way, he will name the wolves' names!) A good shepherd will also single out the wandering sheep and bring him back to the fold; Luke 15:4 speaks of the shepherd who leaves the 99 to go find the one lost sheep. Jesus was busy with the crowds and yet He still gave individual attention to people, like Nicodemus and the woman at the well. It's interesting that the word feed in this verse is in the aorist tense in the Greek, which conveys a sense of urgency to feed them. Of course, this would probably be due to the persecution of the church and the judgment which was falling upon the house of God.

Peter says part of this shepherding of the flock is *serving as overseers,* or taking oversight of them. This means these shepherds are to be aware of or spy out or oversee the flock; they are to take care of it. In the physical realm, when a sheep had a special need like a bruise, a sore, or a briar in his foot, the shepherd would tend to him. At the end of the day, he would examine each sheep to see if it needed special attention. It is rather interesting that Peter is reiterating here what had been told him by the Chief Shepherd three times—when Jesus told him to feed His lambs, to tend to His sheep, and to feed His sheep. These were actually some of Christ's final words to Peter and, of course, final words are of utmost importance—and the ones we sometimes remember the most. Perhaps these words were in Peter's heart and mind often. The apostle Paul mentions something very similar when he is saying goodbye to the elders at Ephesus, in Acts 20:28: "Therefore take heed to yourselves and to all the flock, among which the Holy Spirit has made you overseers, to shepherd the church of God which He purchased with His own blood."

As you do the Questions to Consider that accompany this lesson, hopefully you will notice in Ezekiel 34 the seriousness of shepherds who do not heed this admonition to feed the flock. But listen also to Zechariah 11:17, "Woe to the worthless shepherd, who leaves the flock! A sword shall be against his arm and against his right eye;

his arm shall completely wither, and his right eye shall be totally blinded." Yikes! Those are some pretty scary words for shepherds who don't feed their flock.

The Mindset of the Pastor

1 Peter 5:2b-3

> serving as overseers, not by compulsion but willingly, not for dishonest gain but eagerly; (1 Peter 5:2b)

After Peter gives these shepherds their ministry description, which is to feed the flock, he then moves on to the three-fold mindset that should accompany their ministry. First, he says, *not by compulsion but willingly*, or not because you must, but because you are willing. *The first mindset that should accompany the role of a shepherd is a willing heart.* Peter says don't do it because you feel forced; don't think of the pastorate as a heavy burden that you wish you could get rid of. Ministry is hard work, and yet it should be viewed as a joy, not a burden. I have to say, I loved being a pastor's wife, but I know many who do not love it! Instead of serving because you feel obligated to, serve because you want to; do it willingly, voluntarily. An elder should not pastor because it is a job, but because it is a ministry from his heart that God has called him to. When a man has a pastor's heart, he loves the sheep and serves them because he wants to, not because he has to. This idea of being willing is the same idea Paul mentions in 2 Corinthians 9:7 when he speaks of believers giving their money to the Lord's work: "So let each one give as he purposes in his heart, not grudgingly or of necessity; for God loves a cheerful giver."

The second mindset that should accompany the ministry of an elder is that of being ready to serve the Lord. Peter puts it this way: *not for dishonest gain, but eagerly,* or your translation might say not for filthy lucre, but of a ready mind. A pastor is not to be in the ministry for sordid gain. There should be no greed or fraud on his part. In fact, Peter talks in his second epistle, 2 Peter 2:12-15, about false shepherds who covet and who make merchandise of their sheep. The goal of the pastor should not be making money—and yet he should be paid. Paul makes this very clear in 1 Timothy 5:17-18, where he says, "Let the elders who rule well be counted worthy of double honor, especially those who labor in the word and doctrine. For the Scripture says, 'You shall not muzzle an ox while it treads out the grain,' and, 'The laborer is worthy of his wages.'" He also mentions this in 1 Corinthians 9:7-14.

When I first looked at this, I scratched my head, because I did not understand how these shepherds could get rich—until I put myself in biblical times, and not in 21st century times. If we consider Acts 4:33-37, where the believers are said to lay money at the apostles' feet, and Acts 6:1-4, where they chose men of honest reputation to be the leaders among them, then it makes sense. The temptation for these leaders, entrusted with these monies, would have been to pocket the money like Judas did. John 12:6 says of him, "He was a thief, and had the money box; and he used to take what was put in it." In most churches today, the pastor doesn't see the money, as it is generally handled by a church treasurer—so I guess we'd be wise to keep a close eye on the treasurer! Paul states in Acts 20:33 that he coveted no man's silver or gold or apparel.

Instead of being in the ministry for the money, shepherds are to be in it for the Lord. Peter says they are to do so eagerly, to be of a ready mind. This would be a cheerful shepherd who is not seeking selfish gain. They must find satisfaction in serving God, not in the money which could be gained by it. They should not serve for self-gratification, but for the glory of God and out of response to His love. The third mindset shepherds should have is found in verse 3.

> nor as being lords over those entrusted to you, but being examples to the flock; (1 Peter 5:3)

These shepherds are to be an example. They are not to be lords over those entrusted to them, not even once. Lord means to control or rule, and it has the idea of someone who is strong ruling over someone who is weak. The idea is found in Mark 10:42-43, "But Jesus called them to Himself and said to them, 'You know that those who are considered rulers over the Gentiles lord it over them, and their great ones exercise authority over them. Yet it shall not be so among you; but whoever desires to become great among you shall be your servant.'" The shepherds in Ezekiel 34 ruled harshly, and it says the sheep were scattered because of it. Shepherds should not drive their sheep. Shepherds are leaders, not dictators. They should not lead with intimidation and manipulation. It is important that we remember the elders are called to rule, and we should respect that office and we should obey them, as Hebrews 13:17 tells us to. We also should recognize them and esteem them highly, as 1 Thessalonians 5:12-13 says. We must remember they are leaders, just like a parent is a leader over a child, or a husband over a wife. The child doesn't lead the parent, and the wife doesn't lead the husband—or at least they shouldn't! I know some sheep don't like it when their shepherd warns or rebukes them, and yet that is a necessary part of tending the sheep. Sometimes, sheep get rebellious and they need discipline. You might be asking yourself, "Well, what is the difference between an elder lording over his sheep and me being obedient to those who rule over me?" Lording would involve anything that would be unbiblical and demanding, especially being harsh or brutal. For example, a shepherd who insisted that everyone in his congregation home school or be a registered Republican or mow their yard every week, or tells them where to grocery shop and what to eat and where to get their hair cut—those are examples of lording and they have nothing to do with his shepherding responsibilities. Now, can he give you advice on things that are outside the Bible? Sure! But his calling is to guide his sheep within the parameters given to him by God in His Word. He must be authoritative, for sure, on matters of sin and issues that pertain to God's Word. Peter has already mentioned in chapter four that if any one speaks, it should be as if God were speaking, and this would certainly include pastors (1 Peter 4:11)!

Peter reminds these shepherds for the second time (verse 2 and here) that these are God's sheep that have been *entrusted to them*. The

KJV says God's heritage, and it is a really interesting word; it means the charge allotted to you. It refers to various congregations that God has allotted to different groups of elders by His providential hand. These elders are not to do as they please, so to speak, with their allotted portions. Peter is saying to them: this is not your church; this is God's church, His heritage. I know some pastors who can be pretty territorial about their congregations, like they're the head honcho, but they must remember that the sheep in their fold are God's sheep that He has entrusted to those elders for a brief time. "The pastors of the church ought to consider their people as the flock of God, as God's heritage, and treat them accordingly. They are not theirs, to be lorded over at pleasure; but they are God's people, and should be treated with love, meekness, and tenderness, for the sake of him to whom they belong."[90]

Instead of being a lord over their sheep, elders are to be *examples to the flock*. What does the word *example* mean? It means a stamp, a pattern, or a model. The word primarily refers to the impression left by a stroke, as in John 20:25, which mentions the print of the nails on Jesus's hands. Peter has already used this word when he was speaking of Christ as an example for us to follow in suffering, in 1 Peter 2:21. Christ did not lord things over his disciples but left them His example to follow. Paul said in 2 Corinthians 1:24, "Not that we have dominion over your faith, but are fellow workers for your joy; for by faith you stand." Paul and Peter both placed themselves alongside their flocks, never using the office of elder for personal advantage. How are elders to be examples to the flock? Paul tells Timothy in 1 Timothy 4:12 how to be an example to the flock. He says, "Let no one despise your youth, but be an example to the believers in word, in conduct, in love, in spirit, in faith, in purity." In that brief command, Paul is telling Timothy to be an example in several key areas: in word, which is doctrine; in conduct, which is how you behave; in love, which is agape love, a sacrificial love, which seeks the good of another; in spirit, which is the manner and disposition in which you do something; in faith, which means faithfulness to the flock and to God; and in purity, which means

---

[90]Matthew Henry; Matthew Henry Commentary; PC Study Software; 1993-1997.

purity of body and mind. A pastor must practice what he preaches to set the example for the sheep to imitate.

Now, in case some of these elders are still not convinced that this is how they should behave, Peter reminds them they will give an account someday to the Chief Shepherd. They are not above accountability! This would definitely be a motivating factor behind the elders' behavior. So we turn from the three-fold mindset of the pastor to the motive of the pastor.

The Motive of the Pastor

1 Peter 5:4

> and when the Chief Shepherd appears, you will receive the crown of glory that does not fade away. (1 Peter 5:4)

Peter has already referred to Christ as the Shepherd in 1 Peter 2:25 and now here he calls Him *the Chief Shepherd. Chief* means He is the principle, the head. In John 10, He is called the Good Shepherd; in Hebrews 13:20, He is called the Great Shepherd; in Ezekiel 34:11-16, He is called the True Shepherd. This chief shepherd will *appear,* to judge all ministers and under-shepherds, to call them to account. He alone will judge whether they have been faithful publicly and privately to their ministry. Peter is reminding these elders here that they too will give an account. This is also mentioned in Hebrews 13:17, "Obey those who rule over you, and be submissive, for they watch out for your souls, as those who must give account. Let them do so with joy and not with grief, for that would be unprofitable for you."

If they have been faithful on that day of accounting, they *will receive a crown of glory that does not fade away. Crown of glory* comes from a Greek word which describes the amaranth flower. It was a beautiful flower and was called this because it never withered and it revived if moistened with water—and because of that it became a symbol of immortality. The crowns that athletes were given in the games were made of oak or ivy leaves, and these would wither and fade. But the crown talked about here *does not fade away*—it never withers or fades. The Bible speaks of numerous crowns: a crown of righteousness, in 2 Timothy 4:8; a crown of life, in James 1:12, and again in Revelation 2:10; and in Revelation 3:11, there is a reference to the fact that we are not to let anyone take our crown.

The crown here in 1 Peter is called a *crown of glory.* We are not sure exactly what this is, but it might be a special crown for shepherds. It is interesting that Peter begins with speaking about our inheritance which does not fade away in 1 Peter 1:4, and now he speaks of a crown which does not fade away in 1 Peter 5:4. And so, the faithful shepherd who has fed his flock by careful oversight, who has served willingly, readily, and with a holy example for his sheep to follow, will receive a crown of glory from the Chief Shepherd. What a promise! For those who see their shepherding responsibility as a chore, who are in it for money, glory, and authority—whoa! It will be a sad day when they face the Chief Shepherd; Peter says in 2 Peter 2:1 that they bring upon themselves swift destruction!

We are seeing all kinds of bizarre things going on in the church today, and we have many sick and diseased sheep because we have sick and diseased shepherds. Many leaders in the church are shepherding so they can build names and empires for themselves. Some are striving for the applause of men and for success in their denomination. But all this self-made glory will fade away, unlike the crown of glory that will never fade away. The good and faithful pastor will have no desire for personal glory, but will strive to hear those words from the Chief Shepherd: "Well done, good and faithful servant."A true and godly shepherd will lead by serving and will serve by suffering. That is the way Jesus did it, and this is the only way that truly glorifies Him.

Summary

The meaning of the word pastor is an overseer, one who gives oversight to his flock. The ministry of the pastor is to feed the flock. The mindset of the pastor should be: not because they have to, but because they want to; not for the money, but readily, for the joy of serving God; not as lords, but as examples. The motive for the pastor is the crown of glory he will receive, which will not fade away!

Maybe you're thinking, "Well, this was a most interesting lesson, but it really doesn't apply to me. I am a woman and I don't pastor a church." That's true, and believe me, I am glad you don't pastor a church! But, are you helping your pastor and leaders by supporting them in prayer? Do you always complain to them about everything, or do you encourage your pastor when he's doing a good job? Do you make it easy for him to feed you and care for you by digesting and growing from the things he feeds you?

Those of you who are wives of elders or deacons, do you support your husband in prayer? Do you allow him to shepherd, or do you always complain when he has to go out and minister to some sick sheep? Do you help him in his shepherding responsibilities?

As the wife of an elder for many decades, I would leave you with what I believe to be at least four essential responsibilities for the sheep toward their shepherds:

1. *Pray for them.* Do you pray for your leaders in your church? When is the last time you prayed for them? Do you know what their needs are so that you can pray intelligently for them?

2. *Encourage them.* Does your leadership need encouragement at this time? How have you encouraged them in the past? When is the last time you encouraged your leadership?

3. *Get to know them.* Have you ever spent anytime outside of church with your leadership? Do you know your pastor and his wife, as well as the other elders and deacons and their wives? How much time have you spent with them in the last year? Have you ever had them in your home?

4. *Allow them to make mistakes.* As Peter has already said, love covers a multitude of sins. Are you critical of your leadership and the quirks they might have? If you do have issue with them, have you gone to them in love, or do you spread dissension?

Oh, that all of us would be presented with joy and not grief on that day when our leadership has to give an account for us! While we await that day, may we all endeavor to follow our earthly shepherds as they lead and guide us, while they look to their Chief Shepherd!

Questions to Consider

What Does A Good Pastor Look Like?
1 Peter 5:1-4

1. Read 1 Peter 5:1-4, making note of the qualities that should be present in an elder.

2. Memorize 1 Peter 5:2-3.

3. (a) What other qualities are to be present in elders or deacons, according to 1 Timothy 3:1-13 and Titus 1:5-9? (b) Which of these qualities are the same as what Peter mentions in 1 Peter 5:1-4? (c) Why is it essential that churches choose their leaders based on these qualities? (d) Does your church choose elders based on these qualities?

4. (a) What were the shepherds guilty of in Ezekiel 34:1-3? (b) What "tending" of the flock were they negligent in, according to Ezekiel 34:4? (c) According to Ezekiel 34:5-9, what happened to the sheep? (d) What happened to the shepherds, according to Ezekiel 34:10?

5. (a) Read the remaining portion of Ezekiel 34 (verses 11-31) and summarize what the Great Shepherd did for those scattered sheep. (b) How does this encourage you, for yourself or for others you know who, perhaps, are not in churches where there are faithful shepherds?

6. Peter says in 1 Peter 5:3 that elders are not to "lord" their authority over their flock. Read Hebrews 13:17 and reconcile what you read there with what Peter says in 1 Peter 5:3.

7. What are some ways that the shepherds (or leaders in the church) should set examples for the flock? (You might want to think of how Paul, Peter, or some of the other apostles set examples.)

8. Have you thanked God for the leaders in your church? Do you pray for the leaders in your church? Do you know the ones who shepherd your soul? How much time do you spend with them? How can you pray for the leaders in your church? Write a prayer of thanksgiving for your leaders, as well as a request for them.

Chapter 23

Four Reasons to Avoid Pride
1 Peter 5:5-9

Marian Anderson, who has won worldwide acclaim as a concert soloist, was once asked by a reporter the following question: "What was the greatest moment in your life?" She had had many great moments indeed. Great moments when she became the first African American to sing with the Metropolitan Opera in New York; moments when she became a United States delegate to the United Nations; and then the great moment when it was reported that "a voice like hers only comes once in a century." There were various medals she'd received from countries all around the world, and the time she gave a private concert at the White House. Which of these moments do you think she chose as the greatest moment of her life? None of them! She told the reporter that the greatest moment in her life was the day she went home and told her mother that she would not have to take in washing anymore. Ms. Anderson had never forgotten that her roots reached back into poverty. No amount of public acclaim would ever cause her to forget that her mama took in washing to put food in Marian's stomach. I imagine that every time Marian was tempted to have exaggerated ideas of herself, she looked back to her humble beginnings, and that look would shoot holes in any pride she might have been tempted to possess.

Pride is an awful sin that plagues *every one of us*. In fact, did you know that at the root of every sin we commit is the sin of pride? "Why?" you might ask. Because pride elevates us above others, even above God. Pride says, "I am going to do this my way and not God's way." Pride is an awful sin, and the results, if left unchecked and unrepented of, can be devastating and destructive to God's children. In this lesson, we are going to consider verses 5-9 of 1 Peter 5 and discover four reasons why we should avoid this sin of pride—and they all begin with the letter R for your remembrance. Let's read these verses together.

1 Peter 5:5-9

> Likewise you younger people, submit yourselves to your elders. Yes, all of you be submissive to one another, and be clothed with humility, for "God resists the proud, but gives grace to the humble." ⁶Therefore humble yourselves under the mighty hand of God, that He may exalt you in due time, ⁷casting all your care upon Him, for He cares for you. ⁸Be sober, be vigilant; because your adversary the devil walks about like a roaring lion, seeking whom he may devour. ⁹Resist him, steadfast in the faith, knowing that the same sufferings are experienced by your brotherhood in the world.

Peter now turns our attention from the shepherds to the sheep, in verse 5, and he says:

> Likewise you younger people, submit yourselves to your elders. Yes, all of you be submissive to one another, and be clothed with humility, for "God resists the proud, but gives grace to the humble." (1 Peter 5:5)

The question might come to mind, "Who is Peter referring to when he speaks of the young submitting to the elders?" The word *elders* in the Greek is the same word as in verse 1, *so it seems* that it is the elders of the church to whom the *younger people* are to *submit*, or be subject to. The elders in the church were usually older in age, and the younger members were to be submissive to them. In Hebrews 13:17, the writer to the Hebrews says much the same thing: "Obey those who rule over you, and be submissive, for they watch out for your souls, as those who must give account. Let them do so with joy and not with grief, for that would be unprofitable for you." And then we have 1 Timothy 5:1, where Paul tells young Timothy, "Do not rebuke an older man, but exhort him as a father, younger men as brothers." Those who are younger should be respectful and humble toward the older men, especially the elders in the church. Sometimes young men and women have difficulty honoring and respecting the aged and don't want to be accountable to anyone, so we can understand the admonition here. This is certainly something that is needed in our day, as well; it seems as if obeying any authority has become archaic!

Not only were the younger members to be submissive, but Peter tells them that all of them are to submit to each other. Now you might be wondering if Peter has lost his mind. How can we all *be submissive to one another*, as the *all* here refers to all ages of people and both male and female? Remember the context and the fact that Peter has already admonished them to submit to government in 2:13-17; he has admonished slaves to submit to masters in 2:18; and he has admonished wives to submit to husbands in 3:1. Even husbands are to be submissive in the sense that they obey God in honoring their wives as seen in 3:7; and all of them were to strive for being one in mind, as we saw in 3:8. So, when we put all of that together, it is pretty easy to understand that Peter is saying we should all honor one another by putting others first and considering others more important than ourselves. Submission to one another in this sense takes a lot of humility, which is Peter's next point: he says we are to *be clothed with humility*. As we clothe ourselves with humility, then we will be subject to each other's needs. (But before we look at what that means, look at all these one-another's in 1 Peter: 1 Peter 1:22; 3:8; 4:9; 4:10; 5:5; and 5:14! These virtues are to be demonstrated toward one another and for the benefit of one another.)

What does it mean to *be clothed with humility*? *Humility* has to do with an attitude of our mind. It isn't demeaning yourself; it is simply not thinking of yourself at all. I like how one person defined humility by a story about some children who had built a clubhouse where they could meet and play. They decided to make three rules for their clubhouse: "1. Nobody act big. 2. Nobody act small. 3. Everybody act medium." That's probably a good definition of humility! Acting "big" is a puffed up view of yourself. Acting "small" can sometimes show itself to be false humility; to appear worthless and wormy is really a form of pride because it is still a self-focus. Instead of these, just act "medium," with a view to look at others and seek to minister to others, not even thinking of yourself at all.

Peter says this attitude of humility is something we should *be clothed with*. The word *clothed* means a knot or roll of cloth, which was made by tying or tucking up any part of one's dress. Peter has mentioned something similar in 1 Peter 1:13, where he mentioned that they were to gird up the loins of their mind. Peter probably had in mind John 13, where Jesus laid aside His garments and took a towel and girded Himself to wash the disciple's feet. The laying aside of His garment would indicate that He was getting ready to do some type of work, as He was then dressed as a servant. Jesus illustrates humility to His twelve disciples, and to us, by washing their feet. I imagine Peter never forgot this; remember, he was the one with all the questions and objections during this act of humility from his Lord. Also, we should keep in mind that the slaves in New Testament times would knot a white scarf or apron over their clothing to distinguish themselves from the free men. So Peter is suggesting here that Christians tie humility to their conduct so that everyone is able to recognize them. This doesn't mean we wear a sign that says, "I'm humble!"—that is *not* humility! It is also interesting to consider that the Greek word that is used here for *clothe* referred to another kind of garment, a long, stole-like garment which was a sign of honor and preeminence. This garment they did not tie up in a knot. So when we marry these two ideas together, like Christ, we must put on the apron of humility in serving others, and that very apron of humility, so to speak, becomes the garment of honor for us. "Put on and wrap yourselves about with humility, so that the covering of humility cannot possibly be stripped from you."[91] It is known that some of the early Christians actually sold themselves as slaves, in order that they might preach the gospel to those who were in bondage. That, my friend, is humility!

There is a reason we are to be clothed with humility. Peter says it is because God resists the proud. *So the first reason we should avoid pride is: Resistance from God. God will resist us if we are*

---

[91] Vincent's Word Studies of the New Testament—PC Bible Study Software—1993-1997.

prideful! What does it mean that *God resists the proud?* The word *resist* means to arrange oneself against. It is a strong word, which literally means that God sets Himself in array against us as one that is ready for battle! Pride calls out the armies of God! No wonder the Scripture tells us that pride goes before destruction—because when God calls out for His armies to come against us, we do not stand a chance! We may as well give it up; we are doomed! As 2 Chronicles 13:12 says, if you fight against the Lord, you will not prosper.

The word for *proud* means haughty, or appearing above others. It is the attitude that says,"I am superior to you. I am the standard of excellence, and you fall short of the standard." This person is self-centered, self-sufficient, and ignores their need of God.

I remember meeting a "Christian" woman one time and I will probably never forget her statement to me. She said: "I can't wait for you to get to know me!" That sent up an immediate red flag in my mind! It goes without saying that as I "got to know her," that's exactly what it was. "Me!Me!Me!" was all I got from her. It is hard to be around a person who constantly thinks of themselves and is always talking about themselves, never taking an interest in the needs of others.

So, God resists the proud, but He *gives grace to the humble. Here is our second reason we should avoid pride, that is, in order that we can be a Recipient of God's grace. He gives grace to the humble.* The word *grace* means graciousness or favor. And God gives this to those who are *humble*, to those who are lowly in circumstances or disposition. This is a word which comes from the picture of the Nile River when it's at its low stage. The word literally means not rising far from the ground. It describes the Christian who follows in the humble and low steps of the Lord. This person is very aware of their unworthiness and gladly acknowledges their dependence on God. And to this person God is gracious. James mentions this in James 4:6-10, "But He gives more grace. Therefore He says: 'God resists the proud, but gives grace to the humble.' Therefore submit to God. Resist the devil and he will flee from you. Draw near to God and He will draw near to you. Cleanse your hands, you sinners; and purify your hearts, you double-minded. Lament and mourn and weep! Let your laughter be turned to mourning and your joy to gloom. Humble yourselves in the sight of the Lord, and He will lift you up." Also, Micah 6:8 says, "He has shown you, O man, what is good; and what does the LORD require of you but to do justly, to love mercy, and to walk humbly with your God?" Peter continues on with his theme of humility in verse 6, and says:

> Therefore humble yourselves under the mighty hand of God, that He may exalt you in due time, (1 Peter 5:6)

Perhaps you are wondering, "How is it that you *humble yourselves*?" Do we say to ourselves, "Self, be humbled!"? To understand what Peter means we need to look at the tense of this verb, which is in the passive voice, which means that an outside agent is acting upon the subject of the verb. Peter is referring to these readers as being passive in the *hand of God*, allowing Him to act upon them. In other words, allow yourself to be humbled by Him. This does not mean that you resign yourself to a forced humility; rather, it is a voluntary acceptance of the circumstances that God allows. They were to be submissive to the circumstances that God was allowing. He was using these circumstances to make them more humble. This allowing ourselves to be humbled is a precious thought as we consider that Peter says that we do so under the *mighty* hand of God. This means that our humbling is under the powerful hand of God. The concept of God's *hand* is the idea of hollowness for grasping. It is the idea seen in Exodus 3, where we see not a wrathful hand of God toward the Israelites, but a hand of deliverance, that is, God's hand of almighty power. The mighty hand of God that delivered Israel will also deliver you, if you humble yourself. These readers would have a real challenge, as they were in devastating circumstances. To resist God's dealing in their lives would only cause a worse situation for them. As Christians, we should never resent the circumstances God allows, because we know that the mighty hand of God has dealt us those circumstances. So, dear one, we really have two choices when we're going through difficult times: We can humble ourselves willingly under the mighty hand of God and He will exalt us, or we can exalt ourselves and watch His mighty hand humble us. I don't know about you, but I prefer the first!

This brings us to the third reason we should avoid pride: Raised up by God. We should avoid pride so that God can exalt us in due time. The word *exalt* means to elevate or raise up, and *due time* means in the proper time—when God thinks it is the proper time, not when we think we have had enough and we say to God, "Times up, please!" This would be an encouraging word for Peter's readers, as they could know that God would not leave them in this low and depressed condition. He would raise them from their state of suffering! But, this raising up would take place in His proper time, which would, of course, be the best time. It might be in this present life, but more than likely, for them, it would be in glory, in the life to come, something Peter has emphasized over and over in this epistle. Paul says in Romans 8:18, "For I consider that the sufferings of this present time are not worthy to be compared with the glory which shall be revealed in us." I don't know about you, but this encourages me in the midst of my trials—that when He is ready to release me from them, He will! But my responsibility is to allow myself to be humbled by whatever He thinks is best for me, to perfect and conform me to His will. As you and I allow God's mighty hand to humble us and deal with us, then we have the wonderful privilege that is found in verse 7.

casting all your care upon Him, for He cares for you. (1 Peter 5:7)

The Psalmist states a similar idea in Psalm 55:22, when he says, "Cast your burden on the LORD, and He shall sustain you; he shall never permit the righteous to be moved." When Peter says to *cast all your care upon Him*, it means we are to throw it all upon Him. We don't throw our cares on Him only to take them back, which is what most of us do! We bow in humble prayer to cast our concerns to Him, and when we leave our prayer closet, we do not take those concerns with us. Peter is saying: leave all your cares to Him. Now what is a care? *Care* refers to the state of being pulled apart in different directions. It also has the idea of distraction, worry, anxiety. Now, what would be some of their cares? Probably foremost on their mind would be the care of their physical life: would they live or die? Then, perhaps, their families and friends: will they live or die? Then there would be the concern for adequate food and shelter, which comes with persecution. This is where Jesus' words from the Sermon on the Mount in Matthew 6:25-34 would encourage them.

> Therefore I say to you, do not worry about your life, what you will eat or what you will drink; nor about your body, what you will put on. Is not life more than food and the body more than clothing? Look at the birds of the air, for they neither sow nor reap nor gather into barns; yet your heavenly Father feeds them. Are you not of more value than they? Which of you by worrying can add one cubit to his stature? So why do you worry about clothing? Consider the lilies of the field, how they grow: they neither toil nor spin; and yet I say to you that even Solomon in all his glory was not arrayed like one of these. Now if God so clothes the grass of the field, which today is, and tomorrow is thrown into the oven, will He not much more clothe you, O you of little faith? Therefore do not worry, saying, "What shall we eat?" or "What shall we drink?" or "What shall we wear?" For after all these things the Gentiles seek. For your heavenly Father knows that you need all these things. But seek first the kingdom of God and His righteousness, and all these things shall be added to you. Therefore do not worry about tomorrow, for tomorrow will worry about its own things. Sufficient for the day is its own trouble.

The cares of Peter's initial readers would be likely be very different from ours, as they would be dealing with not only concern for the basic necessities of life but even their own lives. Most of us do not have to worry about food, shelter, or clothing—or our lives. Our cares seem to be more relational, like cares over a husband who doesn't lead spiritually, or a friend or family member who has died; or financial cares, like an overdue mortgage or worries about how we are going to stretch our food budget this month; or health cares, like terminal illness or even a common cold; or family cares, like children who make poor grades or who are rebellious; or even irritants, like appliances that don't work, bad weather, aging, a job transfer, or a move. But regardless of whether we live now or lived back in Peter's day, we all must cast all our cares on Christ. Why? Because, Peter says, He cares for you! This word for care is a different Greek word than the previous one in this verse, and this one means He is concerned for you! He has a watchful interest and affection for us in our cares.

When you think about it, pride is at the root of most of our anxiety. It wounds our pride and it's humiliating to cast everything upon another and be cared for by another. Anxiety is a contradiction to true humility. Why? Because we end up depending on ourselves, which is dangerous and is a failure to trust God! Everything is under His control, so why worry? One man said, "to be overwhelmed with anxiety is to be concerned with self rather than with Him."[92] Worry is condemned, but watchfulness is demanded, as Peter shows us in verse 8:

> Be sober, be vigilant; because your adversary the devil walks about like a roaring lion, seeking whom he may devour. (1 Peter 5:8)

The word sober is not a new word in 1 Peter; Peter has already mentioned it in 1:13 and 4:7. To *be sober* means to be watchful, to be mentally self-controlled, and to abstain from wine. Why would Peter's readers need to be sober? If they were not careful, the cares of this world could overtake them. They needed to be preparing their minds for battle. Peter says they must also *be vigilant*, which means to keep awake, to watch. It has the idea that this watching should be done as if one is in some sort of danger, like walking alone in a dark parking lot. "The moment slothfulness begins, that moment dangers stand thick about us."[93] You might say, "Well, what is the difference between these two words?" Being sober has to do with our ability to look at reality with a clear mind, and being vigilant has to do with a state of watchfulness and readiness. The first adjective describes a person who controls his disposition; the second describes a person's readiness to respond to outside influences. "Sobriety and

---

[92] D. Edmond Hiebert; *First Peter: An Expositional Commentary* (Chicago: Moody Press, 1984), 295
[93] Words by an unknown Puritan.

watchfulness are necessary virtues at all times, but especially in times of suffering and persecution."[94]

Why would these two things need to be in place? Peter says because they have an *adversary the devil, who walks about like a roaring lion, seeking whom he may devour.* Notice that our *adversary*, our opponent, is not our husband or our neighbor; it is *the devil.* Who is the devil? The Greek word for *devil* is diabolos, which literally means to throw over or across, to send over. It has a few connotations: to slander, to accuse, to defame; it was used not only of those who would bring a false charge against someone, but also of one who would broadcast the truth concerning a person but do so with maliciousness and hostility. Of course, the readers here would know what that meant, as their persecutors had slandered them (see 1 Peter 2:12; 3:16; 4:4, 14).

Peter says the devil is walking around like a roaring lion and he wants to devour you. *This is the fourth reason to avoid pride, that is: a Roaring lion is after you! If you remain in a state of pride, a state of rebellion against God, you run a great risk of Satan devouring you!* A *roaring lion* pictures the howl of a beast in fierce hunger. They say that when a lion roars, he is extremely hungry, and that is when he most eagerly seeks his prey. These believers would understand what Peter meant here; many of them had seen or heard of the vicious mauling and devouring of friends and family by lions. Nero made a practice of binding Christians in the skins of animals and letting wild animals kill and devour them. One martyr prayed. "I am God's wheat. May I be ground by the teeth of the wild beasts, until I become the fine white bread that belongs to Christ."[95] Peter describes the devil as *walking about*, which means that he treads all around. It is the graphic picture seen in Job 1:7, "And the LORD said to Satan, 'From where do you come?' So Satan answered the LORD and said, 'From going to and fro on the earth, and from walking back and forth on it.'" And then again in Job 2:2, "And the LORD said to Satan, 'From where do you come?' Satan answered the LORD and said, "From going to and fro on the earth, and from

---

[94] Matthew Henry; PC Bible Study Software—1993-1997
[95] Duane W. H. Arnold, *Prayers of the Martyrs* (Grand Rapids: Zondervan, 1981), 98.

walking back and forth on it." In the physical realm, that's exactly what a lion does; they walk around back and forth looking for prey. My friend, Satan is walking back and forth, seeing which Christians he has the best chance of devouring! Are you aware of his devices? It is interesting to note that lions often hunt at night because they surprise their prey more easily in the dark. Likewise, Satan also usually attacks us spiritually when we are walking in the dark and not in the light.

Peter says the devil is seeking someone in order to devour them. *Seeking* means to plot against life, and *devour* means to drink or swallow down, to gulp entirely. Satan's desire is to kill his victims by destroying their faith. He is constantly on the prowl, looking for someone to devour. In church history, we read about a woman named Biblis, to whom this almost happened. She denied the Lord while she was being tortured, and so the devil thought he had already swallowed her up. She then was subjected to further torture so that she would renounce other Christians, but it is said that "once on the rack she came to her senses and awoke as if from a deep sleep." The story concludes that from then on, she confessed that she was a Christian and was counted among the number of the martyrs.[96]

Paul himself felt that if he did not fight the fight as he should, he himself would be a castaway; he feared going apostate, feared he might deny his faith (1 Corinthians 9:24-27). Satan wants to shake us in our faith, and he wants us to stop believing. "The design of Satan in raising persecutions against the faithful servants of God is to bring them to apostasy, by reason of their sufferings, and so to destroy their souls."[97] It's interesting that in 2 Timothy 4:17, Paul talks about being delivered from the mouth of the lion, which is possibly a reference to Satan or to Nero. "But the Lord stood with me and strengthened me, so that the message might be preached fully through me, and that all the Gentiles might hear. And I was delivered out of the mouth of the lion." Peter would have known

---

[96] Paul Middleton; *A Guide for the Perplexed* (New York: Continuum Publishing, 2011), paraphrased, 72.
[97] Matthew Henry; PC Study Bible Software—1993-1997.

first hand the seriousness of this admonition about the adversary, Satan. Remember what Jesus said to him in Luke 22:31-32? "And the Lord said, 'Simon, Simon! Indeed, Satan has asked for you, that he may sift you as wheat. But I have prayed for you, that your faith should not fail; and when you have returned to Me, strengthen your brethren.'" And my dear sister, Satan desires to sift us as wheat, too! We must be awake and alert to his devices and his schemes to attack us.

There are many ways that Satan attacks us. However, one man helps us with this; he says these attacks can fall under three categories: Persecution, peer-pressure, and preoccupation.[98] Persecution should not take us by surprise—Jesus said it would happen—and yet it surprises some of us. Jesus makes this reality clear in the parable of the soils, in Matthew 13:20-21, "But he who received the seed on stony places, this is he who hears the word and immediately receives it with joy; yet he has no root in himself, but endures only for a while. For when tribulation or persecution arises because of the word, immediately he stumbles." Persecution and trials can catch us off guard, if we are not careful, and so lead us to fall away. Others are prone to peer-pressure and are afraid of losing friends, so they compromise and give Satan a foothold. In regard to peer-pressure, we must strive to please God over man. Paul warns us of this in 1 Corinthians 15:33, "Do not be deceived: 'Evil company corrupts good habits.'" Preoccupation is a big temptation that gets to many of us. Preoccupation with the world can diminish our devotion to God. Things like redecorating our houses, vacations, our kid's soccer games and practices, entertainment, the latest fashions, and even our jobs can preoccupy us with worldly stuff and make it easy for Satan to attack us. "To guard against these attacks, remember that God uses persecution to mature you and bring glory to Himself."[99]

---

[98] John F. MacArthur Jr., *Drawing Near* (Wheaton: Crossway Books, 1993), September 9.
[99] Ibid.

Regarding preoccupation with the world, we must evaluate our priorities and activities carefully. Don't be preoccupied with things. So, pay attention, wake up; your opponent, the devil, is on the move like a roaring lion ready to swallow his prey. And he does so quietly and subtly.

So what should be our response to this roaring lion, Satan? Do we rebuke him, do we bind him, or do we run from him? Actually, Peter says something a bit different. He says,

> Resist him, steadfast in the faith, knowing that the same sufferings are experienced by your brotherhood in the world. (1 Peter 5:9)

In the physical realm, we obviously don't rebuke a real lion, or bind one (unless you have some serious help!), or even run from one—they would most certainly run after us! It is the same in the spiritual realm. Running is the cowardly thing to do; resisting is the courageous thing to do. In Scripture, we are told to flee idolatry, flee youthful lusts, and flee fornication, but nowhere are we told to flee from the devil. That would be futile; he would just run after you. You cannot get away from him, but you can resist him. What does it mean to *resist him*? It means to stand against, to oppose, to be firm and solid against him. As Christians, we should stand firm like a rock, unyielding in the attacks by the enemy. The wonderful thing is that James 4:7 says that as we resist him, he flees from us! When Christ resisted Satan's temptations, in Matthew 4, that is when the devil left Him. The Christian would do well to remember that he cannot fight the devil. He was the most powerful and wise angel God created, according to Isaiah 14. We don't have any power to rebuke him; even in Jude verse 9, it is recorded for us that Michael the archangel, when contending with the devil over Moses' body, would not dare bring an accusation against Satan, but instead said "the Lord rebuke you." If Michael the archangel wouldn't even rebuke Satan, what makes us think we can or should do that? Also, we have a similar situation in Zechariah 3:2, where Joshua the high priest was standing before an angel of the Lord and before Satan. Joshua who was trying to resist him, and it was the Lord who said to

Satan, "the Lord rebuke you." Even Joshua the high priest and the angel did not rebuke Satan! But the Lord did.

Now, you might be wondering, how does one resist Satan? Ephesians 6 tells us how to do so; it explains the believer's spiritual armor that he or she must put on. We won't thoroughly explain all that right here (Get the book, *With the Master in Heavenly Places*, to learn more about how that's done!)[100], but basically, the armor consists of defending ourselves with truth, with the Word, with right living, with a steadfast faith, and with prayer. When a Christian is fully equipped, the devil cannot penetrate that armor, and so he leaves. If your armor isn't in place, then you are vulnerable to the attacks of Satan. If you neglect prayer, worship, Bible Study, accountability, and the other disciplines of the faith, you cannot expect to withstand the devices of the enemy!

Peter goes on to say we resist our enemy *steadfast in the faith*, which means firm in your place. *Steadfast* is a military term referring to a body of heavily-armed infantry formed in ranks and files, close and deep. They aren't moving; they are firm like a rock. Now, the key here to being firm like a rock, to being steadfast, is to have a foundation of something, and Peter says that something is *the faith*. We must be strong in the faith. Peter is not talking about putting strength into what we already believe, but drawing strength from what we believe. It is faith alone that will cause us to be victorious over the enemy. As John says in 1 John 5:4, "For whatever is born of God overcomes the world. And this is the victory that has overcome the world—our faith." Paul says in 2 Corinthians 1:24 that it is by faith that we stand. Most of us want some magical formula to get rid of Satan, but it is our faith that will cause him to flee. This truth would be of great importance to Peter's readers, as many of them had been faced with the option of renouncing their faith and being allowed to live, or confessing their faith and dying for it. They must not deny their faith, Peter is saying, but confess it openly and stand firm in it. And, of course Peter, is talking from experience here; he knew the grief of denying his Lord, of not standing firm in the faith.

---

[100] Susan Heck, *With the Master in Heavenly Places* (Bemidji: Focus Publishing, 2016).

Peter ends with this: *knowing that the same sufferings are experienced by your brotherhood in the world.* Peter is saying that they are not the only ones suffering hardship or pain. He lets them know that their fellow believers have the same common lot. It is similar to what Paul says in 1 Corinthians 10:13, "No temptation has overtaken you except such as is *common to man*; but God is faithful, who will not allow you to be tempted beyond what you are able, but with the temptation will also make the way of escape, that you may be able to bear it" (emphasis mine). In our day, there are other believers in Christ around the world who are suffering, and they are suffering far worse than you or me. We are not alone in our sufferings. There are many who are suffering all around the world; in fact, some in other countries are being killed for their faith. And that is a sign of God's favor, not His displeasure, that Satan is allowed to harass them as he did Job. In fact, such treatment is really an indicator that they belong to the brotherhood of believers.

Summary

Would you say that you have a problem with pride? Let me remind you of the four reasons to avoid it at all costs!

1. *Resistance from God.* God resists the proud! Do you want God's army to come against you? If not, humble yourself under His mighty hand!

2. *Recipient of God's Grace.* Do you want to receive God's grace? Then remember, the next time you are going through difficulties, that He gives grace to the humble.

3. *Raised up by God.* God will exalt you in His time! Do you desire for the Lord to lift you up at the proper time? Then allow Him to use whatever He desires in your life to accomplish His purposes!

4. *Roaring lion is after you.* The devil will try to devour you! Do you want Satan to eat you for lunch? If not, then resist him by being steadfast in your faith!

If a reporter asked you the same question he asked Marian Anderson, "What was the greatest moment in your life?" what would your answer be? Would you think back to a time in your life when you achieved some great accomplishment or reward? Would it be a time when someone recognized you publicly and said some complimentary remarks about you? Would it be when you were the star in a play or a performance of some kind? What would your answer be? Only you can answer that. But, the next time you are tempted to think more of yourself than you should, think back to where you have come from, from the miry pit out of which the Lord lifted you—that does have a way of shooting a hole in our pride.

Questions to Consider

Four Reasons to Avoid Pride
1 Peter 5:5-9

1. Read 1 Peter 5:1-7. (a) Who do you think the "younger" are in verse 5? (b) Who are the "elder"?

2. Memorize 1 Peter 5:7.

3. (a) What does the Lord think of pride, according to Proverbs 6:16-17 and 8:13? (b) What do the following verses say about pride? Proverbs 11:2; 16:18; 21:4, 24; 29:23; Luke 1:51-52; 1 John 2:15-17. (c) How do these verses encourage you to avoid this awful sin?

4. (a) What does the Lord do for those who are humble, according to Psalm 9:12; Isaiah 57:15; 66:2; Matthew 18:4; 23:12; and James 4:6, 10? (b) How do you think people can "humble themselves"? (c) What is the most difficult thing about humbling yourself?

5. (a) Make *three* columns on the back of your paper. Entitle the first column: *Who was proud?* Entitle the second column: *Why were they proud?* Entitle the third column: *What was the result of their pride?* (b) Look up the following verses and then fill in the columns: Genesis 3; Isaiah 14:12-17; Daniel 4:28-37; Acts 12:20-23. (c) Summarize what you learned about pride from those verses.

6. (a) In the following passages of Scripture, who do you see casting their cares on the Lord, and what was the result? 1 Samuel 1:9-19; 1 Samuel 30:1-20; 2 Chronicles 20:1-25. (b) Recall a time you cast your care on the Lord. What was the result?

7. Putting yourself in the shoes of these suffering saints to whom Peter is writing, what would be some of their *cares* that they would need to *cast* on the Lord?

8. (a) How would you define pride? (b) Recall a time when you knew God was resisting you because of your pride. What did you learn during that time that you could pass on to others? (c) How did He break your pride?

9. (a) What are your "cares" this day? (b) Are you casting them upon the Lord? (c) How may we pray for you? Please put your need in a prayer request.

Chapter 24

A Hopeful End

1 Peter 5:10-14

Most of you have probably heard of Elisabeth Elliott, who for a few years was the wife of missionary Jim Elliott. Jim Elliott was one of five missionaries killed in Ecuador by a tribe known, at that time, as the Acua Indians. Mrs. Elliott went through some tremendous trials in her life, including not only the loss of one husband, but two. In the years before her death, she also suffered with Alzheimer's Disease. Without a doubt, she has been a role model of suffering for all of us to follow. She once said something that I have never forgotten: "No suffering is wasted." *No suffering is wasted.* Do you believe that? Peter did! He believed there is purpose in suffering, in persecution, and he ends his letter by sharing with his readers just what that purpose is. We come to the end of Peter's letter to these persecuted Christians, and we see Peter, the apostle of hope, end on a hopeful note, reminding his readers that God is indeed in control. This is a hopeful end, and a great way to end his letter to these readers. Let's read these words together.

1 Peter 5:10-14

> But may the God of all grace, who called us to His eternal glory by Christ Jesus, after you have suffered a while, perfect, establish, strengthen, and settle you. [11]To Him be the glory and the dominion forever and ever. Amen. [12]By Silvanus, our faithful brother as I consider him, I have written to you briefly, exhorting and testifying that this is the true grace of God in which you stand. [13]She who is in Babylon, elect together with you, greets you; and so does Mark my son. [14]Greet one another with a kiss of love. Peace to you all who are in Christ Jesus. Amen.

In our outline for this lesson, we will see that Peter gives his readers six reasons to retain a hopeful attitude under fiery trials—and they will all start with the letter G.

> But may the God of all grace, who called us to His eternal glory by Christ Jesus, after you have suffered a while, perfect, establish, strengthen, and settle you. (1 Peter 5:10)

Peter begins verse 10 with the word *but*, which is a word of contrast. He has just mentioned Satan in the previous verses, and now he mentions God. *God* is in contrast to Satan! In contrast to Satan, the adversary, the roaring lion, who is trying to devour you, we have *the God of all grace*. By the way, this is the only time you will find this title for God in the entire Bible. I find that fact interesting, because these readers would have had a special need for the grace of God as they went through persecution. This title would include the fact that He is also the God of all comfort and He is there to help and to give us hope in every situation. This would be of utmost importance to these readers, considering the persecution they were enduring.

The first reason we have, then, that we should retain a hopeful attitude during trials is: Got God's grace. We have God's grace! The unbeliever does not understand this grace we have as we go through trials, but we as Christians can testify to a grace that is truly unexplainable, that only comes from God. One of my favorite verses in all of Scripture is Hebrews 4:15-16, which states: "For we do not have a High Priest who cannot sympathize with our weaknesses, but was in all points tempted as we are, yet without sin. Let us therefore come boldly to the throne of grace, that we may obtain mercy and find grace to help in time of need." What a comfort!

Peter says this God of all grace *has called us to His eternal glory by Christ Jesus*. The word *called* is more than an invitation; it is a divine summons. This is an effectual call, where the one called is willing to obey. God has divinely summoned us and we have willingly obeyed that call! And He has called us *to His eternal glory*, praise the Lord! This, again, must have been of special significance to Peter's readers, because they could bank on the fact that if they suffered with Him, they would also be glorified with Him. This principle is seen over and over again in 1 Peter, and hopefully that has been apparent to you as you have gone through this study. In just the past few verses, Peter has brought this out. Consider 1 Peter 4:14, which says, "If you are reproached for the name of Christ, blessed are you, for the Spirit of glory and of God rests upon you. On their part He is blasphemed, but on your part He is glorified." And 1 Peter 5:1, "The elders who are among you I exhort, I who am a fellow elder and a witness of the sufferings of Christ, and also a partaker of the glory that will be revealed."

The second reason, then, to retain a hopeful attitude when suffering is: Going to Glory! We know we are going to glory! The road may be difficult, but it leads to glory, and that's what matters. Paul says in Romans 8:18, "For I consider that the sufferings of this present time are not worthy to be compared with the glory which shall be revealed in us." Now, notice that the calling is *by Christ Jesus*. My friend, the only way you and I are going to get to glory is by our union with Christ. That union is an assurance of our destiny, which is glory.

I remember talking with a young lady who told me she believed in the teachings of Christ, yet she also believed Buddhists and other religious people would get to heaven because of the sincerity of their faith. I said, "So then, you really don't believe in the teachings of Christ, because He says 'I am the way, the truth, and the life. No one comes to the Father except through Me'" (John 14:6). Our relationship with Christ, our union with Him, is the only way any of us will ever get to glory. May I pause here and say that if you have never embraced Christ as your Lord and Savior, and if you do not have a personal relationship with Him this day, please don't put it off. This is our last lesson, and I certainly don't know your hearts, but before God, and as your friend in Christ and as your teacher, I beg you if you are not reconciled to God, be reconciled today! If you will hear His voice, do not harden your heart!

After talking about glory, Peter then moves to the theme of suffering once again, and says *after you have suffered a while. A while* may refer to the amount of time they suffered, or it may refer to the degree of their suffering. In other words, our suffering is short compared with eternity, and it is light compared to our eternal weight of glory. Paul says in 2 Corinthians 4:17, "For our light affliction, which is but for a moment, is working for us a far more exceeding and eternal weight of glory." Our suffering is not forever, thankfully! Peter has already said in 1:6 that it is just for a season. *So the third reason we should retain a hopeful attitude during trials is: Grief is brief! Our present suffering is only for a while.* Suffering is for a season, but glory is for eternity.

Peter then goes on to say that suffering is good for us and that is the fourth reason we should retain an attitude of hope during suffering: Growth will happen! We know our trials are building character. Peter describes it like this: *perfect, establish, strengthen, and settle you.* It is interesting that all of these terms are architectural. It is possible that Peter had in mind something he already wrote, in 1 Peter 2:5, "you also, as living stones, are being built up a spiritual house, a holy priesthood, to offer up spiritual sacrifices acceptable to God through Jesus Christ." The imagery here is of a building, and the terms perfect, establish, strengthen, and settle are also words which describe a building.

This same God who grants us grace will, first of all, *perfect* us. This means He will make us complete or thorough. It is a word which means to put in complete joint, like the timbers of a building, to fit together in order and arrange properly. It was used to describe setting right what had previously gone wrong. It is even used in Scripture to describe the mending of a net or the setting of broken bones (see Matthew 4:21, Mark 1:19; and Galatians 6:1). The idea is that suffering, for the believer, will repair and mend any weaknesses in one's character. We are purified or made complete in our maturity through our suffering. As James says in James 1:2-4, trials produce patience in us and make us perfect and complete—which is exactly what Peter is saying in this verse. Trials are for our growth! One martyr understood that suffering perfected him; he wrote, "I thank you, Lord and Master, that you have deemed to honor me, by making *complete* my love for you, in that you have bound me with chains of iron to your apostle Paul" [101](emphasis mine).

The second thing God will do in us through our trials is *establish* us, which means to confirm or set fast, to make solid as granite. Suffering makes one firm in every part. Paul mentions this in 2 Thessalonians 3:3, where he says, "But the Lord is faithful, who will establish you and guard you from the evil one." Suffering will either make one collapse or it will make one build character. God will give these believers the grace that will enable them to resist the temptation to deny their Lord. And He will do the same for you and me. The Christian who is established will not be moved when persecution comes. One martyr prayed this: "Near to the sword I am near to God. In the company of wild beasts I am in company with God. Only let all that happens be in the name of Jesus Christ, so that I may suffer with him. I can endure all things if he enables me."[102]

The third thing the Lord intends to do in our trials is to *strengthen* us. This Greek word actually means to fill with strength, and it has the idea of connecting every part so that there is no danger of any warping or splitting or falling. We really do not know what strength is until we have been put through the fiery furnace. The strength these readers would need would be the spiritual strength to resist Satan and to endure suffering. Peter is assuring them that God will give them the strength to stand firm. One martyr prayed this: "O God who was and is, you willed that I should be born. You brought me to salvation through the waters of baptism. Be with me now and *strengthen* my soul that I will not weaken. Praise to God who has looked upon me and delivered me from my enemies"[103] (emphasis mine).

---

[101] Duane W. H. Arnold, *Prayers of the Martyrs* (Grand Rapids: Zondervan Publishing House, 1991), 40.
[102] Ibid, 58.
[103] Ibid, 24.

The last thing Peter mentions that God is working to accomplish in us in our trials is to *settle* us. This means to fix on a foundation. The Christian who is fixed on a firm foundation will not be tossed to and fro when persecution comes. Through trials, we discover if our faith is genuine or not! The Psalmist penned it well in Psalm 112:7, "He will not be afraid of evil tidings; his heart is steadfast, trusting in the LORD." As one martyred saint prayed, "Let me be *steadfast* in my faith to the end. I have no hope of seeing my brethren again in this life, If they kill me, let me die as a witness to my faith. If I live, let me go on proclaiming it"[104] (emphasis mine). These persecuted Christians would especially need this strengthening to go through the fiery trials they were experiencing.

These are such words of hope that Peter gives, as he writes about these trials producing character. They would hopefully encourage Peter's first readers, just as I hope they encourage you today. No suffering is wasted! Sufferings have been sent by God to perfect and conform us to Christ's image. We won't go through them alone, but with God helping us all along the way. What comfort and encouragement! Peter, too, seems overcome by God's enabling grace to us in our suffering, and so he cries out with a doxology in verse 11.

> To Him be the glory and the dominion forever and ever. Amen.
> (1 Peter 5:11)

This is not the first time Peter has broken out in praise to God. In 1 Peter 4:11, he did this when he was writing of the gifts that God gives us by His ability and for His glory. Here, Peter breaks out in praise to God after writing of God's ability to perfect His people through suffering. In fact, these two doxologies are almost identical in wording. Here, it is simply an expression of Peter's gratitude and praise to God for His grace and help in time of need for these suffering saints. But notice that Peter is careful to give *the glory and the dominion* to God and not to man, for not only the use and enabling of spiritual gifts in 1 Peter 4:11, but also here for God's help

---
[104] Ibid, 23.

in strengthening the believer in their suffering. Sometimes, we think it is our own strength of character that makes us strong, but nothing could be further from the truth! It is all of God, and He gets all the glory. *So, this would be number five of our reasons for remaining hopeful during trials: <u>God gets glory!</u> To Him be the glory!*

A great principle also to bring out here is that we should praise God when we're going through trials. I often think of King Jehoshaphat in 2 Chronicles 20 as he was facing an enormous army coming against him. He did not know what to do, and he even tells the Lord, "I don't know what to do!" But the scriptures tell us that when he and all his people began to sing and to praise the Lord, that is when the Lord acted on their behalf and fought the enemy army in an amazing way! So much so, that it says that there wasn't even one person who remained alive and that it took them three days to collect all the spoils because there was so much of it! (See 2 Chronicles 20.) It's amazing how praising the Lord during trials can change one's attitude. (By the way, for those of you who like detail: the term *glory* has been mentioned 12 times in this epistle, this mentioning being the last one.) Peter now ends this letter by sending greetings in verses 12-14.

> By Silvanus, our faithful brother as I consider him, I have written to you briefly, exhorting and testifying that this is the true grace of God in which you stand. (1 Peter 5:12)

To say that he wrote *by* Silvanus would mean that Silvanus was the channel of that act; it probably indicates that Silvanus was the bearer of the letter. But Silvanus was also likely the amanuensis, the one to whom Peter dictated the letter and by whom it was then sent on its way. It appears that *Silvanus* (or Silas, as he is called elsewhere) was the one who wrote down the words as Peter dictated them, and then took the letter to the ones for whom it was written. In many instances, the New Testament writers dictated their letters to someone else, who then wrote down all that had been dictated to them. This is probably the situation in Peter's case. In Acts 4:13, it was said that Peter and John were perceived by others to be unlearned and ignorant men. Many believe that Peter could not have known classical Greek well enough to write the letter of 1 Peter, so he would have had to have used an amanuensis. It's certainly a strong possibility.

It is also interesting that Silvanus's name means sent. He obviously was a close friend of Peter's, as well as a companion of Paul. How he became acquainted with Peter and why he was with Peter in Babylon is unknown. Peter, however, thought very highly of Silvanus, referring to him as *a faithful brother*, which means that he was trustworthy. Could someone say that of you and me? "She is a faithful and trustworthy sister!"

Peter goes on to say *as I consider him*, which indicates that Peter had a settled persuasion and assurance about Silvanus's character. Peter knew Silvanus could be trusted, and he could highly recommend him.

Peter mentions that he has *written briefly*, which means simply that this is a short letter. It is indeed, especially when you compare it to some other letters like Hebrews, Romans, or 1 and 2 Corinthians. If, by this time, Peter's readers knew of Paul's letters, then they would know that 1 Peter is rather brief; Romans and 1 Corinthians are each four times the length of 1 Peter! Next, Peter mentions two things he has done in this brief letter he has written. He has *exhorted and testified*. To *exhort* would be to use persuasive speech along with encouragement towards one's audience, and here its purpose is to call the readers to face their trials with confidence. Exhorting does not necessarily include comforting and consoling. Peter is saying, "I have called upon you to be faithful, humble, and steady." He has already exhorted the elders in the beginning of this chapter, and you can find plenty more of this exhorting in 1 Peter 1:16; 1:22; 2:1-2, 11, 13, 18; 3:1-4, 7-12, 15-17; most of chapter 4; and nearly all of chapter 5. To *testify* would be to confirm truth. Peter certainly has confirmed a lot of truth in this letter: the doctrine of election; the holiness of God; the benefits of suffering; the importance of the Word, and so much more.

So what has Peter exhorted and testified of? That *this is the true grace of God in which you stand*. This is Peter's twofold purpose for writing his letter: to confirm their faith and hope in God by his apostolic witness of God's saving grace, and to encourage them to stand firm in it. Peter is leaving them here with a final admonition to stand firm as he has already mentioned in 5:9. Notice that Peter mentions that this grace of God is *true*, which means it is genuine. And, certainly, these suffering saints would need to know that God's grace was real in their lives. Then Peter sends another greeting.

> She who is in Babylon, elect together with you, greets you; and so does Mark my son. (1 Peter 5:13)

There is some debate here about what *Babylon* is a reference to. Some think it is referring to the literal city of Babylon, located on the Euphrates. Some think that Peter was in Rome and he is using the name Babylon here as a disguised reference to Rome, in order to protect the church from Nero's persecution. Some think this is a reference to Peter's wife, as he was married and his wife traveled with him (see 1 Corinthians 9:5). They think this because it reads in the Greek, "She who is in Babylon." But the Greek word for church is always in the feminine gender, so I think Peter is referring to the church at Babylon, which is located on the Euphrates. I don't think there are any hidden meanings, and there is no hidden wife. Peter does say this Babylon is *elect together with you*, which means the believers who were in the church at Babylon were also elected. He started with the doctrine of election in 1:2 and now he ends with this same doctrine. Peter says this church at Babylon *greets you*, which means to enfold in the arms.

Not only does the church at Babylon send greetings, but *so does Mark*. Who is this Mark? *Mark* was once a source of contention between Paul and Barnabas, but later became valuable to Paul in ministry, and now to Peter (see Acts 15:37-39 and 2 Timothy 4:11). Why does Peter call Mark his *son*? It is very unlikely that Peter had a son named Mark, though those who claim that she who is in Babylon is Peter's wife, say also that Mark is Peter's son. But history does not verify that Peter had a son name Mark. He is called Peter's son, probably because Peter had something to do with his conversion. In the same way, Paul called Timothy his true son in the faith, in 1 Timothy 1:2. Peter and Mark seemed to have been close; Peter went to Mark's mother's house after being miraculously released from prison (see Acts 12:5-17). We know from Colossians 4:10 that Mark was with Paul in Rome about five years before this time. Just as we mentioned with Silas, why Mark is with Peter at this time is unknown, but we do know from tradition that Mark and Peter had always been closely connected. Peter ends his epistle with verse 14.

> Greet one another with a kiss of love. Peace to you all who are in Christ Jesus. Amen. (1 Peter 5:14)

He exhorts them to *greet one another with a kiss of love*. Now, maybe you're wondering what this *kiss of love* is. In Romans 16:16; 1 Corinthians 16:20; 2 Corinthians 13:12; and 1 Thessalonians 5:26, it is referred to as a holy kiss, which is a bit different than *a kiss of love*. A holy kiss would indicate the expression we show each other because of the holy, spiritual relationship we have with one other. A kiss *of love*, as Peter mentions here, would indicate their brotherly love toward one another.

A good example of this is found in Acts 20:37, where the elders at Ephesus are saying their good-byes to Paul and it says they fell on his neck and kissed him. Another good example is found in Luke 7:36-50. So, *number six on the list of why we should remain hopeful in trials is that in our trials God: <u>Glues us together</u>! Greet one another with a kiss of love!* It really goes without saying that the trials of life should bring us closer together as Christians. I know that with all that is going on in our world today and with the increased persecution, I long and love to be with like-minded believers who will encourage me to press on and will push me closer to Christ!

Now, *a kiss* was a very normal expression of affection for the early church, just as it is in many parts of the world today. Disciples would kiss their Rabbi on the cheek, just as Judas, the disciple, kissed Jesus, the Rabbi, on the cheek. But we know that Judas turned his kiss of love into a kiss of betrayal. Kissing was also a sign of welcome and respect and was an essential part of believers' worship services. It was especially a part of the communion service; kisses were given after the prayer and before the elements were brought in. The kiss would remind them that all wrongs were forgiven and that those who sat at the Lord's Table were indeed one in the Lord. Believers would kiss at a person's baptism; the person being baptized was kissed by the person who baptized them and then by the whole congregation as a sign of welcoming them into the family of God. When an elder was ordained, they were given a kiss in the Lord. When there was a marriage, a kiss would be given by those present. If someone was dying, the dying one would first kiss the cross, and then they would be kissed by all who were present with them. The dead were even kissed before burial. Augustine said, "When Christians were about to communicate, they demonstrated their inward peace by the outward kiss."[105] It was a sign that their souls were knit together with brotherly love, but there was nothing erotic about this kiss.

You might be wondering why we don't kiss each other anymore. Well, like any good thing, if it is not done in moderation and with the proper intent, it can become abused and perverted. By the 4th century, this kiss had become confined to the same sex; the women kissed the women and the men kissed the men. Church history records for us that this practice got out of hand, to the point that "some do nothing but fill the church with noise of kissing."[106] Then there was the other side of it. "There is another—an impure—kiss full of venom pretending to holiness."[107] Because of these things, it eventually became regulated, where men kissed only men and women kissed only women, and the custom gradually dwindled away from there.

Now, let me say this: I think because of the abuse of this practice, perhaps we have swung the pendulum all the way to the other end

---

[105] William Barclay, *The Letters of James and Peter* (Louisville: Westminster John Knox Press, 1976), 279.
[106] Kenneth Wuest, *Word Studies in the Greek New Testament: Volume II* (Grand Rapids: Eerdmans Publishing Company, 1942), 133.
[107] Ibid, 133.

of the spectrum of displaying affection, which is also not good. Our tendency is to do nothing—no touching, no hugging, no affection, as we hold each other at arm's length. Among Christians, there should be love, and it should be shown by action, and part of that action is physical affection, especially toward the singles and the widows and those who are lonely and hurting. It is sad that some of us don't really know one another or love one another, and that some of us don't wish to know one another.

Peter's final words are: *Peace to you all who are in Christ Jesus*. Paul typically ended his letters with "grace be with you," but Peter ends with *peace*. It is most appropriate that Peter ends his letter with a greeting of peace because that is how he started the letter, in 1 Peter 1:2. Jesus said in John 14:27, "Peace I leave with you, My peace I give to you; not as the world gives do I give to you. Let not your heart be troubled, neither let it be afraid." There can always be peace in the storm when we know the One who created the storm. But this peace is for those *who are in Christ Jesus*. That is the only real peace there is, the only peace that is lasting and genuine. Christ is our peace, as Paul says in Ephesians 2:14. This would have been most comforting to those first readers of this epistle as they went through such fiery trials that most of us know nothing of—at least not yet! Finally, Peter says, *amen*, which means so be it!

Summary

As we closeout our study of Peter's first epistle, let me ask you: Do you believe that whatever trial you're going through right now is a waste of time and energy? Do you wish the Lord would release you from the misery you are in? My friend, no suffering is wasted. Peter tells us it is not wasted because:

1. *Got God's Grace! We have God's grace.* Are you experiencing the grace of God right now as you go through your current trial? How have you experienced God's grace lately?

2. *Going to Glory! We know we are going to glory.* Have you meditated on the fact that heaven is far, far better than any trial or suffering you are encountering? Knowing that heaven is coming soon should help us as we go through present sufferings.

3. *Grief is brief! Our present suffering is only for a while.* Does your suffering right now seem like an eternity? My friend, it is but a brief moment in light of all eternity! Soon, it will be over! Be patient and trust the Lord!

4. *Growth will happen! We know our trials are building character.* What character is God building in your life through your current sufferings? What changes have you seen in your spiritual growth as you go through your trials?

5. *God gets glory! To Him be the glory!* Has God been glorified through your suffering or are you trying to get glory for yourself by thinking it is your own strength that enables you to go through your trials? How has God been glorified in your trials?

6. *Glues us together! Greet one another with a kiss of love.* How has your suffering made you more thankful for your brothers and sisters that God has given you to help you and encourage you in your own trials? Are you showing affection to those who are hurting and perhaps need that "kiss of love" from you as they go through their own suffering?

Whatever the Lord allows in your life, my dear sister, it is for your good. "No suffering is wasted," Elisabeth Elliott once said. Be hopeful, my friend, as you go through the fiery furnace with your Master! Remember this: glory is soon to come! And then we will no longer walk through the fiery furnace with our Master, but we will walk with Him in paradise for all of eternity!

Consider the Lillies
Johnny Oravetz

Questions to Consider
A Hopeful End!
1 Peter 5:10-14

1. Read all of 1 Peter and then answer the following questions. (a) What themes do you see repeated in 1 Peter? (b) If you were to give 1 Peter a title, what would it be?

2. Memorize 1 Peter 5:10-11.

3. Blow the dust off your first week's homework, and look back at question one. ☺ (a) Have you grown in your understanding of the verses which you indicated then that you did not understand? (b) What knowledge have you gained of these verses?

4. Summarize 1 Peter 5 in three sentences or less.

5. (a) List all the things Peter has admonished his readers to do to "one another," according to 1 Peter 1:22; 3:8; 4:9; 4:10; 5:5; and 5:14. (b) Why would these commands be especially important in light of their suffering? (c) Are these the things that you are currently doing for the brethren?

6. (a) What do you learn about Silvanus from 1 Peter 5:12? (b) What do the following references in Scripture say about him? 2 Corinthians 1:19; 1 Thessalonians 1:1; 2 Thessalonians 1:1. (Also *skim* Acts 15:40 – 18:5, where Silvanus is called Silas, to see what else is said about him.)

7. (a) What does Peter say about Mark in 1 Peter 5:13? (b) What do you learn about Mark from the following verses? Acts 12:12, 25; 15:36-41; Colossians 4:10; 2 Timothy 4:11; Philemon 23-24.

8. In looking over question 5, what area do you need to grow in? Write down your prayer request to share.